REACHING ALL LEARNERS

REACHING ALL LEARNERS

Understanding Diverse Classroom Populations

FIRST EDITION

Joseph Johnson, Ph.D.

Troy University

cognella® SAN DIEGO

Bassim Hamadeh, CEO and Publisher
Casey Hands, Production Editor
Jess Estrella, Senior Graphic Designer
Alexa Lucido, Licensing Manager
Natalie Piccotti, Director of Marketing
Kassie Graves, Vice President of Editorial
Jamie Giganti, Director of Academic Publishing

Cover images: Copyright © 2012 iStockphoto LP/mbortolino.
Copyright © 2013 Depositphotos/Antonvector.
Copyright © 2015 Depositphotos/tashechka.

Printed in the United States of America.

3970 Sorrento Valley Blvd., Ste. 500, San Diego, CA 92121

TABLE OF CONTENTS

PREFACE

Writing comes more easily if you have something to say.

—Sholem Asch

Of course, the trick with the above quote, I believe, is *knowing when* you have something to say. Take this book, for instance. There are many books out there on how teachers can succeed with diverse student populations. These books can drill down on specific aspects of diversity, such as socioeconomic status or race/ethnicity, or provide broader coverage on a variety of topics that are significant when discussing diversity in modern classrooms. Any of these books that you may pick up will offer some important insights on teaching that can be helpful. So what might I have to add about working with diverse student populations that would make this book worth your time? I hope a great deal.

Diversity takes many forms, and the aim of this book is to cover many of the most significant aspects of diversity in modern classrooms in a concise manner meant to educate future teachers. Topics to be covered include racial and ethnic diversity, the effect of poverty on classrooms and schools, how special education plays a large role in our schools, how English-language learners are a growing part of the student population, and how gifted learners are often not receiving the support they need. All of these topics will be presented in a manner meant to inform future teachers, with vignettes and application scenarios across grade levels. Simple and direct strategies and ideas will be presented to help teachers better support their diverse students. Chapter content is meant to be informative, though not exhaustive, and to generate further discussion on and contemplation of the information and ideas presented in each chapter.

This book was inspired by the future teachers I have tried to support during my career. The discussion and reflection questions in the chapters are all born from actual conversations in classes and seminars. Future teachers want to know what to expect, regardless of how much time they get to spend in a working classroom. Their preservice classroom experiences may have had limited diversity, meaning that, after graduation, their first encounter with a student from extreme poverty or a student learning to speak English might just be their first such encounter. While no book could ever entirely cover the way diversity may present itself to a teacher, it is hoped this text will provide basic foundational knowledge to indeed better prepare teachers for some of the more common forms of diversity.

> One of the biggest complaints I hear from students finishing their student teaching is: "Our classes didn't really prepare us." My response: "If teacher education courses could replicate you being in charge of your own class from 7:30 to 3:30 five days a week, you probably would have been much more prepared for your student teaching."

I've been working with preservice teachers for more than a decade, and as they approach the end of their teacher education program, many students still have unanswered questions. Even with 150 hours or more of field experience and a semester of student teaching, they haven't had the chance to fully experience everything that comes with the teaching profession. And while, as noted, no book can fully prepare any future teacher for every single situation they may encounter, this book is my effort to answer many of the questions I've heard from those entering their own classrooms for the first time. As a proxy for the future teachers, I present Kortney Wicks, a recent graduate with a degree in elementary education who is about to have the interview experience of a lifetime.

Kortney is an amalgam of first-year teachers going through an interview, representative in the grand scheme of all grade levels and content areas, and she will be visiting with Mrs. Frayer, a veteran administrator with many stories about teachers dealing with diverse student populations. Kortney's interview begins and ends the book, and each chapter concludes with her hearing a story about some aspect of diversity and being given questions about that story. The questions are my way to give you, the reader, a chance to process the content of each chapter on a higher level. I hope that as you follow Kortney's interview journey through topics on ethnic diversity, poverty, special education, gifted education, and more, you may glean some information and advice that can indeed help you better work with diverse student populations.

And at the end, I hope you will be able to think, "That guy had something to say."

Joe Johnson

May 2020

INTRODUCTION

Schools in the United States are becoming increasingly diverse as the population of the country itself continues to diversify. Race, ethnicity, socioeconomic status, achievement levels, intelligence, emotional health, and more contribute to the heterogeneous nature of our country and our schools. And those going into teaching, along with those teaching currently, are faced with having to meet the complex needs of students and families that are often very different based on individual circumstances. Those going into education have to ask themselves, "Am I ready to appropriately meet the diverse needs my students are going to bring into my classroom every day?"

Tell me and I forget, teach me and I remember, involve me and I learn.
—Benjamin Franklin

This book hopes to help educators be able to answer that question with a strong yes. In the chapters to follow, multiple types of diversity will be addressed, and ideas will be presented on how educators can better meet the diverse needs of their students. Furthermore, each chapter will contain practical application and discussion activities that readers can use to further engage with the content. Look for the **Pause and Reflect** and **Pause and Discuss** headers as opportunities to think more deeply about the text. Each chapter will also end with a case scenario focused on the core content of the chapter, and to which readers can synthesize and apply the ideas presented in the chapter. Presenting information is only one goal of this text; providing specific and concrete opportunities to apply that information is a goal of equal importance.

Specific Topics Covered in This Text

- Socioeconomic status

- Race/ethnicity

- Gifted students

- Students with disabilities included in general education classrooms

- Students with disabilities primarily educated in separate classrooms/settings

- English-language learners

Each of these topics will be covered holistically but not exhaustively. Additional chapters will focus on the mental health of students and how technology is playing an ever-increasing role in the education of students. These topics will be surveyed to help readers gain a better understanding of these categories while acknowledging that learning about diversity is a lifelong endeavor. Readers' ideas and conceptions about some of these categories may be challenged, and it is hoped that if this occurs, it will open a constructive dialogue or self-reflective process regarding diversity. Everyone has existing schema about what constitutes diversity, and schemas are meant to be malleable as individuals learn new information and synthesize new concepts. The background knowledge that this book should build or fortify will help readers be more mindful of multiple aspects of diversity. That mindfulness can translate to positive actions in providing education in modern classrooms.

Why Does This Matter?

Human beings have a natural inclination toward ethnocentricity (Kinder & Kam, 2009), as has been demonstrated throughout history. And this aspect of our personalities has not always led to positive outcomes when reviewing world relations. Think of any major world conflict between two or more nations as an extreme example. This ethnocentricity can bluntly be characterized as, "We often stick with our own kind." Sometimes that works, and individuals and groups experience great success working in a homogenous society. But the truth teachers have to face is that rarely are their classrooms going to be characterized by the word *homogeneous.*

What is interesting to consider is that while American classrooms are getting more heterogeneous, teachers themselves are not. In 2016 approximately 80% of teachers were Caucasian, and 77% were female (Taie & Goldring, 2018). Compare those percentages with those for students in American classrooms, where trends suggest that by 2024 Caucasian students will make up 46% of the students in American public schools, whereas African American students will make up 15%, and Hispanic students 29% (U.S. Department of Education, 2016). And ethnicity is only one measure of diversity. Statistics are available for the number of students who qualify for free and reduced lunch, for one example, and there is also the crucial factor of multiple achievement levels present in the same classroom (Steenbergen-Hu, Makel, & Olszewski-Kubilius, 2016). Simply put, there are many classrooms in schools today made up of students who represent a vast array of backgrounds. And these backgrounds often influence their attitudes and dispositions toward education.

> *In addition to the robust social science evidence on the positive relationship between student body diversity and academic outcomes, there is a similarly impressive body of research supporting the correlation between campus and classroom diversity and an enhanced ability of students to exhibit interracial understanding, empathy, and an ability to live with and learn from people of diverse backgrounds.*
>
> **—Wells, Fox, & Cordova-Cobo, 2016**

In their book *How to Teach Now*, William Powell and Ochan Kusuma-Powell (2011) devote an entire chapter to the significance of teachers knowing their students as learners. The authors identify numerous student traits that can affect learning, including biological, societal, cultural, emotional, and social factors. Nearly all of the factors identified are outside any teacher's direct control, yet these factors often play a significant role in how a child learns. Teachers must therefore take the time to get to know their students as individuals. "Knowing students means more than merely acquiring social or administrative information. ... To maximize learning, we need to dig deeper than this superficial acquaintance" (Powell & Kusuma-Powell, 2011, p. 21). A superficial acquaintance will not suffice if teachers hope to engage learners at a high level, so having foundational knowledge of the diversity their students represent is a must for all educators.

Any book focusing on teaching diverse student populations would be negligent if it did not mention the concept of culturally responsive pedagogy. While just one facet of diversity, culture has a tremendous effect on everyone. Our culture becomes ingrained in us to the point that we do not really think about it in an active fashion. Rather, it is a subconscious phenomenon, as we are often unaware that we are engaged in anything that may be particular to our own culture. The same goes for students, all of whom are products of a culture. The concept, then, of culturally responsive pedagogy is well summarized by Richards, Brown, and Forde (2007, p. 64), who stated:

> Culturally responsive pedagogy facilitates and supports the achievement of all students. In a culturally responsive classroom, effective teaching and learning occur in a culturally supported, learner-centered context, whereby the strengths students bring to school are identified, nurtured, and utilized to promote student achievement.

If teachers are more *diversity aware* they can better engage in practices that resemble culturally responsive pedagogy.

Helping educators reach every student is the goal of this book. Increasing awareness of diversity in its various forms will be a positive step in reaching that goal. Teachers may not be able to be fully versed in all facets of diversity at all times, but having some basic foundational knowledge about the differences students may present is why nearly all teacher educator programs require a diversity course. As well they should. Teachers need to embrace the diversity of their classrooms if they are fully invested in their students' ability to achieve.

As American author Neale Donald Walsch (2000) wrote, "Build your school around concepts, not academic subjects: core concepts such as awareness, honesty, responsibility, freedom, and diversity in oneness. Teach your children these things and you will have taught them grandly." Teachers can be the ultimate role models and should be modeling attitudes that promote awareness, honesty, responsibility, freedom, and a respect for diversity. This book will strive to help teachers better grasp those attributes and demonstrate them when succeeding with the great diversity in today's classrooms.

Some important takeaways from this introductory chapter include:

- Modern classrooms are becoming increasingly diverse, and there are many ways to identify diversity, including ability levels, socioeconomic status, gender, and race/ethnicity.

- Teachers cannot give in to the ethnocentrism that seems to characterize many human beings.

- Although the student population in the United States is growing increasingly ethnically diverse, the same does not hold true for the vast majority of teachers in American classrooms.

- Teachers can be most effective in the classroom when they get to know their students beyond a superficial level.

- While it is only one type of diversity, cultural diversity is impactful in classrooms, and teachers should engage in culturally responsive pedagogy to ensure they reach the greatest number of students.

- Our schools will benefit from acknowledging that their role is not strictly limited to academics and that teachers have an opportunity to be a profoundly positive influence on students, instilling in those students important values, such as a respect for diversity.

REFERENCES

Kinder, D. R., & Kam, C. D. (2009). *Us against them: Ethnocentric foundations of American opinion*. University of Chicago Press.

Powell, W., & Kusuma-Powell, O. (2011). *How to teach now: Five keys to personalized learning in the global classroom*. ASCD.

Richards, H. V., Brown, A. F., & Forde, T. B. (2007). Addressing diversity in schools: Culturally responsive pedagogy. *Teaching Exceptional Children, 39*(3), 64–68.

Steenbergen-Hu, S., Makel, M. C., & Olszewski-Kubilius, P. (2016). What one hundred years of research says about the effects of ability grouping and acceleration on K–12 students' academic achievement: Findings of two second-order meta-analyses. *Review of Educational Research, 86*(4), 849–99.

Taie, S., & Goldring, R. (2018). *Characteristics of public elementary and secondary school teachers in the United States: Results from the 2015–16 National Teacher and Principal Survey First Look (NCES 2017-072rev)*. National Center for Education Statistics. http://nces.ed.gov/pubsearch/pubsinfo.ap?pubid=2017072rev

U.S. Department of Education. (2016). *The state of racial diversity in the educator workforce*.

Walsch, N. D. (2000). *Communion with God.* Berkley.

Wells, A. S., Fox, L., & Cordova-Cobo, D. (2016). *How racially diverse classrooms and schools can benefit all learners*. Century Foundation. https://tcf.org/content/report/how-racially-diverse-schools-and-classrooms-can-benefit-all-students/?agreed=1

The Interview Begins

Kortney Wicks looked at herself in her car's rearview mirror. She wanted to make sure, one last time, that her hair and makeup were just right. She was nervous but doing her best to show no outward signs. Today was her big day, her first interview for a teaching position. She had not even finished her student teaching semester and felt some pride that she was being considered for a job before she even graduated. Satisfied with what she saw in the mirror, she stepped out of the car and looked toward the school.

South Jameson Elementary was in a small city and only a half-hour's drive from Kortney's university. She had heard of the school but had never been placed there to gain any field experience. As she researched the school, she had learned it was a Title 1 school, with a very diverse population of students. There were more than 400 students in kindergarten through sixth grade, with approximately 65% of those students qualifying for free or reduced lunch. Kortney caught herself for a moment, remembering she should not judge any school by its socioeconomic demographics. She knew it was best to keep an open mind going into an interview and that, as her instructors and cooperating teachers had told her, having preconceived notions about a school and teaching position could hurt a candidate during an interview. Still, she could not help herself as she looked around the perimeter of the school and noticed several dilapidated houses.

Closing her eyes to get her thoughts back on track, Kortney quickly reviewed the practice questions her roommate had thrown at her over the past few days. She felt very comfortable there would be no surprise questions during the interview. She was having a great semester in the classroom and getting very positive marks from her university supervisor. Feedback on her evaluation forms had given her ideas on what strengths she wanted to convey in the interview and also her areas for professional growth. She felt ready. She opened her eyes and started walking toward the school's front entrance.

"Welcome to our wonderful school, where every child has value and a willingness to learn," proclaimed a large banner over the front entrance. The banner was white with bold red letters, and at the end of the welcoming statement was a picture of an eagle. It looked majestic as it appeared to leap off the banner and head for the skies. On the door she was about to enter, Kortney saw a poster. It read, "Be Respectful, Be Responsible, Be Kind, and Be Safe." It reminded Kortney of some of the

Positive Behavioral Intervention and Supports programs she had learned about during her teacher education courses. She hoped South Jameson had such a program up and running. She reached for the button on the intercom to the right of the door, which she had to press to gain entrance.

She was buzzed in after briefly stating why she was there. She walked into the main office and was met by the secretary, who asked her to have a seat, as the principal had been delayed a few minutes. Kortney took the seat and scanned the small, simple office/reception area. There was nothing ostentatious about the area; it seemed designed to serve its purpose and nothing more. There were a few pictures of students and faculty members on the walls, along with more posters encouraging positive thoughts, attitudes, and behaviors. The receptionist remained at her desk, her focus on her computer. Everything was strangely quiet, and no students, teachers, or parents came into the office while Kortney was waiting for Mrs. Frayer, the school principal. The wait was not very long.

Mrs. Frayer strode into the office in a hurry and glanced toward Kortney. She paused a beat and seemed to be thinking about who this person sitting in the office might be. Realization came quickly, and she extended her hand and said, "Ms. Wicks? I'm Rhonda Frayer. Welcome to South Jameson. Let's go in my office and talk." And in less than 10 minutes, Kortney realized she was nowhere near as prepared for the interview as she had originally thought.

The interview had begun normally enough with some small talk about Kortney's student teaching experience and who she knew at various schools in the surrounding area. Mrs. Frayer shared that she had been in education for nearly 30 years and was in her seventh year as the principal at South Jameson. She asked Kortney why she wanted to be a teacher and some general questions about classroom management, working with other teachers, and working with parents. All of those questions had been part of Kortney's preparation for the interview, and she felt she answered all pretty well. Then Mrs. Frayer paused and put down the notepad she had been using to record short notes on Kortney's answers. She leaned back in her chair and asked, "Kortney, please tell me your definition of diversity."

Kortney paused. She had expected some questions about teaching diverse student populations or meeting the needs of diverse learners; she had not expected to be asked so bluntly to provide her own definition of diversity. Her pause lengthened, and she felt that Mrs. Frayer was somehow judging her because she was taking too long to answer. She attempted to buy some time by asking, "Is there a particular type of diversity you mean?"

"No," Mrs. Frayer said. "Just the term *diversity* itself, please."

"Well," Kortney began, immediately regretting starting a sentence with that famously overused delaying term, "I think diversity comes in many forms. We have cultural diversity. We have socioeconomic diversity. We have ethnic diversity. We have diversity based on life experiences. We have educational diversity. It's hard for me to summarize all of those different types in one single answer."

Mrs. Frayer sat forward. "Yes, there are many types of diversity when you start breaking it down into separate categories, including the ones you just listed," she said. "But I'm asking for a holistic overview of the term. What does it mean to you on a foundational level? Think of word association. I say 'diversity' and you think what?"

"Ethnicity," Kortney responded. She was immediately surprised at her answer. Had she not been taught repeatedly that no one should ever try to summarize diversity by starting with racial differences? She had been taught that, and yet her reflexive response had seemingly betrayed some underlying belief she held about what constituted diversity.

Before she could try and recover, Mrs. Frayer held up her hand, indicating Kortney should hold off before continuing. "It's okay, Ms. Wicks. I get that answer a lot, in some form or fashion," she said. "I think a lot of teachers in this building would say the same thing if they had to answer right away. We, and by 'we' I mean society in general, seem to always think about racial diversity first. Do you agree with that, in general?"

Kortney knew her answer had spoken for itself. "Yes, I suppose that is the way we choose to think about diversity, right out of the gate," she said. She was surprised to hear her own voice, how it had grown softer and lost some of the energy and boldness she conveyed in earlier answers. She waited to hear what Mrs. Frayer would say next.

"I'm not trying to intimidate you or confuse you with the question," Mrs. Frayer said. "I have to take the concept very seriously. South Jameson has gotten more diverse in multiple different ways since I became principal. And I'm not just talking about Caucasian, African American, Latino, Asian American, and other ethnic categories. We've got students here from the Sudan, and we've got students here from Ukraine. But that's just one part of it."

Mrs. Frayer paused briefly before continuing. "We can talk about socioeconomic diversity, of course. There's a great deal of that here. I'm confident you looked up that demographic information before you came in for this interview. Don't get hung up on the percentage of students receiving free and reduced lunch. Every school has to deal with that factor. And at the end of the day it doesn't really matter if the students are rich, poor, or middle class, we teach them all. You do know the foundation for public education in the United States, the driving concept?"

Kortney thought for a moment, and said, "Do you mean a free and appropriate public education? FAPE? We did learn about that, but it was in my special education course and I don't recall hearing it much anywhere else."

Mrs. Frayer nodded. "Yes," she said. "FAPE. The idea that we are here to provide all children with an education. It's a concept all teachers must take to heart, I believe, and the most challenging word in that principle, I think, is *appropriate*, because what's appropriate for one is rarely appropriate for all. And that brings me back to diversity."

Mrs. Frayer stood, walked around her desk, and looked at some pictures on her office wall. Kortney could see they were pictures of various classes and noticed they were all sixth grade. She guessed Mrs. Frayer kept them as reminders of the classes that had moved on from South Jameson. After a long moment, Mrs. Frayer turned back to Kortney.

"I'm not trying to make you feel uncomfortable with all of this," she said. "I just want to know that a prospective teacher at my school can view diversity with a capital D. Can get a sense of the idea of diversity being so much bigger than most people realize. When you hear someone talk about a diverse student population, I really don't think they understand what that means. Working here will certainly expose you to broad-scale diversity. Can you handle that, Ms. Wicks? Do you think you can embrace diversity, in whatever form it may take, and teach every student?"

A Teacher's Influence

Dr. Lisa F. Etheridge

Setting the Classroom Scene

Brandon isn't your typical first-grade student. He has struggled to stay on task with his work in the classroom. Some days he has even struggled just to stay in his seat. Brandon is a wonderful kid, but he has struggled this year in first grade. He is a great student at math, but he has struggled with reading and has tried to avoid it. Brandon's teacher, Mrs. Robinson, started working with him one-on-one using beginning sound books. At first, he was reluctant and not happy that they were working together on improving his reading skills. But Mrs. Robinson and Brandon kept at it, and after a few weeks, Brandon was able to read a small book independently. He was so proud! He showed everyone, including his classmates, that he could read. Mrs. Robinson will not soon forget the joy in his eyes, knowing that it stemmed from the fact that he had learned how to read. Mrs. Robinson wants to find that joy in all of her students because she believes there is nothing like seeing the realization of accomplishment in their eyes.

Prereading Questions

1. What qualities or characteristics did Mrs. Robinson possess in the above scenario?

2. Why are the qualities or characteristics listed in your answer to the previous question important for teachers to possess?

3. How did the qualities or characteristics of Mrs. Robinson affect Brandon in learning to read?

Introduction

If you asked a group of students what makes a great teacher, you would most likely get a variety of responses, reflecting the current challenge faced by school administrators and school districts when evaluating the effectiveness of a classroom teacher. Bell, Bell, and Little (2008), however, suggested that effective teachers exhibited some common qualities or traits that, when implemented, can positively influence student learning. The following are the qualities or characteristics they found:

- Contribute to positive academics, attitudinal, and social/emotional outcomes for students.

- Use diverse resources to plan and structure engaging learning opportunities, monitor student progress formatively, adapt instruction as needed, and evaluate learning using multiple sources of evidence.

- Contribute to the development of classrooms and schools that value diversity and civic mindedness.

- Collaborate with other teachers, administrators, parents, and educator professionals to ensure student success, particularly the success of students with special needs and those at high risk for failure.

- Have high expectations for all students and help all students in learning.

This chapter will discuss in detail some of the factors that make up these qualities and characteristics, which effective teachers should possess to positively affect and influence students and student learning.

A teacher affects eternity; no one can tell where their influence stops.
—**Henry Brooks Adams**

Teacher Beliefs

Teachers' beliefs and practices are important for understanding and improving educational processes. They are closely linked to teachers' strategies for coping with challenges in their daily professional lives and to their general well-being, and they shape students' learning environment and influence student motivation and achievement. Furthermore, they can be expected to mediate the effects of job-related policies such as changes in curricula for teachers' initial education or professional development on student learning.

Kagan (1992) defined teacher beliefs as "often unconsciously held assumptions about students, classrooms, and the academic material to be taught" (p. 65). Teacher beliefs may be influenced by life experiences, their preservice education experiences, the students they teach at any given moment, and the school in which they are teaching (Calderhead & Robson, 1991; Walsh, 2006). Teachers' instructional practices are influenced in different ways by these beliefs as they consider methods and materials to provide for effective lessons (Pajares, 1992). Additionally, what teachers say and do in their classrooms is governed by what they think, and teachers' theories and beliefs serve as a filter through which instructional judgments and decisions are made. The beliefs teachers hold not only shape teachers' pedagogy but also shape classroom interactions and decision making (Li, 2013).

Phipps and Borg (2009) noted that teachers' belief systems may outweigh the contents learned in a teacher education program when it comes to the instructional decisions they make about their day-to-day lessons. That said, not all teachers have the ability to articulate their beliefs (Senior, 2006), and not all beliefs articulate exactly what teachers believe (Basturkmen, 2012), as some beliefs may be held with varying levels of conviction (Thompson, 1992).

Pause and Discuss	In a small group, discuss the pros and cons of teacher beliefs. Also, discuss some teacher beliefs that you may have and why. Be ready to share those beliefs and how you believe they could influence your preparation as an educator.

Teacher Attitudes

Teachers have the opportunity to leave an enduring impression on their students' lives. School experiences can mold, shape, and influence how children view themselves inside and outside of school. These school memories have the potential to last a lifetime in students' minds and can play a consequential role with current and future decisions (Gourneau, 2005).

Attitude is a very important attribute for a teacher. It affects students in many ways and can shape their learning experience. As a teacher, you will sometimes have a bad day or experience stress, but responding with a negative attitude will only make matters worse and will not positively affect the students or their learning. According to Florin Sava (2002), teachers' use of humiliation, fear, and intimidation can cause students to develop habit disorders, shyness, withdrawal, and anxiety. In some cases, negative teacher attitudes produce such strong feelings of anxiety that students develop physical symptoms, such as skeletal aches, muscle cramps, lack of energy, upset stomach, and neck tension (Sava, 2001). Such stress-related illnesses not only harm students' physical well-being, they also disrupt students' abilities to focus in class.

Teacher attitudes displayed by effective teachers demonstrate an overall positive attitude that shows genuine caring and kindness, a willingness to share responsibility, a sincere sensitivity to diversity, a motivation to provide meaningful learning experiences, and an enthusiasm for stimulating students' creativity (Gourneau, 2005). We will now take a look at each of these characteristics.

Caring and Kindness

Effective teachers willingly share emotions and feelings (e.g., enthusiasm, affection, patience, sadness, disapproval) and a sincere interest in and caring toward their students. Communication is also valued, and feelings are openly expressed by both the students and the teacher.

Sharing Responsibility

Effective teachers strive to establish a shared environment. An effective teacher must not be overly possessive or need complete control of the students and the environment. It is important to allow students both responsibility and freedom within the classroom community.

Accepting Diversity

Effective teachers know the importance of understanding their students. Effective teachers understand that sensitivity, acceptance, and encouragement are critical when approaching issues associated with student diversity. In addition, effective teachers understand their students without analyzing or judging. It is critical for students to feel positive about themselves as individuals to gain the self-confidence to try new things. Verbally praising a shy or friendless child can be a turning point for that child's self-esteem and confidence level. A child may be born with a talent, but someone—such as a teacher—needs to realize and believe in it or it may never be nurtured. A teacher has the ability to reinforce, support, and appreciate the work and play of their students.

Fostering Individualized Instruction

Effective teachers provide meaningful learning opportunities for all students. When provided with motivating activities and lessons, students become active and independent agents of their own learning. Learning should become an open adventure that does not lead down one straight and narrow path; instead, many roads should be provided that lead to a variety of destinations. Students have the right to travel with an encouraging facilitator or teacher waiting at each roadblock or to challenge with a smile and an optimistic attitude that encourages them to continue their learning adventures. All students need to have a form of individualized instruction and be actively involved in their learning.

Encouraging Creativity

Effective teachers know the importance of stimulating students' creativity. When given the opportunity to be creative, students will take their learning to higher levels and become actively engaged in lessons by contributing ideas and insights. Teachers should capitalize on students' intrinsic motivation, cognitive learning styles, and skill levels. This type of environment will be most conducive to fostering learning.

As you can now see, the attitude of a teacher, either consciously or unconsciously, directly or indirectly, affects students' academic performance. Shittu and Oanite (2015) found that teachers' attitudes highly influence students' interest in learning. Teachers' professional attitude in the areas of communication, classroom management, and pedagogy may be a strong factor that could influence students' academic performance in schools. Positive professional attitudes of teachers will go a long way in bringing about positive performance of the students, while negative attitudes demonstrated by teachers in the classroom will not only bring about subpar academic performance but, more importantly, may bring about negative psychological issues for students.

> *Attitude is a little thing that makes a big difference.*
> —**Winston Churchill**

Write a short paragraph describing your personal experiences with a teacher who demonstrated a negative attitude in the classroom and a teacher who demonstrated a positive attitude in the classroom. Be ready to discuss how the experiences with these two teachers made you feel as a student.	Pause and Reflect

Mindsets

As a teacher, your mindset plays a critical role in how you cope with life's challenges and how others, such as students, perceive you as the teacher. A recent study conducted by Gutshall (2016) surveyed 126 students and seven teachers regarding the teachers' mindsets or the perception of their mindsets in regard to student learning and achievement. The results suggest that a teacher's mindset (fixed or growth) or the perception of a teacher's mindset affects students and their achievements. The results of the study also demonstrate that students both recognize or perceive that teachers have a mindset and also whether that mindset is a fixed or growth mindset. This recognition or perception can either positively or negatively affect students and their abilities to learn and grow (Gutshall, 2016).

Carol Dweck (2006) explained there are two types of mindsets: fixed and growth. People with a fixed mindset tend to create a need for approval. "I've seen so many people with this one consuming goal of proving themselves in the classroom, in their careers, and in their relationships," Dweck (2006, p. 12) stated. Dweck (2006) said a person with a fixed mindset sees every situation as a call for a confirmation of their intelligence, personality, or character. Every situation is evaluated: Will I succeed or fail? Will I look smart or dumb? Will I be accepted or rejected? Will I feel like a winner or a loser? Some examples of teacher behaviors or decisions that illuminate a fixed mindset are: (1) a teacher keeps her intervention or ability groups the same because she says she knows the students and their abilities, and the ability levels of the students will not change; (2) a colleague is asked to teach collaboratively with another grade-level teacher, who responds that he would prefer not to teach collaboratively because he already has everything organized and working well and doesn't need to adjust anything for his students; and (3) after the majority of the students in a class fail a math test, the teacher reviews the test scores and concludes that it was the students' fault because they didn't study for the test.

In growth mindsets, however, people have a desire to work hard and discover new things. They want to tackle challenges and grow as a person. When people with a growth mindset try and fail, they tend not to view it as a failure or disappointment. Instead, they see it as a learning experience that can lead to growth and change. Some examples of teacher behaviors or decisions based on a growth mindset are: (1) a teacher praises her students on the process and effort they took in solving a problem, rather than praising them for simply getting the correct solution; (2) a teacher consistently attends professional development/learning opportunities, and when one of his colleagues asks him why, he replies, "I attend because I need to continually grow and learn and to stay abreast of the latest instructional strategies to teach my students effectively"; and (3) a teacher reflects on the scores of a math test she gave last week in which most of her students failed, and she concludes that she didn't teach the content effectively enough and decides to reteach the content using different instructional strategies.

What Is Your Mindset?

Do you have a fixed or growth mindset? Read the following statements and decide which ones you agree with most.

1. People have a certain amount of intelligence, and there isn't any way to change it.

2. No matter who you are, there isn't much you can do to improve your basic abilities and personality.

3. People are capable of changing who they are.

4. You can learn new things and improve your intelligence.

5. People either have particular talents or they don't. You can't just acquire talent for things such as music, writing, art, or athletics.

6. Studying, working hard, and practicing new skills are all ways to develop new talents and abilities.

If you tend to agree with statements 1, 2, and 5, you probably have a more fixed mindset. But if you agree with statements 3, 4, and 6, you probably have a growth mindset (Cherry, 2020).

Changing Teacher Mindsets

If your result was a fixed mindset from the quiz, the first question that might come to mind as a future teacher is, "How can I change my mindset?" First, let's review the difference between a fixed and a growth mindset. Dweck (2006) defined a growth mindset as the belief that intelligence can be developed. People with a growth mindset understand that they can get smarter through hard work, the use of effective strategies, and help from others when needed. In contrast, a fixed mindset is the belief that intelligence is a fixed trait that is set in stone at birth. Some characteristics of a fixed mindset include sticking with what one knows works, believing putting forth effort is worthless, believing personal failure(s) define who one is, hiding flaws in order not to be judged, tending to give up easily, ignoring feedback from others, viewing personal feedback as criticism, and feeling threatened by the success of others.

Because they are more likely to establish high expectations for students, effective teachers exhibit a growth mindset, making instruction engaging and offering extra help when necessary. Teachers with a growth mindset genuinely believe each of their students is capable of learning the material, and they use strategies to unlock hidden potential. They also believe that mistakes are an essential component of learning. In addition, they believe that failures are temporary setbacks, welcome feedback from others in order to learn, and view others' success as a source of inspiration and information.

Now that we have reviewed what fixed and growth mindsets are, let's take a look at some examples of what teachers in a fixed mindset might say and how they can respond differently using a growth mindset (Kline, 2020).

- Fixed Mindset: **"I'm just not good at technology."**

  - Growth Mindset Responses:

    - "I know that technology is always updating, and I'm choosing to do the same thing."

    - "I teach my students to learn important skills that help their learning, even if these skills are difficult and take time. I need to do the same when learning new technology."

- Fixed Mindset: **"That student is just lazy."**

  - Growth Mindset Responses:

    - "I believe that all children can be motivated, and it's my profession to discover how."

    - "I'm dedicated to trying new ways each day to motivate my students, even the most challenging."

- Fixed Mindset: **"That family just doesn't care."**

  - Growth Mindset Responses:

    - "I know that this family may face realities that I'm unaware of, and I'm working hard to learn more about them."

    - "I'm trying creative ways to connect with this family, as I know how important teacher-family collaboration is for a child's academic and social growth."

- Fixed Mindset: **"I just figured this out, and now we're changing it?"**

  - Growth Mindset Responses:

"I know that change is inevitable, and it's essential that I'm a flexible professional."

"I'm teaching my students to be flexible lifelong learners, and I need to model this when school changes occur."

Fixed Mindset: "**If that student wastes my time, I'll just waste theirs.**"

Growth Mindset Responses:

"Taking away recess does not address nor teach solutions to a student's time-management issues. It's my job to teach specific strategies to support this learning."

"This child struggles with self-management skills. It's my job to teach specific strategies to support this learning."

Fixed Mindset: "**The media is always bashing our profession; there's nothing I can do.**"

Growth Mindset Response:

"How can I use social media to share the positive stories occurring daily in my school?"

Fixed Mindset: "**But this has always just worked fine for me.**"

Growth Mindset Response:

"I'm continually learning new ways to do what's best for my students, not what's best or easiest for me."

As teachers, mindset is the core set of beliefs that become the lenses through which we see, interpret, and respond to our students (Dweck, 2006; Gergen, 2015; McGonigal, 2015). If mindsets are the way we see, take in, and then respond to students, then a growth mindset could be understood as the capacity to notice, seek out, and magnify opportunities for safety, positive relationships, learning, play, and enjoyment (Cherkowski, Hanson, & Walker, 2018). The more we see the world as an opportunity to grow, the more we seem to find opportunities for this to happen.

Pause and Discuss	In a small group, discuss what type of mindset you scored. If you scored a fixed mindset, discuss how you will begin to change your mindset to a growth mindset. Also, discuss why a growth mindset is important to have as a teacher. Be ready to share your responses.

Teacher Self-Efficacy

Teachers' self-efficacy is a powerful influence that explains teachers' behaviors and has an effect on students' motivation and achievement. The construct of self-efficacy evolved out of Bandura's (1997) social cognitive theory, which focused on the ways human behavior is influenced by cognitive processes.

Bandura (1997) proposed four sources of self-efficacy beliefs: enactive mastery experience, vicarious experience, verbal persuasion, and physiological and effective states. The most significant and powerful source of self-efficacy is enactive mastery experiences, or "performance attainments" (Bandura, 1997, p. 399). When a person experiences success in a certain situation, they will hold high expectations of success in similar situations in the future; failures, however, lower these expectations. Obstacles and difficulties inform individuals that successes necessitate persistent effort. "A resilient sense of efficacy requires experience in overcoming obstacles through perseverant effort" (Bandura, 1995, p. 3). An example of enactive mastery experience is providing students with assignments or tasks that progress from easy to difficult levels. Successfully accomplishing progressively difficult tasks helps students realize that they are competent and capable, which in turn raises their expectation levels.

The second source of efficacy that influences the development of efficacy beliefs is vicarious experience (Bandura, 1997). Vicarious experiences are people's judgments about their abilities to successfully perform a task based on the performance of similar others (Bandura, 1997). Observing someone performing a certain task successfully informs the observer that he or she is capable of achieving the same results. Likewise, seeing someone fail decreases the observer's efficacy. Models influence individuals' efficacy beliefs when they see the model as similar to them (Bandura, 1995). An example of a vicarious experience is a preservice teacher teaching a lesson or activity in front of peers in a college class. The college classroom is a safe environment in which to teach a lesson or conduct an activity and receive feedback and to observe other preservice students teach their lessons.

Verbal persuasion is the third source of beliefs about self-efficacy. Through verbal feedback from another person about their performance, individuals' sense of efficacy increases, and they are more likely to put their effort into accomplishing the task (Bandura, 1995, 1997). An example of verbal persuasion is providing positive encouragement and support to students as they work through their assignments or tasks. Examples might include "Great job, Brandon" or "I like how you are trying different strategies to solve the problem, Mary Beth."

Finally, physiological reactions, such as stress and anxiety, influence people's assessment of their abilities (Bandura, 1997). Stress might be interpreted as "signs of vulnerability to poor performance" (Bandura, 1995, p. 4). A strong reaction to performing a task allows one to predict success or failure (Usher & Pajares, 2009). The way people interpret these physiological reactions influences their efficacy beliefs. An example of psychological reactions is to allow preservice students to teach lessons in a variety of environments (field placements) so that they can experience different levels of stress and anxiety in their teaching, which builds their self-efficacy.

Teaching, by its very nature, involves solving ill-defined problems that are complex, dynamic, and nonlinear. Consequently, teacher effectiveness is largely dependent on how teachers define tasks, employ strategies, view the possibility of success, and ultimately solve the problems and challenges they face. Listed below are some ideas that can be implemented to help improve teacher self-efficacy, which in turn will enhance student achievement. This list isn't exhaustive by any means, but by supporting teachers and improving their self-efficacy, teachers will have more influence with students and ultimately improve student achievement.

1. **Show the data:**

For some teachers, the most convincing argument is to see their students' test data, as a whole class, in black and white. If the collective data shows little to no student progress over a period of time, then the teacher needs to reflect on what they could do differently and should bear in mind that the beliefs of teachers profoundly influence what happens in the classroom for students.

> Example: A teacher attends a grade-level data meeting after school. The data show little to no progress of her entire class over the previous 9 weeks. The teacher seems puzzled and begins to reflect on what she could have done differently and what she could change moving forward to help students learn and improve the data.

2. Network and collaborate:

Teachers learn best when learning from other teachers and when their learning is self-directed. This type of professional development could be an opportunity for teachers to take something of their own to network with other teachers and then see how it affects their own learning—or, better yet, student learning. Some teachers believe that networking will help improve their classroom objectives, and by collaborating with other teachers, a teacher can see the effect of efficacy in other rooms.

> Example: The third-grade teachers at ABC Elementary School decide to start a professional learning community in which they will meet each week. Each teacher will be responsible for sharing ideas and instructional strategies with other members and for determining content areas in which they could collaborate with one another.

3. Coaching/reflective questioning:

By using reflective questioning, teachers see how factors within their control can create change with students. For most of us, just being "told" to change won't actually change anything—we need to work through it ourselves from the inside out.

> Example: Even as instructional coaches attempt to come into the classroom and, alongside the teachers, offer support and helpful suggestions to enhance instruction, teachers should ask themselves reflective questions to gain a clear understanding of what went right with the lesson and what they might need to change. Some examples of reflective questions they might ask are:
>
> (1) What did I notice about student learning?
> (2) I wonder what would have happened if I had done … ?
> (3) What did I notice about the instructional strategies I used in connection with student learning?
> (4) How does this information assist me in deciding my next steps?

4. Approach from another angle:

There are other ways to help teachers "see" the possibility of their impact, including student feedback. Listed below are some examples of ways to gather student feedback.

> Examples: student surveys, student exit slips, student conferences, student focus groups

5. **Challenge all excuses:**

As discussions occur within the school and within teams, teacher leaders must not hesitate when challenging the excuses that teachers make. If the conversation begins with "Parents these days ..." we need to hit the pause button and refocus. This should be done with professionalism and kindness, and the practice can stem the tide of teacher efficacy if it becomes part of the culture.

> Example: The grade-level chair calls a meeting to discuss the latest 9-weeks' benchmark data. As the meeting starts, a teacher states that she is tired of dealing with two students and their behavior. She continues to talk about how their parents allow them to do as they please and that there is no discipline in the home. She also says the parents are the reason her test scores are not good. The grade-level chair immediately interjects and professionally states that they are going to focus on the data and how they as a grade level could make changes to better assist the students. The meeting continues and goes smoothly, with no other excuses given.

6. **If possible, remove barriers to success:**

Some excuses can be real barriers to helping teachers improve. When we get into efficacy, we can start to dismiss any excuse as just a teacher's desire not to change. This may be the case, but a teacher might also have a legitimate reason for the suggestion/excuse. As much as possible, we should remove these from the mindset of teachers to help them see what they are doing as meaningful.

> Example: A veteran fourth-grade reading teacher who has 23 years of experience in the classroom is being moved to sixth grade to teach mathematics. While the teacher knows she has been a great teacher in fourth grade, she says she isn't good at math and will not be able to effectively teach the students. The administrator encourages her not to think like that and says she will be just fine in sixth grade. At the end of the school year, the veteran teacher has the highest test scores in the school district for sixth-grade mathematics.

> *Perceived self-efficacy influences the types of causal attributions people make for their performances.*
>
> **—Albert Bandura**

Pause and Discuss

In a small group, discuss how a teacher's sense of efficacy can affect his or her teaching and ultimately influence student achievement. Be ready to share your thoughts.

Professional Development

Today's education policy places a high priority on improving teacher quality and teaching effectiveness in U.S. schools. Standards-based professional learning requires teachers to have deep subject knowledge and the most effective pedagogy for teaching the subject. States and school districts are charged with establishing teacher professional development programs, some with federal funding support, designed to address the significant needs for improved teacher preparation (Blank, 2013).

A review and analysis of the characteristics of professional learning and development follows. While obviously not exhaustive, these characteristics are presented to help establish a basic understanding of professional development for teachers.

1. Content focus

The primary goal of all professional learning is to improve and increase the content knowledge of teachers. Effective teachers stay abreast of new content and skills that they need to know and be able to teach effectively. They willingly attend professional learning opportunities with their students in mind.

2. More time (contact hours) for professional learning

While each state mandates a certain number of professional learning clock hours for teachers to complete every 5 years, effective teachers go above and beyond the minimum expectations. They understand that teaching is a lifelong learning process.

3. Longer duration of professional learning

Years ago, teachers were expected to attend teacher workshops to satisfy their professional learning requirements for their school districts. Today, effective teachers attend professional learning that may include summer institutes with follow-up training during the school year. They also may receive sustained professional development such as coaching and mentoring to improve their teaching practices.

4. Multiple professional learning activities and active learning methods

The most effective professional learning methods that effective teachers participate in include coaching, mentoring, internships, professional networks, and study groups. During this professional learning, teachers may be asked to lead instruction, have a discussion with colleagues, observe other teachers, develop assessments, and develop and participate in professional networks.

5. Learning goals in professional learning design

Effective teachers focus on improving teacher knowledge of how students learn and how to teach the subject or content with effective strategies. They take professional learning seriously and establish goals that directly translate into improvements in curriculum and instruction.

6. Collective participation by teachers

Some schools and districts require entire faculties to attend professional learning opportunities at some point. One of the most effective ways to participate in professional learning, however, is through the use of professional learning communities. In these communities, teachers gain a sense of comradery through the sharing of ideas and suggestions and through meaningful discussion on how to improve their teaching practices.

> Write a short paragraph on the importance of professional development for teachers. Be ready to share two or three important points from your reading.
>
> Pause and Reflect

Conclusion

Education is an important tool that can shape an individual and allow creative opportunity and growth. Teachers are important role models for students and have a significant effect on helping shape, create, support, and establish students' strengths and knowledge. This chapter attempted to provide you with some characteristics that effective teachers possess that in turn positively influence students and student achievement. It is important for all teachers to understand that they possess personality traits, beliefs, mindsets, and attitudes that play a tremendous role in the success of their students.

KEY CHAPTER TAKEAWAYS

Some important takeaways from this chapter include:

- Teacher beliefs are developed from life experiences, preservice experiences, and knowledge.
- Instructional practices and decisions are influenced by teacher beliefs.
- What teachers say and do is influenced by teacher beliefs.
- Teacher attitudes can positively or negatively affect students and student achievement.
- Positive teacher attitudes foster student growth and creativity.
- Negative teacher attitudes stifle student growth and creativity.
- The mindset of teachers influences students and their learning.
- A growth mindset fosters an exploratory classroom that is motivational and creative.
- One way to positively influence teachers' self-efficacy is to network and collaborate with other teachers.
- Effective teachers consistently want to improve their craft through professional development opportunities.

CASE SCENARIO: THE INTERVIEW CONTINUES

"I'd like to get your thoughts on what you think makes a teacher effective," Mrs. Frayer said. Kortney smiled and began to gather her thoughts. She hoped she had answered well so far but was unsure.

"This example is about a fourth-grade teacher who has 18 years of teaching experience," Mrs. Frayer began. "Her departmentalized classroom is a diverse classroom with all ability levels." She then presented the following scenario to Kortney:

Mrs. Roberts was being observed for her yearly evaluation, and Mrs. Frayer noticed that some of the students in the classroom were struggling to understand the math concept Mrs. Roberts was teaching. Mrs. Roberts kept going over problems on the Elmo, explaining step-by-step how to solve the problem. Then she passed out a worksheet and instructed the students to complete it and place it in the basket when finished. Mrs. Roberts began to walk around the classroom and observe the students working, but she never offered to assist those students who were struggling. At the debriefing of the yearly evaluation, Mrs. Frayer asked Mrs. Roberts why she didn't assist the struggling students. "Those are the slow students, and no matter how much you explain it to them, they will not get it," Mrs. Roberts answered. "This is the way I have always taught, and there has never been a problem with it."

WORKING WITH THE SCENARIO

"Needless to say," Mrs. Frayer began, "I was not exactly thrilled with how Mrs. Roberts responded after the observation."

"I can understand why," Kortney said.

"So, given that short story," Mrs. Frayer continued, "what do you think would have been a better response? How would you suggest Mrs. Roberts can change her mindset? And I'm curious if you think there might be any kind of professional development out there that might help Mrs. Roberts."

"Those are some tough questions," Kortney answered.

"Yes, they are," Mrs. Frayer said. "And here are two more. What do Mrs. Roberts's actions say about her beliefs as a teacher, and if you were in my position, what are some ideas you might suggest to her to change those beliefs?"

If you were Kortney, how would you answer Mrs. Frayer's questions?

REFERENCES

Bandura, A. (Ed.). (1995). *Self-Efficacy in changing societies.* Cambridge University Press

Bandura, A. (1997). *Self-Efficacy: The exercise of control.* W. H. Freeman & Co.

Basturkmen, H. (2012). Review of research into the correspondence between language teachers' stated beliefs and practices. *System, 40,* 282–95.

Goe, L., Bell, C., & Little, O. (2008). *Approaches to teacher effectiveness: A research synthesis.* National Comprehensive Center for Teacher Quality.

Blank, R. K. (2013). What research tells us: Common characteristics of professional learning that lead to student achievement. *Journal of Staff Development, 34*(1), 50–53.

Calderhead, J., & Robson, M. (1991). Images of teaching: Student teachers' early conceptions of classroom practice. *Teaching and Teacher Education, 7*(1), 1–8.

Cherkowski, S., Hanson, K. & Walker, K. (2018). *Mindfulness alignment: Foundations of educator flourishing.* Rowan & Littlefield.

Cherry, K. (2020). *Why mindset matters for your success.* Verywell Mind. https://www.verywellmind.com/what-is-a-mindset-2795025

Dweck, C. S. (2006). *Mindset: The new psychology of success.* Random House.

Gergen, K. (2015). *An invitation to social construction* (3rd ed.). SAGE Publications.

Gourneau, B. (2005). Five attitudes for effective teachers: Implications of teacher training. *Essays in Education, 13*, 1–8.

Gutshall, C. (2016). Student perceptions of teachers' mindset: Beliefs in the classroom setting. *Journal of New York Educational and Developmental Psychology, 6*(2), 71–78.

Kagan, D. M. (1992). Implications of research on teacher belief. *Educational Psychologist, 27*, 65–90.

Kline, T. (2020). *Modeling the growth mindset we expect from students.* Changekidslives.org. http://www.changekidslives.org/words-9

Li, L. (2013). The complexity of language teachers' beliefs and practice: One EFL teacher's theories. *Language Learning Journal, 41*(2), 175–91.

McGonigal, K. (2015). *The upside of stress: Why stress is good for you and how to get good at it.* Random House.

Pajares, F. (1992). Teachers' beliefs and educational research: Cleaning up the messy construct. *Review of Educational Research, 62*(3), 307–32.

Phipps, S., & Borg, S. (2009). Exploring tensions between teachers' grammar teaching beliefs and practices. *System, 37*(3), 380–90.

Sava, F. (2002). Causes and effects of teacher conflict inducing attitudes towards pupils: A path analysis model. *Teaching and Teacher Education, 18*, 1007–21.

Senior, R. M. (2006). *The experience of language teaching.* Cambridge University Press.

Shittu, R. O., & Oanite, R. A. (2015). Teachers' attitudes: A great influence on teaching and learning of social studies. *Journal of Law, Policy and Globalization, 42*, 131–37.

Thompson, A. (1992). *Teachers' beliefs and conceptions: A synthesis of the research.* Macmillan.

Usher, E. L., & Pajares, F. (2009). Sources of self-efficacy in mathematics: A validation study. *Contemporary Educational Psychology, 34*(1), 89–101.

Walsh, S. (2006). Talking the talk of the TESOL classroom. *ELT Journal, 60*(2), 133–41.

The Effect of Race/Ethnicity on Learning

Setting the Classroom Scene

Kris Colter was bummed. The school day had ended, but the teachers were having their monthly faculty meeting that afternoon, and this meant no one was going home at a normal time. And this faculty meeting promised to be even duller than most. A professional development session had been added to the end of the meeting, stretching the end time from the normal 4:30 to what honestly felt much worse than only 30 minutes later, 5 p.m. Kris sighed as he walked into the library and looked for his friends/colleagues. He spotted Doug Tomlin and Susan Valian, whom everyone called "An An" because of her alliterative name, toward the back of the meeting area, and he walked over to join them.

As he sat he scanned the room. Sometimes he could get a sense for how a meeting was going to run based on the general mood of the faculty. Just as every class developed its own personality, a school's faculty, when combined in one place, also began to develop a personality. Kris prided himself on reading such personalities, and he was surprised to see his colleagues were not giving off negative or bored vibes. Instead, he noticed a light buzz in the conversations around the room. The small talk would only last until the principal arrived.

"So, what's going on?" he asked his tablemates. "I was expecting this to be pretty bad, but everyone seems oddly cheerful for a faculty meeting."

"Haven't you heard?" Susan responded. "The professional development after the meeting is supposed to be pretty good for once. And given the circumstances, a lot of us want to hear what the speaker has to say."

"Circumstances?" Kris asked, perplexed.

"Buddy, you need to pay more attention," Doug chimed in. "We're getting something like 30 new students next week based on some redistricting issues and some other factors."

"So, what's the big deal about getting more students?" Kris asked. "Our numbers fluctuate from time to time in any given year, and I heard we were getting a particularly large influx. What makes this group so special?"

"It's mostly a cultural thing," Susan answered. "Turns out 25 of the new students are Asian American. A pretty specific ethnic group, I heard, predominantly from South Asia. I think they're called Hmong. When the school board rezoned attendance areas, the new lines put these kids right in our attendance area."

"Guess they, and I mean that collectively, tend to live in the same area once they move in, or their parents moved in," Doug added.

Kris took a moment to let the news sink in, and just before the principal walked in, said, "That's a pretty big shift in our diversity levels. So, this professional development is supposed to get us ready for that somehow?"

"I hope so," Susan answered. "Can't say that many of us are experienced working with Hmong students. And we're all smart enough to know a kid's culture can influence how they learn. I'm hoping this presenter has some good information and advice for us."

Prereading Questions

1. What was the ethnic diversity like at your school? Do you remember ever noticing it or thinking much about it? And if so, what exactly do you remember?

2. Think about your own family and how education was viewed as you were growing up. Did your family emphasize the importance of an education? Were they involved with your school or schools as you progressed toward graduation? What impressions did your family leave on you, specifically in regard to education?

3. Now think outside your family. What do you know about how other cultures or ethnic groups view education? Can you list any specific details about those views? Do you have any experience working with students from different ethnic backgrounds? If so, what do you remember about their ideas and values regarding education?

Introduction

As noted in the introduction of this book, the racial and ethnic diversity in American classrooms continues to increase with each passing year. Also as noted in the introduction, this stands in stark contrast with the steady lack of diversity among the teachers working in the classrooms. This "ethnic divide," if you will, in schools between the student population and the teachers is not a situation that will be resolved by a sudden and drastic increase in teacher diversity. Therefore, it is significant that teachers have a working knowledge of the role race and ethnicity often play in a child's education.

It would be remiss to disregard how issues of race and ethnicity can be—and unfortunately often are—sensitive matters. That is true around the world, and in the United States there is a long history of discriminatory and segregationist practices built on racial divides. It was not until 1954, in the landmark *Brown v. Board of Education* Supreme Court ruling, that school segregation was declared unconstitutional. The court's 1954 decision overturned an earlier ruling from the late 19th century that had established the concept of "separate but equal" (though not in regard to schools, the ruling was used to justify having separate schools for African American students and also separate restrooms in public buildings and restaurants, for example). In 1954 the Supreme Court acknowledged that separate almost never means equal.

And although our nation prides itself on being a "melting pot" that blends diverse races and cultures, there are still obvious signs that, in spite of its illegality, de facto racial segregation is still occurring. An interesting aspect of that reality is how it occurs by individual or family choice, rather than being blatantly implemented by a group or organization. Sociologists have been studying the concept of "white flight" for more than 50 years, as an example of segregation by choice, and have noted evidence that some movement from one school to another is driven by racial factors (e.g., Fairlie & Reisch, 2002). The preceding is not meant to criticize any particular group but rather to note that race/ethnicity is an ongoing, impactful facet of education in modern times. Schools do not have the luxury of ignoring sensitive social matters, including racial/ethnic differences, that may play a significant role in the learning process for most students.

All of this begs a legitimate question: What role does race/ethnicity play in how a child learns? And related to that question: What should teachers know and do in regard to racial/ethnic differences in learning aspirations, preferences, and styles? The remainder of this chapter will attempt to provide basic answers to both of those critical questions. To begin to provide those answers it is necessary to state that race/ethnicity does indeed play a role in education and that teachers should possess a working knowledge of how they can best provide instruction for students from specific racial/ethnic groups.

Education, in the broadest of truest sense, will make an individual seek to help all people, regardless of race, regardless of color, regardless of condition.
—George Washington Carver

A Few Points to Ponder

Before diving fully into how race and ethnicity play a role in education, it is appropriate to provide some context. Table 3.1 presents some interesting data and research results that pertain to educational performance by various ethnic groups, along with educational aspirations of those same groups. The statistics and research evidence presented do not tell the whole story but do provide a basic framework on which to build a knowledge base for race/ethnicity in education.

TABLE 3.1 Education Data and Research Findings for Various Ethnic Groups

	Asian American	African American	Caucasian	Hispanic/ Latino
GRADUATION RATE, 2015–2016 (NCES, 2018B)	91%	76%	88%	79%
PERCENTAGE READING AT OR ABOVE PROFICIENT LEVEL IN EIGHTH GRADE IN 2017 (NCES, 2018A)	55%	18%	45%	23%
PERCENTAGE PERFORMING MATH AT OR ABOVE PROFICIENT LEVEL IN EIGHTH GRADE IN 2017 (NCES, 2018A)	61%	13%	44%	20%
PERCENTAGE OF ADOLESCENTS INCLUDING HIGHER EDUCATION AS A FIVE-YEAR GOAL (TURCIOS-COTTO & MILAN, 2013)	NA	73%	80%	57%
PERCENTAGE OF STUDENTS IN K–12 CLASSROOMS IN THE UNITED STATES IN 2016 (NCES, 2018A)	5%	15%	49%	26%

The data presented in Table 3.1 show some stark differences between ethnicities in just a few areas of education. Significant gaps exist between the reading and math performance in eighth grade when comparing Asian American and Caucasian students with African American and Hispanic/Latino students. A notable discrepancy can be seen in the graduation rates between these four groups as well. Efforts continue to identify causes of the achievement and graduation gaps that exist between Caucasian students and their African American and Hispanic peers (Asian American students are outperforming Caucasian students, so the gap is reversed in that instance), and teachers will play a critical role in closing those gaps for their ethnically diverse students.

Race/Ethnicity and Education

Entire books have been written about the role ethnicity plays in education. A good example is the 2003 work by David Gillborn, *Race, Ethnicity and Education: Teaching and Learning in Multi-ethnic Schools.* In the preface, Gillborn (2003, p. xi) writes:

This book is about "race" in schools. It is about the day-to-day interaction, conflict and negotiation between teachers and pupils of different ethnic backgrounds. It is about education in an unequal society where many white people believe that the best way to handle ethnic diversity is to ignore it.

In this instance the author, right out of the gate, acknowledges the delicacy of his book's topic but does not shy away from it. Gillborn proceeds to recount what he learned during 2 years of intensive study at an inner-city, multiethnic school. Gillborn (2003) compared what he observed during those 2 years with earlier and ongoing research on the role ethnicity plays in education, and he was not surprised to learn that role was significant.

So, what exactly is the role race and ethnicity play in education? Two significant effects have been noted. First, they affect how students respond to curriculum and instruction, and second, they affect teachers' opinions on how these students learn and, very importantly, how much they are capable of achieving (Hawley & Nieto, 2010). Examining those two effects for a moment reveals how they are invariably intertwined. The manner in which a student responds to instruction is going to influence a teacher's opinion on how that student learns; that is a natural reaction from an educator, to form an impression of a student based on that student's reactions to the instruction provided. Focusing on the second effect first brings us to a very sensitive yet validated matter when it comes to ethnicity and education—implicit bias.

Implicit bias has been described as our attitudes or beliefs toward a group of people that occur on a subconscious level. Harvard University has an online implicit bias test, though it is called the Implicit Association Test (IAT). The IAT is available to the public and may be accessed at https://implicit.harvard.edu/implicit/takeatest.html. It is described briefly in the section that follows. Many people who take this particular test are incredulous with the results and often criticize the formatting of the test. The researchers behind this instrument have gone so far as to have a warning statement on the home page, basically stating that if you are worried you might not like the results, maybe you should not take the test.

> **The Harvard Implicit Association Test (IAT):** To take the test, you are tasked with sorting words into two categories, one on the left side of the screen and one on the right. To move words to the left, you push the E key, and to move words to the right, you push the I key. The first part of the test asks you to sort words associated with concepts, and in the second part you sort words related to evaluation. The third part of the IAT asks you to sort words by both concept and evaluation. These words appear and disappear quickly, giving you little time to think before you click a key. And at this point, the test is seeking to assess your subconscious thoughts, not the ones you may provide when given time to consider the pictures more fully. The test provides scores indicating the degree to which we subconsciously hold bias toward particular groups. There are scores for bias toward gender, religion, a disability group, an ethnic group, and a few others.

Implicit bias is vastly different from explicit bias, which is revealed through blatantly prejudicial or discriminatory behaviors. Implicit bias is more insidious in how it lurks beneath the surface, influencing our actions in ways we are unaware of (and if all of this sounds familiar to fans of Malcolm Gladwell, he included an entire section on implicit bias in his 2006 book, *Blink*). The reason implicit bias is part of the discussion on how ethnicity affects education is because, while no teacher will admit to having implicit bias toward ethnically diverse students, research suggests it is a very real factor in how teachers treat these students.

No one is suggesting all teachers are closet racists. The point made in the first chapter, that we are all products of our own cultures, however, is valid. And the truth is, cultures clash, often along racial lines. Again, these clashes are not constant and do not involve everyone, but in education it is negligent to ignore how teachers' perceptions affect their ethnically diverse students. As an example, in a review of 39 research studies, Tenenbaum and Ruck (2007) found that teachers did, on average, have lower expectations for African American students and, furthermore, were more likely to give these students discipline referrals. The research did not explain why teachers treated those students differently, as that answer may be ever elusive, but the results were unfortunately consistent across the studies. Additional research has backed the results found by Tenenbaum and Ruck (e.g., Godsil et al., 2014), and this has increased awareness of the effects of implicit bias on ethnically diverse students.

Switching the focus away from teachers' perceptions, it is necessary to consider how ethnically diverse students respond to instruction, the other component of how race/ethnicity affects education. A good starting point for this content lies in what researchers have termed "race-based social stressors," which include perceived discrimination (the anticipation of discrimination based on one's ethnic group) and stereotype threat (the stress of wanting to perform well to overcome the negative expectations associated with one's ethnic group; Clark et al., 1999; Major & O'Brien, 2005; Miller & Kaiser, 2001). It is interesting to note that the race-based social stressors noted in the research often have physiological effects, which in turn may affect motivation along with cognitive functions, including executive processes such as attention and memory (Levy et al., 2016). Race-based social stressors are not a new phenomenon, though the research on their effects on education has gotten more widespread over the past decade.

Levy et al. (2016) proposed a holistic model that looked at race-based social stressors in combination with additional stressors, including socioeconomic status and resource availability, to demonstrate how those stressors could negatively affect a student's academic achievement, educational aspirations, and physical and mental health (see Figure 3.1).

As the model depicts, the effects of race-based stressors can go beyond just academic achievement. Note how the combination of race-based social stress, recent socioeconomic status-based social stress, and resources all contribute to perceived stress. The perceived stress leads to numerous psychological and biological stress responses, all of which may play a part in a minority student's educational performance. And those responses lead to life outcomes, which are linked to opportunities, including those involved in social and career networks, and one's options based on the economic and policy climate. Though complex, the model proposed by Levy and her colleagues (2016) does provide a comprehensive picture of how a minority student's overall development can be influenced by race-based stressors. The good news is the researchers also found that, long term, a type of resilience was demonstrated by minority students who had found effective emotional and mental coping mechanisms for dealing with stress (Levy et al., 2016). That is a positive for teachers looking to help minority students overcome the potential negatives associated with race-based social stressors.

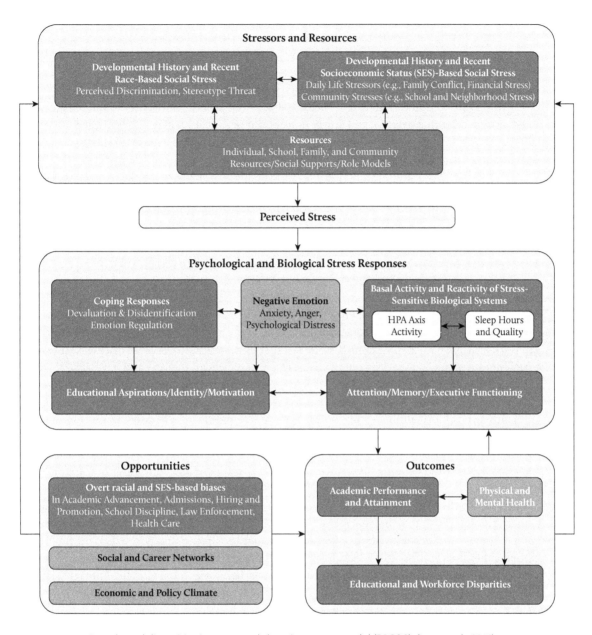

FIGURE 3.1 Race-based disparities in stress and sleep in context model (RDSSC). (Levy et al., 2016)

A last point about the model just cited is to pose the question: Why are race-based social stressors so uniquely impactful for ethnically diverse students? Look at the first two boxes in the RSDSS model and note that both lead with developmental history. If students grow up and attend schools in a society that either directly or indirectly marginalizes their ethnic group in any way, that experience shapes how those students think about and perceive education. It is by no means an absolute certainty that just because a student belongs to a particular ethnicity, they will experience race-based social stressors. But too many of these students appear to experience those stressors, and the ongoing data collections show that our schools are not making adequate progress in closing the achievement gap between certain racial minority groups and Caucasian students.

If we acknowledge that internal factors such as perceptions and stress affect how students learn, we should also consider that parental and family perceptions of education may also influence students from diverse ethnic backgrounds. In his ecological systems theory, Urie Bronfenbrenner proposed four systems in a child's environment that affect how that child develops: the microsystem, the mesosystem, the exosystem, and the macrosystem. The first level, the microsystem, includes a child's family as the first level of influence (Bronfenbrenner, 1994). This theory notes just how critical a role a child's immediate family, in whatever form, will play in how that child develops and matures. So, what does research suggest on how families influence education?

There was an interesting finding in a research study addressing the educational aspirations that parents of various ethnicities had for their children. The study found there was little difference between those aspirations, as parents of all ethnicities wanted a good education for their children, and the overwhelming majority wanted their children to obtain a bachelor's degree or even higher (Spera, Wentzel, & Matto, 2009). Asian American parents had the highest response rates, indicating they wanted their children to achieve either a master's degree or a doctorate. These high educational goals by the parents stand in stark contrast with discouraging historical statistics that indicate African American and Hispanic students are more likely to drop out of school than their Caucasian peers and have a lower level of education attainment (e.g., De La Rosa & Maw, 1990; Goldenberg, 1996; Hodgkinson, 1992; Kao & Tienda, 1995; Soloranzo, 1992). A specific disconnect between parental expectations and ultimate school outcomes among Hispanic families can be noted in the following statistic: In 2008, 18.3% of Hispanic American youth left school without a high school diploma, which is nearly twice the dropout rate of African Americans and four times that of Caucasians (Snyder & Dillow, 2010).

Take that statistic for Hispanic American students for a moment and consider it in conjunction with two aspects of Hispanic culture. Hispanic families often embrace the concept of *familismo*, the idea that loyalty to the family should take precedence over one's personal desires, including educational attainment (Halgunseth, Ispa, & Rudy, 2006). This "family first" mentality may influence how many Hispanic American students ultimately do pursue higher education. Hispanic families also embrace the concept of *ser bien educado*, which literally translated means "to be well educated" but has a deeper meaning for Latino families that includes being a good person (Halgunseth, Ispa, & Rudy, 2006). Do the concepts of *familismo* and *ser bien educado* actually work against each other in Hispanic culture in regard to higher education? That is a question that merits more research.

There is additional research that focuses on familial perceptions of education and their expectations for their children, and while not all of it is positive (e.g., Hossler and Stage [1992] found that some minority parents who had negative educational experiences were less likely to be engaged in schools or fully supportive of their children's educational efforts), the majority suggests that most families want their children to succeed in school. Families, therefore, are not the main source of the race-based social stressors previously discussed; that source is society, a grand and sprawling component of human existence. Can educators influence society? Absolutely, but that starts with the individual students in the classroom. Helping ethnically diverse students feel less stress about education and become more engaged in the process can only be viewed as a noble and proper goal for all teachers.

The interplay of race/ethnicity and education is complex. What did you read in the preceding section that surprised you? Was there information presented with which you were already familiar? How does the information affect your perceptions of teaching students from different racial/ethnic backgrounds? Do you feel it will be challenging for you to adjust your instruction to fully support students of different ethnicities? What might some of those challenges be?

Pause and Reflect

The Teacher's Role

Parents and schools should place great emphasis on the idea that it is all right to be different. Racism and all the other 'isms' grow from primitive tribalism, the instinctive hostility against those of another tribe, race, religion, nationality, class or whatever. You are a lucky child if your parents taught you to accept diversity.

—Roger Ebert

It should be clear by now that teachers can play a dramatic role in the educational experience, and ultimate success, of ethnically diverse students. This is something that will need to be accomplished in spite of the "diversity gap" noted in the introduction between teachers (80% Caucasian) and students (51% ethnic minority groups). It should be noted that teachers alone are not responsible for closing the racial divides that still exist in this country, though they will play a significant role in that process. Doing their part will require teachers to do more than suppress implicit bias and demonstrate an attitude of acceptance of all cultures. Before ideas are presented on how teachers can support students from different ethnic groups, a brief note is needed on the practice of demonstrating respect for other cultures.

There are those who, in an attempt to embrace ethnic diversity, make bold proclamations, saying things such as, "I don't even notice color." While nobly intended, such statements would also suggest a person does not notice the unique characteristics that ethnic groups share as a culture. This is not to suggest everyone should walk around saying things such as, "You're African American. I understand your culture emphasizes music as a means of communication." But that understanding, of a true facet of African American culture, can be held without necessarily being stated. You can notice color, a part of ethnic diversity, as long as you respect that everyone is an individual, though everyone is also a product of their culture to a large degree. We do not simply lose our cultures as we grow up, though how much we embrace our own culture's values may shift over time. Teachers may need to examine their own cultural values and determine how best to incorporate those values into culturally responsive pedagogy.

How can teachers effectively support ethnically diverse students? Table 3.2 presents five fundamental approaches that will serve as a good starting point. There are multiple evidence-based practices to support ethnically diverse students, so those presented should be viewed as foundational.

TABLE 3.2 Methods for Teachers to Engage Ethnically Diverse Students

Study mindfulness-based interventions. (Bluth et al., 2016)	Research continues to demonstrate that when ethnically diverse students are taught coping and self-regulation skills, there are numerous benefits, including in academic performance and mental and physical health.
Engage in culturally responsive, organized after-school activities. (Simpkins et al., 2017)	Schools that design after-school activities designed to appeal to the cultural interests of ethnically diverse students have begun to notice improvements in these students' overall engagement in the education process.
Consider the ideas of restorative practice. (Gregory et al., 2016)	Restorative practice is an educational program consisting of 11 essential practices meant to be implemented school-wide and designed to build better working relationships with students to improve engagement and behaviors (program overview available at http://www.safersanerschools.org/).
Build culturally responsive practices into literacy instruction. (Toppel, 2015)	Teachers should consider the learning and communication styles of culturally diverse students when planning cooperative learning and engagement strategies that promote literacy.
Establish your classroom as a caring learning community. (Butler, Schenellert, & Perry, 2016; Gay, 2013)	Create in your classroom a community of learners in which diverse cultures are recognized, valued, and celebrated. Such environments allow teachers to respectfully discuss diversity in a way that broadens their students' cultural awareness.

All of the strategies will require teachers to keep an open mind on how best to work with culturally diverse students. So much of the success in working with diverse populations comes down to attitude and disposition, concepts covered more thoroughly in Chapter 2. Students will know how much a teacher cares by how the teacher treats them and teaches them. Paying respect to their cultural strengths, and appealing to them during instruction, is the first major step toward success with ethnically diverse students.

Pause and Discuss

With a small group, discuss the following: Do you believe that most teachers are well prepared to teach in multiethnic classrooms? Why or why not? Do you agree that teachers can have a profound effect on the educational achievement of ethnically diverse students? Why or why not? What methods of engagement presented above make the most sense to you? Why? And lastly, do you think that society itself is becoming more culturally responsive? Justify your response.

Conclusion

This chapter has presented a great deal of information regarding the interplay of race/ethnicity and education. Schools and teachers must accept that race/ethnicity do play a role in education, and a great deal of that role stems from perceptions held by both teachers and ethnically diverse students. Changing those perceptions in a positive fashion takes effort and commitment and, above all, an awareness of how actions, attitudes, and ideas are presented by and received by teachers and ethnically diverse students. Taking steps to diminish the achievement and graduation gaps that have plagued this country for far too long are a must in modern education. Teachers will have a very important say in ultimately closing those gaps and helping their ethnically diverse students succeed in multiple aspects of life.

KEY CHAPTER TAKEAWAYS

Some important takeaways from this chapter include:

- Although it remains a sensitive issue, the role of race/ethnicity in education cannot be ignored by teachers and school systems.

- Statistics and research show dramatic differences between ethnic groups in terms of both academic achievement and school completion.

- Race/ethnicity affects education in two specific ways: how ethnically diverse students receive and respond to instruction and how teachers view these students' abilities to achieve.

- The controversial yet well-documented existence of implicit bias, having judgments of or opinions about a particular group on a subconscious level, plays a role in how teachers perceive the capabilities of ethnically diverse students.

- The educational perceptions of ethnically diverse students may be influenced by race-based social stressors, which can play a significant role in these students' motivations and cognitive processes, including attention and memory.

- As students' microcultures, families often have significant influence on how children develop, mature, and ultimately view education.

- Despite the fact that many parents of all ethnicities want their children to attain a higher degree of education, there is still a significant disparity between the number of Caucasian students who go on to postsecondary education and the number of their minority peers who do so.

- Teachers can play a powerful role in the educational and personal lives of their ethnically diverse students.

- Most culturally responsive teaching practices will reflect a high degree of respect for ethnic cultures, including the strengths and values those ethnicities bring to the classroom.

A teacher's attitude is perhaps the most important—and often the first—step toward success when working with students of diverse ethnicity.

CASE SCENARIO: THE INTERVIEW CONTINUES

Mrs. Frayer took a long moment before asking her next question. She leaned back slightly in her chair, and Kortney was surprised to see the principal close her eyes, though just briefly. Mrs. Frayer then leaned forward, opened her eyes, and placed her hands on the desk in front of her. She took a breath.

"I realize we've ventured into some interesting areas so far in this interview," she began, "and that none of your practice interviews could have prepared you for the kinds of questions I'm asking or situations I'm describing. That's probably good for you, in a way. I don't like rehearsed answers; I want to know someone's honest responses. Being direct like this helps me achieve that goal in an interview."

Kortney could only nod.

"And this next one is a bit touchy these days," Mrs. Frayer continued. "I'm afraid it's been a little touchy throughout history. At times it's been quite a divisive area, in a lot of different ways. So I'll start by asking you this—do you have any good friends that aren't white?"

Kortney was taken aback. Mrs. Frayer had been spot-on that none of the practice interviews had included the kinds of questions she had been fielding, and this one was no different. *Did she just ask me if I have any friends who aren't White?*, Kortney thought. She was trying to formulate a response when Mrs. Frayer held up a hand.

"Once again I'd like to tell you a story about why that question comes up," she said. She then leaned back in her chair and told the following story:

A few years earlier, a fourth-grade teacher was guiding her class through a unit on civic responsibility. Part of that unit dealt with what it meant to be a citizen, an active member of a community. As luck would have it, that particular classroom was one of the most ethnically diverse in the school and included several students who were the children of recent immigrants to the United States. The teacher thought she could use this diversity as a talking point for her students. She could point out how the diverse class represented a diverse community and how each ethnicity represented there also represented a unique culture. She went about this for 3 days before she received the first parent complaint.

The email took the teacher by surprise. It read, "Why are you making my son feel unwelcome in your class? He comes home these past 3 days and says you keep telling everyone why he is different. We want our son to enjoy school, not be afraid a teacher is going to single him out or pick on him." This was not an email the teacher had anticipated, as she thought she had been very clear that she was pointing out how different races can come together in a community. Had she been singling students out in some way by making that point? She did not have long to consider that idea before a second parent complaint was delivered, this time in person.

Arriving in the office, the teacher saw the mother and father of one of her students. Stepping in to the principal's office to talk, the parents shared a concern similar to the one in the email. "Our daughter is a good girl," the mother said, "but she has been very upset the past few days. She says you are teaching the class about citizenship, and we haven't even become citizens yet."

"It makes her feel uncomfortable," the father continued. "And she says you keep pointing out different cultures, saying how our culture values this or that more than some others. Our daughter doesn't like that kind of attention, and also, some of the things you've been saying about our culture aren't even true in our family."

The teacher was very shaken by what she was being told. She had always viewed herself as open-minded toward and accepting of all ethnicities and their cultures. And she had never before received such complaints about her teaching. Then again, she had never had a class quite as diverse, and it was dawning on her that perhaps she had been overemphasizing some aspects of ethnicity and culture. She had been using her students as examples. She thought she had been doing so in a respectful manner, but the email and the two visitors strongly suggested otherwise.

WORKING WITH THE SCENARIO

Mrs. Frayer looked steadily at Kortney. "This is just one of many delicate issues we'll be discussing in this interview," she said. "I'd like to pose some follow-up questions if you're okay with that."

Kortney, still processing the story she had just heard, nodded. "Yes, that will be fine," she answered.

"Very good, then," Mrs. Frayer said. She then asked, "Do you think the teacher was doing anything wrong? Why or why not? In your opinion, were there any signs of implicit bias in the teacher's instructional practice?"

"Implicit bias?" Kortney asked.

"A pretty deep topic in and of itself, but don't let that hold up your responses," Mrs. Frayer said before posing more questions. "If you were tasked with covering a citizenship standard in an ethnically diverse class, would you choose to focus on how different ethnicities are often citizens of the same community? And if so, how might you approach that topic? If the parents from my story came to you and you were that teacher, how would you defend your actions or explain yourself?"

Kortney was taken aback by the slew of questions. Mrs. Frayer sensed her unease.

"Don't worry," Mrs. Frayer said. "These are more discussion-type questions to let me see how you think about things. The last one is this—based on the information you have, can you propose a different approach for the teacher to use that honors ethnic diversity without drawing unwanted attention to particular students?"

If you were Kortney, how would you answer the questions posed by Mrs. Frayer?

REFERENCES

Bluth, K., Campo, R. A., Pruteanu-Malinici, S., Reams, A., Mullarkey, M., & Broderick, P. C. (2016). A school-based mindfulness pilot study for ethnically diverse at-risk adolescents. *Mindfulness, 7*(1), 90–104.

Bronfenbrenner, U. (1994). Ecological models of human development. *Readings on the Development of Children, 2*(1), 37–43.

Butler, D. L., Schenellert, L., & Perry, N. E. (2016). *Developing self-regulating learners*. Pearson.

Clark, R., Anderson, N. B., Clark, V. R., & Williams, D. R. (1999). Racism as a stressor for African Americans: A biopsychosocial model. *American Psychologist, 54*, 805–16. http://dx.doi.org/10.1037/0003-066X.54.10.805

De La Rosa, D., & Maw, C. E. (1990). *Hispanic education: A statistical portrait, 1990.* National Council of La Raza.

Fairlie, R. W., & Resch, A. M. (2002). Is there "white flight" into private schools? Evidence from the National Educational Longitudinal Survey. *Review of Economics and Statistics, 84*(1), 21–33.

Gay, G. (2013). Teaching to and through cultural diversity. *Curriculum Inquiry, 43*(1), 48–70. http://doi.org/10.1111/curi.12002

Gillborn, D. (2003). *Race, ethnicity and education: Teaching and learning in multi-ethnic schools.* Routledge.

Gladwell, M. (2006). *Blink: The power of thinking without thinking.* Back Bay.

Godsil, R. D., Tropp, L. R., Goff, P. A., & Powell, J. A. (2014). *Science of inequality, volume 1: Addressing implicit bias, racial anxiety, and stereotype threat in education and healthcare.* Scholarly project. https://equity.ucla.edu/wp-content/uploads/2016/11/Science-of-Equality-Vol.-1-Perception-Institute-2014.pdf

Goldenberg, C. (1996). Latin American immigration and U.S. schools. *Social Policy Report, 10*(1), 1–32.

Gregory, A., Clawson, K., Davis, A., & Gerewitz, J. (2016). The promise of restorative practices to transform teacher-student relationships and achieve equity in school discipline. *Journal of Educational and Psychological Consultation, 26*(4), 325–53.

Halgunseth, L. C., Ispa, J. M., & Rudy, D. (2006). Parental control in Latino families: An integrated review of the literature. *Child Development, 77*(5), 1282–97.

Hawley, W. D., & Nieto, S. (2010). Another inconvenient truth: Race and ethnicity matter. *Educational Leadership, 68*(3), 66–71.

Hodgkinson, H. L. (1992). *A demographic look at tomorrow.* Institute for Educational Leadership.

Hossler, D., & Stage, F. K. (1992). Family and high school experience influences on the postsecondary educational plans of ninth-grade students. *American Educational Research Journal, 29*(2), 425–51.

Kao, G., & Tienda, M. (1995). Optimism and achievement: The educational performance of immigrant youth. *Social Science Quarterly, 76*, 1–19.

Levy, D. J., Heissel, J. A., Richeson, J. A., & Adam, E. K. (2016). Psychological and biological responses to race-based social stress as pathways to disparities in educational outcomes. *American Psychologist, 71*(6), 455–73.

Major, B., & O'Brien, L. T. (2005). The social psychology of stigma. *Annual Review of Psychology, 56, 393–421.* http://dx.doi.org/10.1146/annurev.psych.56.091103.070137

Miller, C. T., & Kaiser, C. R. (2001). A theoretical perspective on coping with stigma. *Journal of Social Issues, 57*, 73–92. http://dx.doi.org/10.1111/0022-4537.00202

NCES (National Center for Education Statistics). (2018a). *The nation's report card.* U.S. Department of Education.

NCES. (2018b). *Public high school graduation rates.* https://nces.ed.gov/programs/coe/indicator_coi.asp

Simpkins, S. D., Riggs, N. R., Ngo, B., Vest Ettekal, A., & Okamoto, D. (2017). Designing culturally responsive organized after-school activities. *Journal of Adolescent Research, 32*(1), 11–36.

Snyder, T. D., & Dillow, S. A. (2010). *Digest of education statistics, 2009.* NCES 2010-013. National Center for Education Statistics.

Soloranzo, D. G. (1992). An exploratory analysis of the effects of race, class, and gender on student and parent mobility aspirations. *Journal of Negro Education, 61*, 30–44. doi:10.2307/2295627

Spera, C., Wentzel, K. R., & Matto, H. C. (2009). Parental aspirations for their children's educational attainment: Relations to ethnicity, parental education, children's academic performance, and parental perceptions of school climate. *Journal of Youth and Adolescence, 38*(8), 1140–52. doi:http://dx.doi.org/10.1007/s10964-008-9314-7

Tenenbaum, H. R., & Ruck, M. D. (2007). Are teachers' expectations different for racial minority than for European American students? A meta-analysis. *Journal of Educational Psychology, 99*(2), 253.

Toppel, K. (2015). Enhancing core reading programs with culturally responsive practices. *Reading Teacher, 68*(7), 552–59.

Turcios-Cotto, Viana Y., & Milan, S. (2012). Racial/ethnic differences in the educational expectations of adolescents: Does pursuing higher education mean something different to Latino students compared to White and Black students? *Journal of Youth and Adolescence, 42*(9) (2013), 1399–1412.

The Effect of Poverty on Learning

Setting the Classroom Scene

Carol Danforth was with her fifth-grade class, reviewing the concept of figurative language as the school day drew to a close on a Friday. Her students were cooperating, mostly, but she knew they were all ready for the weekend. Their eyes kept darting to the clock in the front of the room. Carol had often thought of removing it because it was so often a distraction at particular times. But in the end she knew she needed it herself. She wrapped up the review by asking for two more examples from student volunteers, then told the class to gather their things to take home.

As the students were putting papers in their backpacks, Carol reminded three of them to go to the cafeteria right away, even a few minutes before the bell rang. The three students acknowledged this request with silent assent, nodding their heads but not making eye contact with Carol. This was the usual pattern for the end of the day on Friday, and Carol felt a familiar emotional pain. Knowing why those three students had to go to the lunchroom often broke her heart.

The three kids from Carol's class were part of a group of nearly 30 students at the inner-city elementary school that had to visit the lunchroom before going home for the weekend. Carol's school qualified as a Title I school because the vast majority of its students, more than 70%, qualified for free and reduced lunch. In the simplest terms, these students came from poor families. Carol had not fully understood the ramifications of that qualification, being classified as a Title I school and working with so many students growing up in poverty, until early in her first year at the school.

Six weeks into that school year, Carol had finally asked a fellow teacher, one who had been at the school for more than 10 years at that time, why some students visited the lunchroom before getting on the buses at the end of the week.

"We send them home with sandwiches and whatever other snacks we can scrounge up," her colleague replied.

"Why on earth do we do that?" Carol had responded, honestly confused.

"Because we're pretty sure that's the only food they're going to get over the weekends," her colleague answered, a troubled look crossing her face.

Prereading Questions

1. What makes a school qualify as Title I? How do you think these distinguishing characteristics affect the teachers and students at a Title I school?

2. How do you feel knowing that some schools have to send food home with students on Fridays to ensure they get food on the weekends? Do you think this would affect how you treat those students while you teach them?

3. Describe your definition of poverty. Be specific, and include any personal experiences you have had in working with individuals living in your definition of poverty. You do not have to include names or other identifying information, just the experiences you may have had. Do you feel these experiences will help you better relate to students and families living in poverty?

Introduction

> *Poverty is not just a lack of money; it is not having the capability to achieve one's full potential as a human being.*
>
> —**Amartya Sen**

Poverty affects education. That is an indisputable fact, demonstrated repeatedly by research efforts going back several decades. While the notion that a poor student is destined to achieve at a lower academic level than a student not living in poverty is false, the plain truth is that a student in poverty will always have a much greater chance to underachieve. And poverty affects some students in nearly every school. There are a large number of schools and school districts, however, where the number of students living in poverty make up more than half the student enrollment. There are cities in the United States, with very large student enrollments between kindergarten and 12th grade, where more than 70% of the students qualify for free and reduced lunch. Qualifying for free and reduced lunch is just one indicator of poverty, but it is a very common metric applied to determine the level of poverty in any school.

The exact effects of poverty on a child's education and educational performance have been studied for years. Although there is great variability on the level of effect, there is little doubt there is an effect, and often a negative one. Seminal books, including *A Framework for Understanding Poverty* by Ruby Payne (1995) and *The Shame of the Nation* by Jonathan Kozol (2005), have painted stark pictures of the drastic and damaging long-term effects of poverty on both students and school systems. The efforts of these two authors and many more have created insight into the problem and in many instances offered some guidance on how best to help students overcome economic disparity and find academic success. The guidance and ideas are not easy and require a high level of commitment and diligence from everyone working with students from poverty.

A sad truth about poverty in modern America is that it is often grimly accepted as a person's or family's destiny. It is difficult to discuss poverty, as it has almost become a shameful secret in our society—the fact that in one of the richest countries in the world there are a large number of people and families living in dire economic circumstances. We are somehow, as a nation, embarrassed that we have not won the War on Poverty begun under President Lyndon Johnson in the 1960s. But that feeling cannot keep teachers from understanding that some of their students will come from poverty. And that status will require something extra from the teacher for those students to succeed.

This chapter will review some of the most significant characteristics of students and schools dealing with poverty. While not meant to be exhaustive, this coverage should provide some foundational knowledge for how socioeconomic disparities can affect students, schools, and teachers. Following this coverage, information will be presented on methods and practices that have been effective for teachers and schools seeking to best help students from poverty. These ideas should be considered a starting point, as there is no cure-all guaranteed to help any student from a poor socioeconomic background. Teachers working with disadvantaged students must be willing to continue to learn new methods and even develop their own strategies to help these children find success in their classrooms.

The Effects

To begin this section, it is appropriate to provide some definitions. For example, what socioeconomic conditions indicate a student is living in poverty? What makes a school Title 1? What exactly is academic achievement? As these and other terms will all play a significant part in the discussion of students coming from poverty, they should be clearly defined (unless otherwise noted, the definitions in Table 4.1 are developed by the author).

TABLE 4.1 Definitions Associated with Discussing Poverty

Term/Phrase	Definition
Poverty	An economic status distinguished by the inability to pay for basic needs. In 2019, the federal government established that the poverty threshold for a family of four was an annual income of $25,750 (U.S. Department of Health and Human Services, 2019).
Title I school	Any school providing education to a significantly high percentage of students living in poverty.
Academic achievement	A holistic term referring to a student or students' academic performance on various measures of academic ability (including reading comprehension, written expression skills, and mathematical computation skills). While standardized testing is a common way to examine academic achievement, it is not the only measure.
Achievement gap	A prolonged and obvious discrepancy, or gap, noted between two or more groups on traditional measures of academic achievement (most notably standardized tests).

On Students

In the early 21st century, the U.S. Department of Education completed a long-term study that focused, in part, on how students living in poverty performed on standardized tests. The study's findings were stark. The research indicated that students from poverty tend to score below average on standardized tests and across grade levels, students who live in poverty score significantly worse on standardized tests when compared with students from middle- or upper-class families, and schools with the highest percentage of students living in poverty scored significantly below schools with lower percentages of such students (U.S. Department of Education, 2001). These results suggested a negative trend, as research conducted a decade earlier found that while students living in poverty ranked, on average, in the 19th percentile (meaning 81% of other students did as well or better on the assessments examined in the study), students from families with middle- to upper-class incomes ranked, on average, in the 66th percentile (Sum & Fogg, 1991). That 47-point gap is significant when considering the academic achievement of students living in poverty. A more recent example can be found in the analysis of ACT scores conducted by a major metropolitan newspaper in the spring of 2019. It found that, in the metropolitan area covered by the newspaper, the average ACT score was 24.6 at a school with a poverty rate of 3.6%, while at a school with a poverty rate of 86.5%, the average was 14.9 (these statistics are real, but out of respect for the school systems, no identifying reference is being provided).

There are additional research findings that demonstrate the academic struggles of many students from poverty. For example, students from low-income households are at increased risk for underperformance in reading, compared with their more affluent peers. Multiple studies and government reports have noted the achievement gaps in reading performance associated with poverty (e.g., Hernandez, 2011; Lacour & Tissington, 2011; Rampey, Dion, & Donahue, 2009; Reardon, 2013). A specific example of this achievement gap can be found on the eighth-grade reading scores from the National Assessment of Educational Progress (NAEP) from 2009. For students in eighth grade, scores on the NAEP reading measures indicated the average reading achievement of students from low-income households was 1.25 standard deviations below that of students from middle- and upper-income households (Rampey, Dion, & Donahue, 2009; Reardon, 2013). In the world of research statistics, being more than one standard deviation away from the average, especially more than one standard deviation below the average, is considered statistically significant. And that is not good news in regard to the reading skills of students living in poverty.

There are other negative effects of poverty on students. One large-scale study (Evans, 2016) noted that children growing up in poverty

- are more likely to have reduced spatial short-term memory (the ability to recall things seen shortly after viewing them),
- are more likely to engage in antisocial and aggressive behaviors,
- are more likely to feel powerless when compared with their middle-class peers, and
- experience higher levels of chronic physical stress, which may continue into adulthood.

Those findings mirror the results of an earlier study (Jensen, 2009) that noted children raised in poverty are more likely to display

- impatience and impulsivity,

- gaps in politeness and social graces,

- inappropriate emotional responses, and

- less empathy for the misfortunes of others.

These studies suggest the effects of poverty on students go beyond just the academics in school. There are negative social, emotional, and physical effects as well.

> *Childhood, after all, is the first precious coin that poverty steals from a child.*
> **—Anthony Horowitz**

And while the research has remained frighteningly consistent in the academic achievement gap between students from poverty and those not in poverty, research has had a tougher time indicating what specific aspects of poverty may hinder a child's academic performance. One study found an interesting correlation based on the number of books in a child's home. The more books available to a child, the better his or her academic performance tended to be (Evans, Kelley, & Sikora, 2014). Students living in poverty simply do not have access to as many resources, and it is harming them academically. This same concept holds true for technology. As some school districts dive headlong into "flipped classrooms" (an educational approach in which students are given work to do at home, then return to school to discuss/apply/synthesize the information learned at home) or "one-to-one" computer access (schools with the resources to do so buying laptops or tablets for students to utilize), students without internet access at home are often left to flounder.

The long-term effects of growing up in poverty go beyond just school performance. Multiple studies have found that students from poverty have an increased risk of dropping out of school (e.g., Baydu, Kaplan, & Bayar, 2013). That's significant when you consider the multiple negatives associated with that outcome. High school dropouts earn on average $9,200 less per year than those who graduate high school and are three times more likely to be unemployed than those who graduate college (Burrus & Roberts, 2012). Furthermore, these students are much more likely to be living in poverty compared with high school graduates (Bridgeland, Dilulio, & Morison, 2006), and this is consequential as those with lower levels of education also tend to be less healthy (Lleras-Muney, 2005).

A new concept was introduced to the study of poverty over the past 20 years, and that is "generational poverty." This term is an acknowledgment that poverty often, unfortunately, remains the status for a family from one generation to the next. Jensen (2009) defined generational poverty as occurring in families in which "at least two generations have been born into poverty. Families living in this type of poverty are not equipped with the tools to move out of their situations" (p. 2). Just the fact that we have to acknowledge poverty being "handed down" in some families is sad to consider.

Poverty affects students in multiple negative ways. The research findings, though unfortunate, are consistent and clear. Students coming from poverty are at a disadvantage, and this disadvantage adversely affects both their academic performance and in too many instances their interpersonal relationships and long-term life outcomes. But poverty is not an academic death sentence. As we will see in a later section of this chapter, teachers and schools have the capacity to have a profoundly positive effect on students living in poverty.

On Teachers

There is an emotional and cognitive toll enacted on teachers who work with large numbers of students living in poverty. These teachers often find themselves having to provide a higher degree of care for and attention to these students. There is a popular concept known as "filling someone's bucket" (McCloud, 2007), which fundamentally means a person takes the time to provide positive reinforcement and praise to someone else to make that person feel better about himself or herself. You are filling someone's bucket when you compliment a person or try to boost their self-confidence. But everyone also needs to have their own "buckets" filled, as the process cannot play out one way all the time. To apply this concept to teachers working with students from poverty, these teachers may find themselves constantly filling the buckets of their students but not always having their own buckets replenished. This can be emotionally draining for teachers, especially when they are truly invested in their students' success.

And the above matters for teachers because they can play a powerful role in the life of a student living in poverty, for good or ill. For example, teachers who fall prey to deficit ideology, the tendency to define a student by her or his perceived weaknesses rather than apparent strengths, can be destructive toward that student's success in a classroom, as teachers' diminished expectations can have a negative effect on student learning (Gorski, 2011). And teachers who become negative or cynical in regard to students from poverty begin to lose their effectiveness as educators. The worst-case scenario for a teacher working with many students from poverty is the development of compassion fatigue, which can then lead to burnout.

The concept of compassion fatigue relates to a caregiver's reduced willingness to provide empathy (Adams, Boscarino, & Figley, 2006), and enough compassion fatigue over time can contribute to burnout, "a syndrome of emotional exhaustion, depersonalization, and reduced personal accomplishment that can occur among individuals who do 'people work' of some kind" (Maslach, 2003, p. 2). Much research has gone into teacher attrition rates, and the statistics are not good when examining how many teachers stay in the profession for more than 5 years. Burnout has been cited as one reason teachers leave the profession, though there are numerous others. Still, given the extra demands associated with serving students from poverty, the chances are increased that teachers tasked with that responsibility may feel extra stress. And unfortunately, that extra stress may lead some teachers to ultimately leave the classroom.

On Schools and School Systems

A recent study by EdBuild (2019) found a troubling economic fact when considering the effects of poverty on schools and school systems. The study found that larger school districts received $23 billion less than smaller school districts. Think about that for a moment. That is $23 billion, more than the gross domestic product of some nations. And that is significant to any discussion on poverty because the larger the school district, the greater the likelihood of it having a large number of Title 1 schools. While the EdBuild study chose to focus a large part of its analysis on the racial demographic differences between large school districts and small school districts, it also included reference to the fact that the larger school districts (average size of 10,000 students) served a larger number of students from poverty, compared with smaller school districts (average size of 1,500 students). This only makes sense, as logic dictates that the larger the school system, the greater the likelihood of there being more students from poverty enrolled in its schools.

This funding discrepancy serves as just one point of discussion when regarding the influence of poverty on schools and school systems. Heavily populated urban centers often have the highest number of Title 1 schools and therefore the highest number of students achieving at a lower academic level than their more affluent peers. And although larger cities have more citizens to contribute to the tax base that funds local schools, if the majority of families sending students to a particular school are living in poverty, their contributions to the funding mechanisms for that school are not going to be substantial. In many urban school systems, there are schools where the number of students qualifying for free or reduced lunch exceeds 70%, even 80%. That is a very high number of students who, as covered earlier, are more likely to struggle academically and face other significant life challenges.

And urban centers are not alone in dealing with large percentages of students from poverty. Many rural communities may have smaller schools, compared with larger cities, but still deal with serving large numbers of students coming from poverty. Ultimately, there is not a "one size fits all" system for generalizing which schools or school systems will deal with the most poverty, but the general consensus is that larger school districts in larger cities will experience the effects of poverty the most. The next most affected school systems will be small-town, rural school systems without strong tax bases for funding schools.

It seems that only a small percentage of school systems have found themselves fortunate enough to avoid the damaging effects of poverty. According to the EdBuild study (2019), "small districts can have the effect of concentrating resources and amplifying political power. Because schools rely heavily on local taxes, drawing borders around small, wealthy communities benefits the few." The debate over school funding inequalities takes up journal articles, chapters, and entire books. While the problem is acknowledged, the solutions to it remain elusive.

What does all of this mean for schools and school systems? Most research efforts focusing on poverty have dealt mostly with the students in the schools. Very little research exists examining what are the exact effects on a school when it has to provide educational services to large numbers of students from poverty. But research is not always needed to demonstrate the obvious. Some things are simply clear and easy to identify, and the effects of poverty on schools fall into that category.

To understand where students are going, you have to know where they come from. ... A zip code can tell you so much more about where a child is going to end up than any other fact that you can learn about that child.
—**Anthony Abraham Jack, assistant professor in the Harvard Graduate School of Education, on how real estate values and property taxes are correlated to school resource availability and, ultimately, student success (Bell, 2020).**

To begin to understand the effects of poverty on a school, consider the following two fictional examples, School A and School B, both K–6 elementary schools. Although the information presented in Table 4.2 is not from actual schools, it is an amalgamation of the vast discrepancies that do exist between some schools in the real world:

TABLE 4.2 Schools Comparison—Which is Better?

	School A	School B
YEAR BUILT	2000	1975
ENROLLMENT	215	385
STUDENT-TEACHER RATIO	16:1	23:1
DEMOGRAPHICS	Caucasian: 79% African American: 12% Hispanic: 4% Asian American: 4% Other: 1%	Caucasian: 42% African American: 33% Hispanic: 22% Asian American: 2% Other: 1%
PERCENTAGE OF STUDENTS QUALIFYING FOR FREE OR REDUCED LUNCH	15%	74%
PERCENTAGE OF STUDENTS QUALIFYING FOR SPECIAL EDUCATION	8%	19%
BUILDING FACILITIES	Well maintained and modern, with a wide lobby area, an auxiliary gym in addition to the main gym, and a half-mile walking track around the playground area. Science classrooms have designated laboratory space, and there are two computer labs. Each wing of the building has bathrooms for students, and there are four separate bathrooms available for teachers.	Exterior is beginning to show serious signs of disrepair, and interior classrooms are also in need of upgrades. Desks are still being used from the late 1980s, and a few pieces of playground equipment have been marked off limits. Only four bathrooms are available for students, plus one for faculty members. The cafeteria is housed adjacent to the auditorium, with some tables being placed onstage.

(continued)

LIBRARY	Spacious and carpeted, with study carrels and designated reading areas. Annual book drive keeps the shelves stocked with abundant reading choices for students.	Cramped, with only eight cabinets of books and five tables available for students to use. Dependent on donations to maintain an adequate supply of reading materials.
TECHNOLOGY RESOURCES	District budget has funds earmarked for technology, so each classroom has a SMART Board® and Elmo. In addition to the computer lab, there are two carts of computers available for teachers to check out and use in class.	No computer lab, and classrooms have two or three computers available for students to use. These are rapidly becoming outdated, as are the computers teachers use for keeping grades and other pertinent files. All classrooms are still using chalkboards.
AVERAGE YEARS OF EXPERIENCE PER TEACHER	Fifteen teachers, with an average of 17 years' experience.	Nineteen teachers, with an average of eight years' experience.
PERFORMANCE ON STATE REPORT CARD (A STANDARDIZED SCORE DERIVED FROM MULTIPLE ACADEMIC MEASURES)	92—more than 76% of students in grades three and five are reading at or above grade level, with a similar percentage performing at or above grade level in mathematics.	63—less than half the students in both third and fifth grades are reading at grade level or performing on grade level in measures of mathematical skills.

Based on the information presented in Table 4.2, which school is in the best position to provide its students with a proper and full education? School A is the obvious choice, even if School B is staffed entirely with award-winning, highly effective teachers. And that boils down to resource availability. Schools and school systems with more resources are simply better able to serve their students. And the fact is that schools such as School A are in the vast minority in this country.

Pause and Discuss	In a group, share your understanding of what constitutes poverty. As a group, come up with a list of characteristics you may associate with a student living in poverty. Furthermore, if you have any particular experiences in working with individuals or students living in poverty, share those experiences. Be willing to share your responses and explain the rationale behind your thinking.

Pathways Forward

The best way to fight poverty is to empower people through access to quality education.

—John Legend

It is quite fortunate that the political and government leaders in this country recognize the growing number of students in poverty as a national crisis and are taking bold steps to address the problem in a direct fashion. The preceding sentence is pure fiction. And that is a shame. The truth is that the government (note: *government* in this context is a broad, nationwide term referring to national, state, and local governments in a holistic fashion) likes to talk about the value of education more than it does spending money showing how much it values education. Recent national news has featured more stories on teachers striking for better pay and teaching conditions (lower student-teacher ratios, for example) than on state and local governments increasing funding for education. A recent national gathering for special education teachers even had as its theme "Doing more with less." So if schools and teachers cannot trust in a new and robust financial commitment to fighting poverty and equipping schools to support students from poverty, in what might they trust to help these students?

For Teachers

An important first step for teachers is to ensure they have developed proper self-management strategies when faced with stress. The truth is that teachers need to take care of themselves before they can best take care of their students. Coping strategies that help teachers alleviate the extra pressures and burdens often associated with supporting students in poverty are therefore a must. In their book *Emotional Intelligence 2.0*, Bradberry and Greaves (2009) offer several simple strategies to develop self-management skills. A sampling follows:

1. Smile and laugh more: This requires a conscious effort to engage in feelings and emotions of happiness and to display those feelings.

2. Set aside some time in your day for problem solving: Obstacles and adverse situations will present themselves, so have some time allotted to consider solutions to challenges.

3. Take control of your self-talk: A metacognitive skill, our inner dialogue can have a profound effect on our attitudes and actions. Positive self-talk is therefore very important for our self-determination and commitment.

4. Focus your attention on your freedoms, not your limitations: Although it is easy to become cynical and give in to negativity, it is very important to stay focused on the positives to keep our dispositions properly aligned.

5. Put a mental recharge in your schedule: "Brain breaks" are a commonly used tool to help students refocus and stay on task; the idea holds merit for teachers too.

Although simplistic, these five strategies can yield strong, positive results for anyone's mental well-being. But taking care of themselves emotionally is just one step teachers have to take. Table 4.3 presents some suggested strategies for teachers to support their students from poverty.

TABLE 4.3 Strategies for Teachers Working With Students From Poverty

Emphasize a growth mindset (previously discussed in Chapter 2).	Students from poverty often demonstrate a fixed mindset, the idea that they are bound by inherent limitations (Claro & Loeb, 2017). Conversely, promoting a growth mindset, the idea that we achieve through persistence and effort, can have positive effects on student learning (Claro, Paunesku, & Dweck, 2016).
Teach self-determination skills.	Closely related to the growth mindset, the strategy of teaching self-determination skills can be consequential for students from poverty. Helping these students set and monitor progress toward goals, develop action plans, and understand personal accountability can help these students improve both academically and socially (Dawson & Guare, 2018).
Promote literacy enjoyment.	Research has demonstrated that incorporating literature representative of popular culture can have a positive effect on students' reading achievement (Vera, 2011). Teachers should therefore seek out books and stories that engage their students by appealing to their popular culture interests.
Build trusting relationships with students.	Many low-income students have negative encounters with those in authority, so teachers need to be mindful of building trust with these students (Gorski, 2017). This may require addressing instances of bias or bullying affecting these students in a direct and supportive manner.
Incorporate movement and exercise during teaching and learning.	Getting students active in the learning process, literally physically active, can be a factor in promoting good health. Teachers should explore ways to promote kinesthetic learning experiences because research suggests healthier learners are better learners (Basch, 2011).

There are multiple other strategies available to teachers who work with students from poverty, so consider the five listed in Table 4.3 as a starting point. Teachers will benefit from building their strategy tool kits to meet the unique needs of their students from poverty. That will be an ongoing process, but everyone has to start somewhere. The five strategies presented can all be implemented simply enough, making them an appropriate starting point.

Imagine for a moment that your first teaching job is at a Title 1 school, and more than 70% of the students in your classroom qualify for free and reduced lunch. The computer you are given to use is on its last legs, and many of the desks in your classroom are broken. What strategies will you use to maintain your own self-determination in regard to helping your students? How will you avoid a deficit ideology about your students when they underachieve academically? How will you work to change the mindset of your students from poverty from one of fixed to one of growth? Write your answers and be ready to share them if called upon to do so.

Pause and Reflect

Conclusion

Jessica Bartholow of the Western Center on Law and Poverty stated, "I can tell you that poverty's cruelty not only permeates a child's body, but their spirit too" (California State Government and Child Poverty, 2018). There is great and powerful truth in those words, truth that no teacher working with a child from poverty can ignore. Although the statistics are daunting and so many aspects of poverty have such a damaging effect on a student's education, teachers must endure. To keep a student from becoming part of those negative outcomes, teachers and schools must be empathic while instilling in children from poverty a will to learn. For while poverty is cruel, one way of escaping its dire clutches is through education. And few children from poverty are going to be able to navigate that pathway to a better life on their own.

KEY CHAPTER TAKEAWAYS

Some important takeaways from this chapter include:

- The rate of students living in poverty has steadily increased over the past several decades.

- Research has consistently demonstrated that students from poverty perform worse on most measures of academic achievement than their peers not living in poverty.

- There are multiple negative effects of poverty on students beyond academics. Children raised in poverty often display socially inappropriate behaviors and experience more physical stress than their peers not living in poverty.

- Teachers who work with large numbers of students from poverty may themselves experience negative professional effects, including burnout.

- Teachers who work with students from poverty must avoid deficit ideology, viewing a particular student based on their perceived weaknesses rather than apparent strengths.

- Teachers working with large numbers of students from poverty face emotional risks that may include compassion fatigue, which then can lead to burnout.

- Schools in high-poverty districts face particularly significant struggles in meeting the needs of their students.

- Schools that do not receive adequate funding in turn lack adequate resources to educate all students.

- Teachers need self-management strategies to better cope with the stresses involved with supporting large numbers of students from poverty.

- Teachers need to incorporate instructional strategies to help their students from poverty achieve at a higher level.

- Strategies to support students from poverty should go beyond academics to include methods to promote self-determination, build trust, and create a growth mindset in these students.

CASE SCENARIO: THE INTERVIEW CONTINUES

Kortney could literally feel her head swimming. She had heard that phrase often enough but could not say for certain she had ever felt it so strongly in her own life. Mrs. Frayer's stories and questions had thrown her off balance, and she was struggling to get back. She attempted to rein in her racing mind, awaiting Mrs. Frayer's next question or story.

"How much experience do you have working with poor students?" Mrs. Frayer asked. "And I'm not using *poor* as an adjective meaning low quality. I'm using it in the financial sense. Students without means, students who are impoverished, students from low socioeconomic homes. In sum, students whose families don't have a lot of money."

"I'm afraid I don't have a lot of experience with students like that," Kortney answered, "but I do have some. There was a school where we went for field experience and there was a family everyone knew. The kids from that family would wear the same clothes three times a week. It was sad."

Mrs. Frayer leaned forward then, a somewhat grim expression on her face. "Yes, *sad* is a good word for it, I think," she said. "And speaking of sad, here's another story for you." As was her habit, Mrs. Frayer leaned back slightly in her chair before beginning the story.

Coach Roberts and Coach Sims sat at basketball practice one afternoon, watching half the team shoot layups off bounce passes on one end of the court, while the other half took elbow jumpers off a pass from the right top of the key on the opposite end. Roberts was the head coach for basketball and Sims the head coach for football, and Roberts had been an assistant for the football team the past two seasons. In the football season that had recently ended with the team going 5–2, the best player had been Junior Higgins, a running back. Junior was playing basketball, too, and was proceeding to hit a lot more shots than he missed on his end of the court.

"So," Roberts began, "what do you think of my idea? That kid could use some better shoes."

"Can't argue that point," Sims agreed. "You got a pair in mind?"

"I do indeed," Roberts answered. "We split them 50/50, and I'll give them to him quiet-like. I know he doesn't want the attention."

"Works for me," Sims said. "Go ahead and get them. I'll have my half for you tomorrow."

So, Coach Roberts went ahead and bought a pair of basketball shoes for Junior. They were not the best on the market by any means but were much better than the ones Junior had been using in practice. Junior was thankful and humble, as Coach Roberts had expected. Junior wore the shoes for almost two weeks. It was only a few days before the first game of the season, and at practice that day Coach Roberts saw that Junior was no longer wearing the new shoes. He waited until after practice and asked the young man where they were.

Junior looked embarrassed and tears formed in the corners of his eyes. Coach Roberts grew immediately concerned and took Junior into the coaches' office, away from the rest of the players who were filing away from the court and into the locker room. He closed the door and turned to Junior.

"Tell me what happened, Junior."

"Coach, these guys in my neighborhood have been talking about my shoes for the past week, and then yesterday …" His voice trailed off.

"What yesterday?" Coach Roberts asked.

With a clear effort to keep his composure, Junior seemed to pull himself together. "Yesterday three guys jumped me before I could get to my house," he said. "Two of them had knives, and they took my shoes."

WORKING WITH THE SCENARIO

"Put yourself in Coach Roberts's position, please," Mrs. Frayer said. "You have a student who has just informed you he has been attacked and robbed, at knife-point. You know this particular student does not have a lot of money and comes from what many consider to be the rough part of town. Still, you are shocked that this has happened to one of your students. I have a few questions for you based on all of this."

She paused briefly and then asked, "How would you respond to Junior's story? What would you say to Junior to try and make him feel better? What other actions would you want to take? Who would you want to tell about what happened to Junior?"

Mrs. Frayer paused again, then continued. "And along those same lines, imagine Junior is a student in your class, and you have gotten word about what happened to him. Is there anything you would want to do for Junior? How would you treat him the next time he was in your class? And the last question here is, do you think teachers have a responsibility to show extra care and concern for any student who might come from a poor socioeconomic situation who experiences such a dramatic event?"

Kortney sat for a moment, collecting her thoughts.

If you were Kortney, how would you answer the questions posed by Mrs. Frayer?

REFERENCES

Adams, R. E., Boscarino, J. A., & Figley, C. R. (2006). Compassion fatigue and psychological distress among social workers: A validation study. *American Journal of Orthopsychiatry, 76*(1), 103–8.

Basch, C. E. (2011). Healthier students are better learners: A missing link in school reforms to close the achievement gap. *Journal of School Health, 81*(10), 593–98.

Baydu, M. M., Kaplan, O., & Bayar, A. (2013). Facing the influence of poverty on graduation rates in public high schools. *Procedia—Social and Behavioral Sciences, 84,* 233–37.

Bell, W. K. (2020, August 2). *What will the new school year look like? Start with unequal.* www.cnn.com/2020/08/02/opinions/united-shades-of-america-public-school-w-kamau-bell/index.html

Bradberry, T., & Greaves, J. (2009). *Emotional intelligence 2.0.* TalentSmart.

Bridgeland, J. M., Dilulio, J. J., & Morison, K. B. (2006). *The silent epidemic: Perspectives of high school dropouts.* http://www.civicenterprises.net/pdfs/ thesilentepidemic3-06.pdf

Burrus, J., & Roberts, R. D. (2012). Dropping out of high school: Prevalence, risk factors, and remediation strategies. *R&D Connections, 18*(2), 1–9.

California State Government and Child Poverty. (2018). *State poverty task force issues plan to end deep child poverty.* https://www.endchildpovertyca.org/press-release-child-poverty-task-force-recommendations/

Claro, S., & Loeb, S. (2017). *New evidence that students' beliefs about their brains drive learning.* https://www.brookings.edu/research/new-evidence-that-students-beliefs-about-their-brains-drive-learning/

Claro, S., Paunesku, D., & Dweck, C. S. (2016). Growth mindset tempers the effects of poverty on academic achievement. *Proceedings of the National Acudemy of Sciences, 113*(31), 8664–68.

Dawson, P., & Guare, R. (2018). *Executive skills in children and adolescents: A practical guide to assessment and intervention.* Guilford.

EdBuild. (2019). *Nonwhite school districts get $23 billion less than White districts despite serving the same number of students.* https://edbuild.org/content/23-billion

Evans, G. W. (2016). Childhood poverty and adult psychological well-being. *Proceedings of the National Academy of Sciences, 113*(52), 14949–52.

Evans, M. D. R., Kelley, J., & Sikora, J. (2014). Scholarly culture and academic performance in 42 nations. *Social Forces, 92*(1), 1573–1605. https://doi.org/10.1093/sf/sou030

Hernandez, D. J. (2011). *Double jeopardy: How third-grade reading skills and poverty influence high school graduation.* Annie E. Casey Foundation. http://eric.ed.gov/?id=ED518818

Gorski, P. C. (2011). Unlearning deficit ideology and the scornful gaze: Thoughts on authenticating the class discourse in education. *Counterpoints, 402,* 152–73.

Gorski, P. C. (2017). *Reaching and teaching students in poverty: Strategies for erasing the opportunity gap.* Teachers College Press.

Jensen, E. (2009). *Teaching with poverty in mind: What being poor does to kids' brains and what schools can do about It.* ASCD.

Kozol, J. (2005). *The shame of the nation: The restoration of apartheid schooling in America.* Broadway.

Lacour, M., & Tissington, L. D. (2011). The effects of poverty on academic achievement. *Educational Research and Reviews, 6*(7), 522–27.

Lleras-Muney, A. (2005). The relationship between education and adult mortality in the United States. *Review of Economic Studies, 72*(1), 189–221.

Maslach, C. (2003). *Burnout: The cost of caring.* Prentice-Hall.

McCloud, C. (2007). *Have you filled a bucket today? A guide to daily happiness for kids.* Ferne.

Payne, R. K. (1995). *A framework for understanding poverty.* aha! Process.

Rampey, B. D., Dion, G. S., & Donahue, P. L. (2009). *NAEP 2008: Trends in academic progress.* NCES 2009–479. National Center for Education Statistics.

Reardon, S. F. (2013). The widening income achievement gap. *Educational Leadership, 70*(8), 10–16

Sum, A. M., & Fogg, W. N. (1991). The adolescent poor and the transition to early adulthood. In *Adolescence & poverty: Challenge for the 1990s* (P. Edelman & J. Ladner, Eds., pp. 37–110). Center for National Policy Press.

U.S. Department of Education. (2001). *The longitudinal evaluation of school change and performance (LESCP) in Title I schools.* Government Printing Office.

U.S. Department of Health and Human Services. (2019). *HHS poverty guidelines for 2019.* https://aspe.hhs.gov/poverty-guidelines

Vera, D. (2011). Using popular culture print to increase emergent literacy skills in one high-poverty urban school district. *Journal of Early Childhood Literacy, 11*(3), 307–30.

Learners With Special Needs in General Education Classrooms

Setting the Classroom Scene

Mrs. Jonas has been a teacher for 15 years, primarily in lower elementary grades, where she has taught kindergarten, first grade, and third grade. She is about to begin her second year teaching a third-grade class and considers herself a veteran and effective teacher. During her career she has generally had very few students with Individualized Education Programs (IEPs) in her classrooms, mainly because in her school system the majority of students are not fully evaluated for special education services until their second-grade year. In fact, Mrs. Jonas has never had a class with more than two students with IEPs. Until this year.

During the workdays prior to the school year starting, Mrs. Jonas is given her class roster and notices that four of the students have an asterisk by their names. She knows the asterisk means the student qualifies for special services, either due to being eligible for special education services, being noted as at risk, or being identified as an English-language learner (ELL). She knows an asterisk may mean gifted but also knows this is rare in the lower elementary grades. She asks some questions about her roster and is surprised to learn that all four of the students have IEPs. Two of the students have qualified for special education services with a specific learning disability in reading, one has been diagnosed with autism spectrum disorder and qualifies for special education, and the fourth has a hearing impairment that requires special education services. Mrs. Jonas has not dealt with this degree of special education diversity in one class before and has to take a moment to ponder what these students' needs will mean for her teaching.

Prereading Questions

1. What are some of the issues confronting Mrs. Jonas? Why would she think this class may pose a unique set of challenges for her?

2. Consider the issues you identified in your preceding answer. How do you think these issues could play out in the classroom? How do you think you would handle your first time having a class of students with such a diverse range of abilities?

3. How would you describe the diversity Mrs. Jonas is encountering in her classroom? Is it merely educational diversity, or are there other facets of diversity represented in the class?

Introduction

> *Special education doesn't mean a student is incapable of learning. It means that they need different supports in order to succeed.*
>
> **—Pramod Kumar Sidar**

Mrs. Jonas is representative of many teachers across the country and around the world who find themselves teaching classes with multiple students receiving special education services. And while many teacher education programs require at least one class with a specific focus on special education, these classes alone are insufficient to fully prepare general education teachers to support students with a wide range of disabilities who are often taught in general education classrooms. This chapter will begin with a brief history of special education and the laws that guide its provision in the United States, followed by a review of the 13 categories of disability under federal law. The chapter will then close with a review of some common evidence-based practices that teachers can utilize to support students with special needs before presenting a scenario to review the chapter content.

The origins of modern special education can actually be traced back to early 19th-century France. Several of the early tenets of special education were established by Jean-Marc-Gaspard Itard when he attempted to teach speech to a young boy found abandoned in the countryside outside the village of St. Sernin in southern France (Nawrot, 2014). The child, found naked and covered in scars and believed to be 11 or 12 years old, was given the name Victor. He became a bit of a sensation, being nicknamed the "Wild Child" as he apparently had grown up outside of society and was unable to speak. Itard utilized several instructional techniques influenced by Enlightenment philosophers in an attempt to teach Victor to talk (as Itard and many of his contemporaries believed, spoken language was the fundamental key to learning [Nawrot, 2014]). Itard's student Eduoard Seguin continued his mentor's efforts in his own attempts to teach children who were considered uneducable (Spaulding & Deanna, 2010).

The methods of Itard and Seguin helped establish the following principles, many of which can still be seen commonly applied in special education today (Daniel, 2018):

- Individualized instruction

- Sequenced instruction

- Emphasis on stimulation of senses

- Meticulous arrangement of the child's environment

- Immediate reward for correct performance

- Tutoring in functional skills

- The idea that every child can improve to some degree

These seven principles put great significance on the individual nature of special education, as the first concept demonstrates. Students with special needs require individualized instruction that is designed to help them have the greatest access to the general education curriculum. Unfortunately, this type of education has not always been provided in the United States, where special education took quite some time to take hold as a formal practice.

Special Education Law: A Brief History

In the United States, special education was not formalized through federal law until the late 20th century. In the 19th century, students who might now be recognized as qualifying for special education services were often kept out of the schools (a distinct exception can be found in the establishment of schools for the deaf and schools for the blind). This practice of exclusion continued into the 20th century, though advocacy groups for excluded students began to form and formally request more state support for students with special needs. In conjunction with the civil rights movement and after the desegregation ordered by the *Brown v. Board of Education* Supreme Court ruling, in 1954, it appeared that the overt and covert discrimination against individuals with disabilities might be addressed by federal and state laws. This was not the case until 1975, when the landmark Public Law 94-142 (PL 94-142) was passed (United States, 1975).

Titled the Education for All Handicapped Children Act, PL 94-142 was an incredibly consequential piece of federal legislation that legitimized the right of all students with disabilities to receive a free and appropriate public education (FAPE). PL 94-142 included additional guiding principles that are still of paramount importance in the provision of services for students with disabilities. After its initial passage in 1975, this special education law was periodically revised to address additional issues and concerns pertaining to the needs of students with disabilities. Table 5.1 provides an overview of the significant portions of the original law and its subsequent revisions (Smith & Tyler, 2018).

Special education law in the United States is not static. As evidenced by the routine revisions in Table 5.1, the law is updated from time to time to better support students with special needs. It has been some time since the most significant revisions to the law, in 2004, but history suggests revisions may be coming in the near future. These changes may be very significant or offer subtle changes to the provision of services for students in special education. Either way, the law will continue to influence how teachers must support and instruct the approximately 14% of American students who qualify for special education (NCES, 2017).

Pause and Discuss

In a small group, review the history of special education law in the United States as just presented. Discuss among yourselves which three specific parts/revisions to special education law have the most significant effect on you, directly, as a classroom teacher. Be ready to share why you picked those three parts/revisions and how you believe they should influence your preparation as an educator.

TABLE 5.1 Special Education Law and Revisions Since 1975

YEAR	Law and Significant Components
1975	Public Law 94-142, Education for all Handicapped Children Act –Guaranteed a free and appropriate (FAPE) public education to all students with disabilities in their least restrictive environment (LRE). LRE should always be the child's general education classroom with the proper provision of accommodations and modifications, and LRE would not be that original classroom only if the child's needs justify her or his removal for more intensive support. –Established procedural safeguards for students receiving special education services, most significantly the right to due process for parents who believed their children were not receiving appropriate supports. –Established the right of each child receiving special education to have an individualized education program (IEP). –Established the practice of nondiscriminatory evaluation to determine whether a child has a disability. –Guaranteed a parent's or guardian's right to access a child's educational records.
1986	Public Law 99-457 –Added the requirement that infants and toddlers are to be covered by special education law. This in effect ensured that children and students in the United States are covered by special education law from birth to age 21. –Mandated the provision of an Individual Family Service Plan (IFSP) to children younger than kindergarten age who have a verified disability and qualify for special education services.
1990	Public Law 101-476 –One of the most important parts of this amendment was the renaming of the law to the Individuals with Disabilities Education Act, or IDEA. This name change is reflective of person-first language, wherein someone is not identified by a disability or characteristic in the nomenclature. It is the respectful way to talk about students with disabilities, not an "autistic kid" or "those sped students." –This revision also added transition plans to the services provided for students meeting special education eligibility. Transition plans are meant for older students with disabilities and are specifically designed to aid those students in transitions from secondary schools to life in postsecondary education, career, or community settings. –For the first time, autism was added as a disability category under federal law. –Also, traumatic brain injury was added as a disability category.
1997	Public Law 105-17 –Formally added attention-deficit/hyperactivity disorder (ADHD) to the other health impairment disability category. (Not without controversy, it should be noted. ADHD is a disorder characterized by inattention, impulsivity, and/or hyperactivity, and those symptoms have to impair a child's learning for the child to qualify for special education. The idea that an ADHD diagnosis alone will qualify a student for special education is inaccurate.) –This revision also added specific language to special education law regarding functional behavioral assessments (FBAs) and behavior intervention plans (BIPs). Specifically, the law was revised to require that schools have formal documentation via an FBA of the causes and consequences of a student's disruptive behaviors, and if those behaviors were disruptive enough a BIP would need to be created to teach the child positive behaviors through modeling and reinforcement, and other means. –Made transition plans, which had been a separate document, a formal part of a student's IEP.

(continued)

	Public Law 108-446
2004	–One of the more significant changes wrought by this revision was that special education teachers had to be highly qualified. This stemmed from the 2001 law, No Child Left Behind, which had first brought up the highly qualified requirement. In sum, highly qualified means a teacher is certified to teach in a particular area or grade level. –This revision also mandated that all students with disabilities had to participate in required district-wide or statewide assessments or be given an alternative assessment of some sort. Efforts to exclude students from special needs with widespread standardized testing were ended by this part of the law. –The process for how learning disabilities are identified was changed. In the past, a discrepancy between a child's IQ score and performance on a standardized assessment in reading, math, or writing could qualify a student for special education. This revision of the law emphasized that eligibility could not be determined on the basis of one test. Additional evidence is required for students to be considered eligible for special education with a specific learning disability.

Disability Categories Under the IDEA

While it has changed over time, the list of disabilities under the IDEA is one of the most important aspects of the law. No student may receive special education services unless they meets the eligibility criteria established for each category. As of 2016, approximately 9% of all students between ages 6 and 21 in the United States were receiving special education services (U.S. Department of Education, 2018). That is more than six million students. Table 5.2 provides a listing of the disability categories, with a brief description of the primary characteristics of the disability, from the U.S. Department of Education (2018).

TABLE 5.2 Disability Categories and Descriptors From the U.S. Department of Education

Disability	Descriptors
Autism	Often referred to as autism spectrum disorder (ASD), this is a developmental disability affecting verbal and nonverbal communication and social interaction. It is usually evident before age 3, though children older than 3 can still be diagnosed with autism. Communication and social interaction deficits have to negatively affect educational performance for a child to qualify for special education services. Additional signs of autism include engagement in repetitive activities and stereotyped movements, resistance to any change in daily routine or schedule, and sometimes extreme responses to environmental stimuli.
Deaf-blindness	The presence of both severe hearing and visual impairments. Causes such severe communication and educational needs that these students cannot be accommodated in special education programs geared for students with only one of the two impairments.

Adapted from: U.S. Department of Education, "Disability Categories and Descriptors from the U.S. Department of Education," 40th Annual Report to Congress on the Implementation of the Individuals with Disabilities Education Act, 2018.

Deafness	Means a hearing impairment so severe that the child is impaired in processing linguistic information through hearing, either with or without amplification. This linguistic processing deficit must be severe enough to negatively affect a child's educational performance for the child to qualify for special education services.
Emotional disturbance	Condition signified by one or more of the following characteristics over a substantial period and to such a significant level that the characteristics adversely affect a child's educational performance: Problems with learning or mastering curriculum that cannot be explained by intellectual, sensory, or health factors. Problems with creating and maintaining satisfactory interpersonal relationships with peers and teachers. Abnormal behavior or feelings under normal circumstances. Continually pervasive mood of depression or unhappiness. Development of physical symptoms or fears associated with either personal or school difficulties.
Hearing impairment	Means an adversity in hearing, whether permanent or fluctuating, that causes obvious detriment to a child's educational performance.
Intellectual disability	Means substantially below average general intellectual functioning. This below average intellectual performance exists together with serious deficits in functional and adaptive skills and behaviors. These characteristics are generally evident during a child's developmental period and clearly impair the child's ability to learn.
Multiple disabilities	Means the combination and presence of two impairments, such as intellectual disability-deafness or intellectual disability-orthopedic impairment. Much like deaf-blindness, the presence of multiple disabilities in a child requires the provision of special education services at a higher and more intensive degree than if only one of the two impairments were present.
Orthopedic impairment	A severe orthopedic impairment that negatively affects a child's educational performance. The category includes impairments caused by congenital anomalies, impairments caused by disease (e.g., poliomyelitis, bone tuberculosis), and impairments from other causes (e.g., cerebral palsy, amputations, and fractures or burns that cause contractures).
Other health impairment	Characterized by having limited strength, vitality, or alertness that results in limited alertness toward the educational environment and is due to chronic or acute health problems, including asthma, diabetes, attention deficit hyperactivity disorder, epilepsy, or several other specific conditions; and adversely affects a child's educational performance.
Specific learning disability	A dysfunction in one or more of the basic mental and neurological processes involved in understanding or using language, in either spoken or written formats. The dysfunction may appear as an imperfect ability to read, write, listen, or speak, or to do mathematical calculations. Specific learning disabilities may include dyslexia and dysgraphia.
Speech-language impairment	A communication disorder, including stuttering or other impaired articulation, that adversely affects a child's educational performance. Speech-language impairments can manifest as either expressive or receptive language disorders.

(continued)

Traumatic brain injury	An injury to the brain caused by an external physical force. The injury results in psychosocial impairment and/or functional disabilities that adversely affects a child's educational performance. Traumatic brain injury applies to open or closed head injuries resulting in dysfunction in one or more areas pertaining to learning, including cognitive functioning, language use, memory, attention, and several others. It should be noted that the symptoms and characteristics of Traumatic Brain Injury may resemble those of other disability categories but that the etiology, or cause of the problem, is more evident based on brain trauma.
Visual impairment	Visual impairment including blindness is an impairment in vision that, even with corrective measures, negatively impacts a child's educational performance. The term includes both partial sight and blindness.

Everybody is a genius. But if you judge a fish by its ability to climb a tree, it will live its whole life believing that it is stupid.

—Albert Einstein

It is important to understand that for all of the 13 categories briefly described in Table 5.2, the concept of "educational impairment" is necessary for a student to receive special education services. One way to think about that aspect is to consider the following phrase: "There is no disability without impairment." That means, for example, that while everyone may feel sad, angry, anxious, or impulsive from time to time, unless those feelings are continuous and cause definitive impairments in daily life activities, then the term *disability* is inappropriate. Making it specific to education, "There is no disability requiring special education without educational impairment."

> Write a short paragraph describing your experiences with any of the disabilities categorized under the IDEA. The experience can be from any point in your life and does not have to be limited to interactions in a school setting. Be ready to discuss what the experience taught you about that particular disability.

Pause and Reflect

Inclusion

The concept of including students with special needs in regular education classrooms is broadly referred to as inclusion. Inclusion as an educational movement was an effort to end segregation practices that excluded learners with special needs from what should have been their regular education classroom if no disability were present. The process of inclusion took some time to gather momentum, but there was an obvious shift toward this practice in the 1980s (Mittler, 2000; Opretti & Belalcazar, 2008). Inclusion as a practice is imperfect; that is, while the concept of including students with disabilities in general education classrooms as much as possible is generally agreed to be the best practice, the logistics of ensuring resources and teacher training at appropriate levels for inclusion to work are often quite variable and differ between schools and school systems.

Inclusion requires that learners with special needs be provided with appropriate adaptations, accommodations, and modifications to support their access to and participation in the general education curriculum. Unfortunately, based on multiple factors, the mechanisms to provide these supports to learners with special needs are not always easily incorporated into regular education classrooms (Fuchs, 2010). Research has been consistent in identifying barriers to inclusion (Cheminais, 2013). Although these barriers may be called different things, they can generally be included in the following broad concepts, described by Worrell (2008):

- Negative teacher perceptions: This one boils down to educators themselves having a bad impression of inclusion. For whatever reason, they do not feel positive about the practice, and these attitudes can negatively affect the implementation of true inclusion.

- Lack of knowledge regarding special education law and procedures: A common theme, and not surprising based on the lack of special education courses required in most teacher education programs, lack of knowledge is absolutely a barrier to effective inclusion. Teachers already have a great deal of responsibility and often feel that being expected to practice inclusion is one more challenge, given what they know or do not know about special education.

- Poor collaboration: A problem in many professional and personal relationships, the lack of working together in true collaboration can impede inclusion. Education professionals must communicate effectively for inclusion to truly benefit not only students with special needs but all students in an inclusive classroom.

- Lack of administrative support: There is a strong notion that inclusion can only work if school administrators provide the proper support system for it. Teachers often think school administrations do not fully understand what inclusion requires and therefore do not provide all of the training and materials necessary for the practice. School administrators are hard-pressed with all the issues affecting a school, and they face a challenge in fully supporting the implementation of inclusion.

- Limited instructional repertoire: This barrier goes back to the perceived lack of knowledge concerning special education and its practices. Teachers know that students with special needs require interventions and accommodations, but they often feel underprepared to provide these services. They do not believe they have the instructional methodologies that will most help students with special needs, and most believe they were not adequately prepared by their teacher preparation programs to have those strategies.

- Inappropriate assessments: This barrier is created by the often intense demands of conducting routine assessments on students to determine their progress through the curriculum. Differentiating assessments and individualizing them to best assess learners with special needs takes time and cognitive energy. This additional demand of effective inclusion is just one more reason that inclusion is often put into practice at a high level.

- Conflicting schedules and time management: This last barrier to inclusion is based on the fact that general education teachers and special education teachers do not always have the same schedules. It is therefore difficult to establish routine meetings necessary to ensure the provision of special education services to students in the general education classroom. All teachers have a finite amount of time for planning and instruction, and planning for the provision of accommodations and modifications to students with special needs does take time. Teachers often find it difficult to manage their time even without considering students with special needs; having to individualize instruction for those students in conjunction with special education teachers does present a time management challenge.

By now it should be clear that the practice of inclusion is an ongoing challenge for schools and teachers. Yet despite all of the acknowledged difficulties in creating a truly inclusive school, there are many parents and educators who push for the concept of full inclusion. Full inclusion is different from inclusion in one dramatic and critical way, as full inclusion is based on the idea that all students with special needs will spend all of their time in general education classrooms. Those who believe in full inclusion believe strongly that the obstacles to inclusion can and should be overcome and that students with special needs can and should receive all proper supports in the general education classroom. There is little evidence to suggest such an approach is truly what is best for all students with special needs, but the idea of full inclusion still has many advocates. In the end it is truly a matter of opinion. One could argue both sides, that some inclusion is better than none and that full inclusion is the best possible path. What is not a matter of opinion is that in schools today, more than half of the students receiving special education services spend approximately 80% of their time in general education classrooms (U.S. Department of Education, 2018). That means, simply, that nearly all teachers will work with a student with an IEP at multiple points in their careers.

Write your opinion on inclusion. Include in your statement what you know about the practice and how you feel about its implementation. If you agree with or have experienced any of the barriers included in the preceding section, document those in your statement. Justify your position with facts and evidence and also as much personal experience as you can.

Pause and Reflect

Evidence-Based Practices for Inclusion of Students With Special Needs

If a child cannot learn in the way we teach, we must teach in a way the child can learn.

—Ivar Lovaas

Knowing that nearly all teachers will work with students with special needs means that teachers should have some resources to better serve these students. To introduce this section of the chapter, it is necessary to review the concept of differentiation. Although there are multiple definitions for differentiation, to summarize, it means teachers are using a variety of instructional arrangements—strategies, resources, materials—to address their students' individual learning strengths and challenges (Dobbertin, 2012; Salend, 2016; Van Garderen & Whittaker, 2006). A good way to view differentiation is to understand that you can fundamentally differentiate a lesson's content, process, and product. *Content* refers to the instructional materials you are utilizing to support students' engagement in teaching or learning activities; *process* refers to the specific pedagogical practices a teacher utilizes during instruction; and *product* refers to the student work or assessments produced from the instruction. Modifying any or all of those three facets of teaching gets to the heart of differentiation, and differentiated instruction is a key method in supporting all learners, including those with special needs (Beecher & Sweeny, 2008).

This section began with differentiation because practicing differentiation requires that teachers implement evidence-based practices (EBPs) into their instructional repertoire. An EBP is an instructional method that has a research—or evidence—base, suggesting it is effective for teaching a certain skill or concept or for teaching a specific group of students based on particular needs (Cook & Odom, 2013). The remainder of this section will present a diverse group of differentiation strategies that teachers can use when designing lessons and implementing them in the classroom. The assumption for all the following ideas is that the students with special needs who are placed in general education classrooms can be successful given appropriate supports. The ideas presented are by no means exhaustive but rather starting points to consider when supporting those students receiving special education services in a general education classroom.

Adapting Instruction

Students with special needs often benefit from the same type of teaching that benefits all students. Ample evidence suggests, however, that students with special needs in inclusive classrooms achieve at a higher level when teachers make a plan to accommodate their specific needs. Adapting instruction for students with special needs involves accommodations, which are changes in input and output processes in teaching and assessment, and/or modifications, which are changes to content (Polloway, Epstein, & Bursuck, 2002). It is important to note the distinction between an accommodation, which is considered an adjustment or change to environmental factors in the classroom, and a modification, which is a change to the materials used during instruction. Some examples of evidence-based instructional adaptations include adjusting the pace of instruction to individual learners (Greenwood, Delquadri, & Hall, 1984), appealing to multiple learning styles via multisensory approaches (Gallavan & Kottler, 2012), and providing immediate individual feedback to a specific student with a disability (Hattie & Temperley, 2007).

A very effective technique for students with information-processing deficits is to incorporate visuals. Visuals are representations of material that do not require reading and are easily understood by simply viewing them. For example, Webster (2018) shares the method of using "a lot of cards for my students with autism, to teach sight vocabulary, attributes, safety signs and to evaluate new vocabulary" (para. 2). The use of visuals is driven by the notion that teachers can present information in multiple ways, including illustrations, models, and technology. These multiple means of representation give more students access to the content, especially students who may struggle to understand content presented in more traditional formats. Multisensory opportunities may include tasting foods from different cultures, watching videos, listening to music, or having manipulatives available that represent specific curricular content. Movement is an active strategy that is particularly useful for kinesthetic learners.

Adapting Assignments

Adapting assignments falls under the modification category of instructional adaptations. Adaptations are often necessary to ensure that students with special needs have the greatest success with the general education curriculum. There are multiple ways to adapt assignments. Evidence-based approaches include breaking academic tasks into smaller steps (Alexander & Judy, 1988), shortening assignments (e.g., Nowacek & Mamlin, 2007), incorporating modeling into instruction (e.g., Ledford & Wolery, 2013), and using materials at an instructional level more appropriate for a child's capabilities (Treptow, Burns, & McComas, 2007). The choices teachers make when adapting assignments should always be based on the particular needs of the student receiving the support, and consideration should be given to how that support is directly tied to instructional goals. Adaptations do require cognitive effort from educators. The driving idea behind making adaptations should always be what is best for the student or students. It may take a little time and some degree of trial and error before teachers can themselves become adept at adaptations.

Teaching Learning Skills

Many students with special needs display deficits in selecting and deploying learning strategies (e.g., Hamlett, Pellegrini, & Conners, 1987; O'Neill & Douglas, 1991), which means these students often benefit a great deal from having such strategies taught and supported in the general education classroom. In fact, strategy instruction is one of the most researched practices in supporting students with special needs, and the evidence strongly suggests it is a very effective method for helping these students. Students with special needs benefit when they are explicitly taught study skills, learning skills, and test-taking skills (Reid, Lienemann, & Hagaman, 2013). It is important to note that these skills do vary and that skills for taking a test are clearly going to be different from skills used to learn new material. An example of a learning strategy is the reading strategy RAP: Read a paragraph, ask what is the main idea and two supporting details, and paraphrase the main idea and two supporting details (Hagaman, Luschen, & Reid, 2010). The strategy usually involves a series of steps students can apply to a learning task, much as the three parts of the RAP strategy. Equipping students with disabilities with a variety of strategies—and there are many well-researched strategies that can be considered evidence based—should assist those students a great deal in learning new content.

Varying Instructional Grouping

Teachers often utilize group work during instruction. This idea of having students work together in small groups is based on the overall concept of cooperative learning. Cooperative learning centers on group-learning activities in which reinforcement and success are based upon the group's performance rather than the individual student (Smith et al., 2006). In true cooperative learning, heterogeneous small groups work together to achieve a group goal. And very important, it is understood that each member of the group must contribute for the group to succeed (Slavin, 1987). Educators have viable options for how to vary instructional groups in their classes. One popular and effective method is class-wide peer tutoring, which has shown positive effects on reading comprehension and fluency (Greenwood et al., 2001) and mathematics (Fuchs et al., 2001). A second method is peer-assisted learning strategies, which have been effective in both reading (McLeskley, Rosenberg, & Westling, 2010) and mathematics (Slavin & Lake, 2008).

A word of caution should be noted when considering using collaborative learning approaches to support learners with special needs. Teachers should not overburden students without disabilities and expect them to assume too much responsibility in the learning of their peers with disabilities. While cooperative learning is an effective method for differentiating instruction to support all learners, it should not be viewed as the best method for helping students with special needs. It is one approach and is always most effective when all the students understand why cooperative learning is being used and what the exact expectations for the groups and/or partnerships may be. Teachers should be judicious in how they implement varying instructional grouping. It works, but it should only be used with proper consideration to the needs of the entire class.

> Activity: In a small group, pick a grade level and academic subject, then find a standard that fits the grade and content area. Using that standard, create an assignment and assessment appropriate for the grade level chosen. Then, apply at least three of the evidence-based practices already cited to (1) **teach the curriculum (process)** associated with the assignment, (2) make a **modification to the materials (content)** you will use in your instruction or to the assignment itself, and (3) make a **modification to the assessment (product)** you created. By doing these three things, your group will address the three basic ways teachers can differentiate instruction.

Conclusion

Covering the history of special education and its laws, the different disability categories under federal law, and the concepts of inclusion and evidence-based practices often takes entire textbooks. This chapter attempted to provide a broad yet useful overview of the many facets of special education. A basic understanding of how special education affects schools and individual students is a fundamental piece of knowledge for all educators. While obviously not exhaustive, the content of this chapter was meant to establish the beginnings of that foundation.

KEY CHAPTER TAKEAWAYS

Some important takeaways from this chapter include:

- Special education is founded on the guaranteed right of all students to receive a free and appropriate public education.

- That means that no student can be denied an education, and that is a particularly important safeguard for students with disabilities, who have had an unfortunate history of exclusion until the past half century.

- It is also important to remember that while there are laws governing the provision of special education, the day-to-day services provided to students with special needs falls to many different people associated with school systems.

- Those individuals need a basic working knowledge of the characteristics of disabilities but also need to know some basic instructional practices for helping those students succeed in our schools.

- Evidence-based practices for supporting learners with special needs in a general education classroom include adapting instruction, adapting assignments, explicitly teaching learning strategies, and using flexible grouping.

- The concept of teaching every student is ultimately a noble calling of acceptance. When teachers accept and embrace their role in supporting the various needs of students with disabilities, they become a powerful force for learning for those students.

CASE SCENARIO: THE INTERVIEW CONTINUES

"I'd like to get your thoughts on another example of a diverse classroom," Mrs. Frayer said.

Kortney nodded her assent. She was beginning to sense an ebb and flow to how Mrs. Frayer presented these stories and then awaited the responses. She hoped she had been answering well so far, but she wasn't sure. Some of the stories Mrs. Frayer was telling were really on unfamiliar ground for Kortney.

"This example is about a class," Mrs. Frayer began. "It is fairly representative of a lot of classes, but what makes this story unique is that the teacher in this classroom, Mrs. Vinson, was facing a class like it for the very first time." And then the principal presented the following scenario to Kortney.

The class has 14 male students and 10 female students, with nine of the students qualifying for free and reduced lunch. Four of the students are receiving special education intervention services; two for specific reading disabilities, one for ASD, and one for hearing impairment. Standardized testing indicates students in the class are reading on a range covering early first-grade to just short of fifth-grade levels. The students with IEPs are all below grade level in reading and in math, and the student with ASD has a BIP due to sporadic outbursts of temper. These instances are generally caused by changes to the student's routine schedule. The child with a hearing impairment is scheduled to receive 30-minute speech-language services twice weekly. The students with reading disabilities are pulled from the class three times a week, for 30 minutes each time, to work on reading interventions with a special education teacher.

Beyond the learning differences present in the class, there is cultural diversity. Exactly half the class, 12 students, are Caucasian, while seven are African American, four are Latino, and one is Asian American. The students have distinct personalities, with a few being very shy and reserved while an equal number are very talkative. The school assigns classes differently each year, so the exact group of students has never been in the same room before. It is evident that Mrs. Vinson will need to be very proactive in working with her students based on the wide range of needs and ability levels present in the class.

This wide range of ability levels is especially of concern to Mrs. Vinson as her students approach the state reading test. She has about one month before the test is administered, and she is already worried about her students' performance. Her daily assessment records, both informal and formal, indicate that her students who started the year behind their peers have not made good progress to improve their reading abilities. Furthermore, she has noticed two of her students slipping a bit; their recent progress in reading has tapered off when compared with the students in class who are, as a group, making adequate progress toward the next reading level. Mrs. Vinson is beginning to wonder what specifically she can do to improve her class's performance on the reading test. She knows she needs a course of action she can follow to ensure she is doing everything possible to help her students.

WORKING WITH THE SCENARIO

"There you have it," Mrs. Frayer said. "Quite the interesting class for Mrs. Vinson. And based on that example, I have a couple of questions for you."

"Yes, ma'am," Kortney answered. "I'll do my best."

"Very good," Mrs. Frayer responded. "With whom can Mrs. Vinson work to help her students' reading performance? And how can she go about making that collaborative effort work? Lastly, are there some strategies she could use on her own that might help her students?"

If you were Kortney, how would you respond to the questions posed by Mrs. Frayer?

REFERENCES

Alexander, P. A., & Judy, J. E. (1988). The interaction of domain-specific and strategic knowledge in academic performance. *Review of Educational Research, 58*(4), 375–404.

Beecher, M., & Sweeny, S. M. (2008). Closing the achievement gap with curriculum enrichment and differentiation: One school's story. *Journal of Advanced Academics, 19*(3), 502–30.

Cheminais, R. (2013). *How to create the inclusive classroom: Removing barriers to learning.* Routledge.

Cook, B. G., & Odom, S. L. (2013). Evidence-based practices and implementation science in special education. *Exceptional Children, 79*(2), 135–44.

Daniel, P. H. (2018). *Exceptional learners: An introduction to special education.* Pearson.

Dobbertin, C. (2012). Just how I need to learn it. *Educational Leadership, 69*(5), 66–70.

Fuchs, D., Fuchs, L. S., Thompson, A., Svenson, E., Yen, L., Al Otaiba, S., & Saenz, L. (2001). Peer-assisted learning strategies in reading: Extensions for kindergarten, first grade, and high school. *Remedial and Special Education, 22*(1), 15–21.

Fuchs, W. W. (2010). Examining teachers' perceived barriers associated with inclusion. *SRATE Journal, 19*(1), 30–35.

Gallavan, N. P., & Kottler, E. (2012). Advancing social studies learning for the 21st century with divergent thinking. *Social Studies, 103*(4), 165–70.

Greenwood, C. R., Arreaga-Mayer, C., Utley, C. A., Gavin, K. M., & Terry, B. J. (2001). ClassWide peer tutoring learning management system: Applications with elementary-level English language learners. *Remedial and Special Education, 22*, 34–47.

Greenwood, C. R., Delquadri, J., & Vance Hall, R. (1984). Opportunity to respond and student academic performance. *Focus on behavior analysis in education*, 58–88.

Hagaman, J. L., Luschen, K., & Reid, R. (2010). The "RAP" on reading comprehension. *Teaching Exceptional Children, 43*(1), 22–29.

Hamlett, K. W., Pellegrini, D. S., & Conners, C. K. (1987). An investigation of executive processes in the problem-solving of attention deficit disorder-hyperactive children. *Journal of Pediatric Psychology, 12*, 227–40.

Hattie, J., & Timperley, H. (2007). The power of feedback. *Review of Educational Research, 77*(1), 81–112.

Ledford, J. R., & Wolery, M. (2013). Peer modeling of academic and social behaviors during small-group direct instruction. *Exceptional Children, 79*(4), 439–58.

McLeskley, J., Rosenberg, M. S., & Westling, D. L. (2010). *Inclusion: Effective practices for all students.* Merrill/Pearson.

Mittler, P. (2000). *Working towards inclusive education: Social contexts.* David Fulton.

NCES (National Center for Education Statistics). (2017). *Students with disabilities.* https://nces.ed.gov/programs/coe/indicator_cgg.asp

Nawrot, E. (2014). "Victor the wild boy" as a teaching tool for the history of psychology. *Teaching of Psychology, 41*(3), 237–41.

Nowacek, E., & Mamlin, N. (2007). General education teachers and students with ADHD: What modifications are made? *Preventing School Failure, 51*(3), 28–35.

O'Neill, M. E., & Douglas, V. I. (1991). Study strategies and story recall in attention-deficit disorder and reading disability. *Journal of Abnormal Child Psychology, 19*, 671–92.

Opretti, R., & Belalcazar, C. (2008). Trends in inclusive education at regional and interregional levels: Issues and challenges. *Prospects, 38*(1), 113–35.

Polloway, E. A., Epstein, M. H., & Bursuck, W. D. (2002). Homework for students with learning disabilities. *Reading and Writing Quarterly, 17*, 181–87.

Reid, R., Lienemann, T. O., & Hagaman, J. L. (2013). *Strategy instruction for students with learning disabilities* (2nd ed.). Guilford.

Salend, S. J. (2016). *Creating inclusive classrooms: Effective, differentiated, and reflected practices.* Pearson.

Slavin, R. (1987). Ability grouping and student achievement in elementary schools: A best-evidence synthesis. *Review of Educational Research, 57*(3), 293–336.

Slavin, R. E., & Lake, C. (2008). Effective programs in elementary mathematics: A best-evidence synthesis. *Review of Educational Research, 78*(3), 427–515.

Smith, D. D., & Tyler, N. C. (2018). *Introduction to contemporary special education: New horizons* (2nd ed.). Pearson Education.

Smith, T. E. C., Polloway, E. A., Patton, J. R., & Dowdy, C. A. (2006). *Teaching students with special needs in inclusive settings* (4th ed.). Pearson.

Spaulding, L. S., & Deanna, L. (2010). The history of special education: Lessons from the past, implications for the future. *Faculty Presentations and Publications, 158*. http://digitalcommons.liberty.edu/educ_fac_pubs/158

Treptow, M. A., Burns, M. K., & McComas, J. J. (2007). Reading at the frustration, instructional, and independent levels: The effects on students' reading comprehension and time on task. *School Psychology Review, 36*(1), 159–66.

United States. (1975). *Public law 94-142: Education for all Handicapped Children Act of 1975*. U.S. Government Printing Office.

U.S. Department of Education. (2018). *The fortieth annual report to Congress on the implementation of IDEA*. U.S. Government Printing Office.

Van Garderen, D., & Whittaker, C. (2006). Planning differentiated, multicultural instruction for secondary inclusive classrooms. *Teaching Exceptional Children, 3*(3), 12–20.

Webster, J. (2018). Differentiation in special education: Differentiating instruction for success. Retrieved from http://specialed.about.com/od/integration/a/root.htm

Worrell, J. L. (2008). How secondary schools can avoid the seven deadly school "sins" of inclusion. *American Secondary Education, 36*(2), 43–56.

6

Learners With Special Needs Receiving Services in Separate Settings

Setting the Classroom Scene

Ron Franklin was driving to work on a Wednesday morning in late February. Ron is a special education teacher at Northwest Middle School, and his teaching assignment is running the self-contained classroom for students with emotional-behavioral disorders and a few students with ASD whose symptoms include occasional violent outbursts. He has been doing this job for 3 years and has found a happy medium in dealing with students who most teachers do not want in their classes. He understands. The behaviors he has to manage each day would be very disruptive to any classroom. He is thinking about this, how he has managed to remain effective in working with a challenging student population, when he rounds a curve and sees Billy Scott up ahead, waiting for the bus to pick him up in front of his house.

"Just one day," Ron thinks, "just one absence, please." Ron cannot help the thought as it surfaces, and he sighs audibly as he passes Billy. Thankfully, Billy does not know what vehicle Ron drives, so there is no recognition. In his 3 years Ron has not had to deal with any student quite as disruptive or disrespectful as Billy. Billy refuses to do his work, picks fights with other students in the classroom, uses inappropriate language, and even mocks Ron and the full-time aide assigned to the classroom. Ron has tried multiple approaches to alter Billy's behavior and attitude for the better, including implementing behavior contracts with rewards and incentives, adjusting the daily routine in the class to be more appealing to Billy, and even resorting to outright bribery on more than one occasion. Nothing has worked so far. Just yesterday in the middle of a math lesson, Billy crumpled up his paper and threw it on the floor, proclaiming loudly, "I ain't doing this crap anymore."

And it is because of this ongoing pattern of behaviors that Ron had thought "just one absence." For in addition to his prevailing negative and disruptive behaviors and attitude, Billy has another distinguishing feature. He has perfect attendance. Billy has arrived at school every day since August, and he has been a terror in Ron's classroom and even in the lunchroom and gym. His behaviors have never gotten to the point of an out-of-school suspension, though he has been given in-school suspension more than once. And so Ron drives on, knowing that today will most likely resemble the rest of the school year. He will have to deal with Billy.

Prereading Questions

1. Think back to the previous chapter and the content on special education law. Think particularly about the concept of FAPE, free and appropriate public education, and LRE, least restrictive environment. Based on the short vignette just presented, do you believe that such self-contained classrooms are necessary in today's schools? Be prepared to explain the reasoning behind your belief.

2. Do you have any experience with students or children who display negative behaviors or very bad attitudes? How have you dealt with these children? Have you observed any effective means to better manage or even change their behavior patterns?

3. With the little you know about Ron, what do you think of his job? How would you feel if your daily routine as a teacher involved dealing constantly with students such as Billy? How do you believe you would handle the disruptions and disrespect from a student such as Billy or any other student?

Introduction

The job of Ron Franklin from the opening vignette is a possible extreme—though very realistic—example of the teaching roles played by special education teachers who work with students in self-contained settings. The concept of a self-contained classroom is very specific to special education in the sense that it describes a class only for students with disabilities. These disabilities do not necessarily have to be behavior disorders or other conditions that include disruptive behaviors, but many self-contained classrooms are populated by students with things in common with Billy. Fortunately for the majority of students receiving special education services, there are other viable options than a self-contained classroom where they spend the entirety of their school day.

This chapter will cover the service provision options for students with special needs who require more direct and intensive supports than are available to them through inclusion in a general education classroom. Concepts including resource rooms and pull-out services will be introduced and explained, along with the other service options that include special schools and any necessary itinerant services provided at a student's home. There is a continuum of placement options for students with special needs, all driven by the individual child and their specific learning needs. That continuum includes options outside of the regular classroom, and that should not be viewed negatively by those who favor inclusive practices.

Educating students with special needs outside of a general education classroom should not be viewed as segregation. These students should only be removed from their regular classroom when absolutely necessary—when the academic or behavioral evidence indicates this is the best path for their educational success. General education teachers should not think that because a student is "pulled" from the classroom the teacher's role in the child's education is somehow diminished. Teachers have a role to play for these students, whether they are general or special education, and this chapter will help clarify those roles.

Placement Options for Students With Special Needs

The continuum of placement options for students receiving special education services ranges from the absolute least restrictive environment, which is the general education classroom in which the student would be placed were no disabilities present, to special schools designed to support students whose disabilities are more severe and require a much higher degree of intervention and support. The different placement options have created the concept of service delivery models (Eppler & Ross, 2014), which include in their descriptions where students with special needs may receive services. Determining which is the most appropriate placement for a student is an individualistic process. In some cases the answer to the placement question is very obvious, while in others that answer requires more diligent data collection and analysis to justify a placement decision. Placement options matter, as more than half of the students receiving special education services spend approximately 20% of their time in classrooms that are not general education (U.S. Department of Education, 2019). The remainder of this section will provide a brief overview of the continuum of placement options for students receiving special education services.

The General Education Classroom

Special education law is very clear about the preferred placement for a student receiving special education services and spells out the concept of least restrictive environment very concretely. The law, according to the U.S. Department of Education (2017), states:

Each public agency must ensure that—

(i) To the maximum extent appropriate, children with disabilities, including children in public or private institutions or other care facilities, are educated with children who are nondisabled; and

(ii) Special classes, separate schooling, or other removal of children with disabilities from the regular educational environment occurs only if the nature or severity of the disability is such that education in regular classes with the use of supplementary aids and services cannot be achieved satisfactorily.

The preceding language is very clear about the first choice of placement for any student with a disability, but the very first part of the requirements holds a great amount of significance. "To the maximum extent appropriate" suggests that schools should always consider what is appropriate for a particular student. As reviewed in Chapter 5, an inclusive setting is not always the best placement for a child with a disability, especially if in that inclusive setting the child cannot receive the level or intensity of supports they require. The general education classroom would be the most appropriate placement if a student with a disability is provided necessary accommodations and modifications and demonstrates that he or she can succeed in that classroom with those supports.

There is one concept that bears mentioning in this section, and that is mainstreaming. Mainstreaming is the practice of integrating students with disabilities into general education classes, as appropriate, in order to best meet individual needs for the least restrictive environment (Scruggs & Mastropieri, 1996). Mainstreaming is very similar to inclusion, with the exception that students with disabilities can be mainstreamed for only parts of their school day. They may spend half the day in classes only for students with disabilities and the other half in general education classrooms. While it is referenced less frequently than in the past, the practice of mainstreaming does still occur. Saying a student is mainstreamed for particular courses is an accurate statement, given the meaning of mainstreaming. How the term is used and exactly what it means will vary from school to school.

> *There is evidence that students with more seriously impaired reading require more time in intervention to meet grade-level standards.*
> **—Vaughn, Denton, and Fletcher (2010, p. 438)**

"Pull-Out" Services

The next placement option for students with disabilities involves students spending the majority of their day in a general education classroom but being "pulled out" for intervention and remediation services based on their specific academic needs. The term *pull-out* refers to a student going to a non-general education setting to receive services (Smith, Tyler, & Skow, 2017). And while that definition could extend to self-contained or special schools, it is generally meant to describe students who spend only part of their time outside of a general education classroom. These students may require more intensive intervention services in reading, mathematics, or written expression, and their schedule of being pulled from the regular classroom is often dependent on the special education teacher's schedule and availability. This means that pull-out services may not be a daily occurrence but could occur two or three times a week. The frequency and intensity of pull-out services should always be based on the student's individual needs. Lastly, pull-out services are not always academic in nature. Some students with special needs qualify for occupational therapy or speech-language therapy, as two examples, and will be pulled as necessary to receive these services.

At this point it should be noted there is some debate about the effectiveness of pulling students for special education services (e.g., Zigmond, 2003). Research studies going back more than 40 years have tried to determine whether students qualified for special education services are, in fact, better served outside the general education classroom. While some studies found that this process did appear to support academic growth for these students, other studies found contradictory evidence. What the research has continued to suggest is that the level of intensity of services provided, and the methodology in which those services are provided, are much greater indicators of success for students with disabilities (Cook & Schirmer, 2003). And a rational conclusion one could reach is that the more intensive services a student may need, the easier it will be to provide those services outside of a general education classroom.

Resource Classrooms

Resource classrooms are fairly synonymous with the concept of pull-out services and are meant to provide services and support to students with special needs for 20% to 60% of the school day (Smith, Tyler, & Skow, 2017). While that upper percentage may seem high, there are not a great number of students receiving special education services who require that amount of time outside the general education classroom. How a particular school or school system chooses to utilize the resource room approach is quite variable. At one level are schools where students with special needs may request to access support in the resource room, and only when they, the students, feel that support is necessary. A somewhat more formal approach to the resource room would be, for example, if students requiring testing accommodations always went to the resource room to complete required assessments. And perhaps the most systematic use of the resource room is when that location is the identified place for students to receive pull-out interventions on a regularly scheduled basis.

Self-Contained Classrooms

Perhaps one of the more controversial separate settings is the notion of the self-contained classroom, which exists to serve only students with verified disabilities who are placed in one classroom for the majority of their school day. Mr. Franklin's class from the opening vignette is such a self-contained classroom. And the reason for that setting being considered controversial is that it is viewed as a very segregated way to provide services for students with disabilities. It is almost a "school within a school," given how these classrooms are designed to provide nearly all academic instruction to students placed in them.

Self-contained does not mean the students spend their entire day in one classroom. Students with such a placement do go to lunch, recess, and even some classes when their abilities support those options. While elective classes, such as art or computer science, are often the first choice for letting these students be educated with their nondisabled peers, they are by no means the only choice. Once again it comes down to the students' abilities and capacity for success with supports in a general education classroom. General education teachers are often given the opportunity to teach these students. To do so they must provide differentiated instruction, accommodations, and modifications as necessary (refer to the final portion of Chapter 5 for specific strategies).

Special Schools

In some instances, students with low-incidence disabilities (certain disability categories affecting less than 5% of students in special education) will need placements in special schools. Appropriate examples of such schools include schools established to provide services for blind or deaf students or schools whose primary function is to serve individuals with more severe intellectual disabilities. There are states that have established such schools, such as the Alabama Institute for the Deaf and Blind, also known as the Helen Keller School, or the North Carolina School for the Deaf. These institutions exist to support students who require constant levels of intensive support and intervention, a level of support that most school systems are unable to provide at an adequate level.

Issues involving provision of services to students with more intensive needs can lead to difficult situations. If no special school is available or accessible to a student who would be best served in a special school, then the home school district must bear the "burden" of providing the appropriate level of supports. The term *burden* is not meant to demean the needs of students with more profound disabilities but rather to acknowledge that most school systems, for a variety of logistical and personnel reasons, simply lack the resources to provide such a high degree of services to one student. The ramifications of such situations are beyond the scope of this text, but acknowledging there are times when schools struggle to meet the needs of a few students with more severe disabilities is proper in the context of fully understanding placement options. The placement decisions are not always easy and sometimes require creative solutions.

> *The pupils' accounts of their special school experience appear to suggest a much broader notion of inclusion, which views the school as only part of the community to which they belong and as instrumental in preparing them for lifelong inclusion. The pupils' experiences were characterized by achievements, progress and independence, rather than isolation and oppression.*
> **—Allan and Brown (2001, p. 208)**

Home Services

This final section will briefly note there are times when teachers may be tasked with going to a student's home to provide educational services. This actually occurs more often for students who have experienced a health crisis, such as an accident or long-term sickness, and had to miss multiple days of school. In these instances, a teacher might be asked to go to that student's home and provide remediation. Such arrangements often involve the teacher receiving extra pay for working outside the normal school day to support a student. The vast majority of these situations do not involve students in special education, so home services are not even listed as a placement option on the placement continuum. Teachers do not have to provide these itinerant-style services and have the right to refuse the option if they see fit to do so. Teachers should be aware, though, that there may be a time when a student misses several days, even weeks, of their class, and a possible solution to helping that student recover that lost learning time will be the teacher visiting the child's home.

Consider the placement options just reviewed. What do you believe should be the most important factors when determining the least restrictive environment for a student? How would you feel about "hosting" a student from a self-contained classroom in your class? Do you believe most teachers are prepared to provide appropriate accommodations and modifications for students who spend most of their time in a self-contained setting? And finally, how do you feel about teachers possibly having to visit a student in the student's home to provide educational services? Be prepared to explain the rationale behind your answers.

Pause and Reflect

Educational Approaches for Students Served in Separate Settings

There are numerous ways in which educational services can be provided to students who are being educated outside of a general education classroom. As previously noted, teachers in general education classrooms can support students with special needs by providing differentiated instruction, including the strategies covered briefly in Chapter 5. Also, schools that embrace and practice inclusion often support coteaching as a service delivery model. In coteaching, a special education teacher and general education teacher work together as a team to teach a heterogeneous class of students with and without disabilities. If inclusion is not the least restrictive environment for a student with special needs, other service provision methodologies are utilized in separate settings. This section will cover how decisions are made concerning where students with special needs will receive services, the types of instructional services they receive in those separate settings, and the specialized curriculum available for students in separate settings.

Determining Factors

Deciding which service delivery model is the best fit for a student involves a great deal of focused assessment and data collection. If a student is pulled from his or her general education classroom, the preferred setting according to federal law, the IEP team has to provide a justification statement as to why this removal is necessary. Evidence used to decide a student's placement is presented in Table 6.1 (Turnbull et al., 2016).

TABLE 6.1 Determining Factors in Placing a Student in a Separate Setting

Evidence	Description
Standardized test results	Only one part of the eligibility and placement equation, standardized test results still serve a valuable purpose when comparing a student's progress with that of their peers. Schools are now frequently conducing universal testing two or three times a year, meaning there is more standardized assessment data available to the IEP team when planning services for a student with special needs.

Curriculum-based assessments	Curriculum-based assessments are most commonly student work samples, which can include tests, quizzes, or progress-monitoring probes. These work samples all stem from the curriculum being covered in the general education classroom and can provide additional comparative data for how a student with a disability is performing compared with their nondisabled peers.
Observations	In situations in which behaviors are part of the placement consideration, observation data is often a valuable piece of evidence in the decision-making process. Observations can be formal, conducted by the school psychologist, psychometrician, or a special education teacher using a proven observation technique; or informal, which can include notes made by the classroom teacher. In cases where observation data is utilized, the more data collected, the better.
Functional skill assessments	For students with more severe disabilities, functional skills are a significant consideration in placement decisions. Functional skills include basic life skills such as hygiene, food preparation, choosing appropriate clothing, and handling common household tasks. Functional skills assessments are standardized and formalized, and they provide very important information concerning a student's ability to handle, at an appropriate level, many of life's basic functions.

The sources of evidence in Table 6.1 are not exhaustive but do feature common methods used to determine a student's placement. There are other methods available, depending on a student's specific circumstances. And it must be noted very clearly that no placement decisions can be made without involving a student's parents or guardians. Special education law is very clear on how parents or guardians are to be included in any placement decisions.

Instructional Methods

> *DI (or Direct Instruction) is backed by research and is proven to transform all students into confident learners, including at-risk, EL, special education, and at-level students. In DI, skills are introduced gradually, reinforced, and continually assessed, so no student can fall behind. Content is delivered via scripted and quickly paced lessons, while teachers correct errors immediately and motivate students with positive reinforcement.*
>
> **—Hill (2017)**

If a student qualifies to be pulled from a general education classroom, they are clearly in need of more intensive instruction and supports in order to make progress through the curriculum. Having a student placed in a separate setting can make it easier for special education teachers and interventionists to provide the more individualized instruction these students require. The exact methods for how instruction is delivered should be determined based on the student's needs and strengths and will be quite variable. Despite that variability, there are a few instructional systems and techniques that can often be found being utilized in separate settings. These include the following:

Common Instructional Practices in Separate Settings

Direct/explicit instruction: The practice of direct or explicit instruction has long been a method for teaching students with special needs, though there has been some debate as to what the terms actually mean. In simplest terms, direct instruction means a teacher is providing instruction aimed straight at one student, with a clearly defined focus on a set of skills or subskills or a clearly defined knowledge base. More recently, there has been an attempt to operationally define the concept of explicit instruction. Hughes et al. (2017, pp. 141–142) identified five critical components that characterize explicit instruction:

- Segment complex skills.

- Draw student attention to important features of the content through modeling/think-alouds.

- Promote successful engagement by using systematically faded supports/prompts.

- Provide opportunities for students to respond and receive feedback.

- Create purposeful practice opportunities.

These aspects of explicit instruction clearly emphasize the "explicit" terminology associated with the instructional practice. It is a teaching model that requires great attention to detail and is clearly aimed at providing proper supports to students with special needs.

- Small group instruction: Students who receive services in a separate setting may or may not be on similar ability levels, but in many cases a small group of students with similar academic needs may be pulled together to receive intervention or remediation services. In such cases, the students are often taught using the same principles found in explicit instruction. Looking back at the five core components of explicit instruction, it should be clear that those practices can and often are utilized when teaching small groups of learners with special needs.

- Systematic instruction: This instructional approach has much in common with explicit instruction but has some distinguishing features that make it more applicable for students with moderate to severe disabilities. Systematic instruction incorporates the principles of applied behavior analysis and supports teaching on topics ranging from academic skills to functional living behaviors. The system relies on breaking a skill down to its individual components, then identifying which prompts or cues are most effective for teaching each of those components and letting a student build the entire skill through repetition and review. Systematic instruction is characterized by task analysis, identification of antecedents and consequences, identification of attentional cues and responses, prompts, and instructional trials (Collins, 2012). All of those facets require diligence in development and application because one key to the success of systematic instruction is the fidelity with which it is implemented.

- Specific content-based instructional programs: There are multiple instructional programs available for special education teachers to utilize when providing services to students with special needs. In reading, the Orton-Gillingham approach is a well-known method (e.g., Sayeski et al., 2019), as is *Reading Street* (Scott Foresman, 2013). For writing, there are programs such as *Writing by Design K8* (Certified Education Consultants, 2014) and *Redbird Language Arts and Writing* (McGraw-Hill, 2019). And for math, programs include *Touch Math* (2019) and *EnvisionMath 2.0* (Scott Foresman, 2016). There are multiple programs available, and those listed are just a sampling to demonstrate that schools and teachers do have some options when seeking instructional programs for specific academic areas. The feasibility of any of these programs, none of which is free, is entirely dependent on the resources of a school district and the preferences of the teachers who will utilize the programs.

Special Curricula

Acknowledging the varying ability levels and diverse needs of students with disabilities, special curricula have been designed to support these students' specific learning needs. The type of special curriculum utilized will vary from state to state but is almost always created in an effort to grant these students as much access as possible to the general education curriculum. Special curricula go beyond the instructional methodologies described in the preceding section and are more holistic in nature, addressing multiple facets of a child's education. There are no example programs similar to the ones listed in the preceding academic programs because each state has its own curriculum standards. Therefore, special curricula are driven by state standards and will vary from state to state.

Special curricula are often defined by their standards having different names to differentiate them from the general education standards. This nomenclature includes alternative standards or extended standards, as two examples. Regardless of the state, however, special curriculum is most often provided to those students with moderate to severe disabilities who will struggle greatly in accessing the general education curriculum. The changes to the curriculum are not meant to replace the general standards but rather to make them more accessible to students with more intensive needs. Just as teachers should be knowledgeable of the instructional methods available in separate settings, they too should have a sense that special curricula do exist for students who need them.

Pause and Discuss

The preceding content has covered many different methods for how students in separate settings may be taught. Share your responses to the following questions with another student. What do you believe are the most important factors to consider when determining the best methods for teaching these students? Why do you think those are the most significant? Do you have any experience with any of the approaches, methods, or programs mentioned? And if so, what is your opinion of them? And think briefly about special curricula. Do you think there needs to be a separate curriculum for students with moderate to severe disabilities? Is this fair to those students? Be prepared to explain the rationale behind your answers.

Conclusion

Perhaps the most significant idea pointed out in this chapter was in the section on pull-out services, which noted it is not necessarily where a child receives services for special education but rather how those services are provided that makes the greatest difference. A teacher's role may be quite variable when it involves working with or supporting a student placed outside a general education classroom. But all teachers should have a working knowledge of the placement continuum that exists for students whose needs exceed what can be provided in the general education classroom. Teachers should also have some knowledge about the different instructional methodologies and programs that may be offered in those settings.

Students with disabilities present a wide range of ability levels and functional skills. While the hope is clear that these students can be served in their general education classrooms, the fact is that these students often do have needs that cannot be adequately met in those classrooms. It is proper that school systems are able to provide a continuum of placements, ranging from intermittent pull-out services to special schools where available. Determining which placement is best for any particular student will always come down to that student's unique situation, abilities, and needs.

KEY CHAPTER TAKEAWAYS

Some important takeaways from this chapter include:

- There is a placement continuum available for students with special needs.

- The most preferred least-restrictive environment is the student's regular classroom.

- Multiple factors are considered when determining which placement option is best for a student.

- One of the most important determining factors is the level of supports a student requires.

- Teachers working with students in separate settings have multiple instructional approaches available to support these students.

- Special programs exist that can support students in separate settings in improving their reading, written expression, and mathematics skills.

- States have in place special curriculum for students with moderate to severe disabilities who are unable to successfully navigate the general education curriculum.

CASE SCENARIO: THE INTERVIEW CONTINUES

"Interview lasting a lot longer than you expected?" Mrs. Frayer asked.

Kortney, still reeling mentally from all the questions and different scenarios she had been pre-sented, nodded. "Yes, ma'am," she answered. "I can honestly say this has gone on longer than I expected, and none of my interview preparation really got me ready for some of the things you've asked or described."

"I wouldn't expect any mock interviews or online interview suggestions to really prepare anyone for how I conduct my interviews," Mrs. Frayer said. "Part of this process is letting me see how a candidate can deal with the stress of unexpected questions. And these different scenarios I've been pitching at you? They are all steeped in reality and come from my own experiences." She stopped talking then and opened a drawer in her desk. She took out a blue file folder and briefly skimmed its contents before she continued. "This next one is an interesting and unique case," she began. "It's not something my teachers encounter often, but it can and has happened, so I need to know what you think about it and how you might respond." She placed the folder back in the drawer she had opened and then told the following story:

A student with a long history of violent outbursts and aggressive behaviors had been placed in a self-contained classroom early in his fifth-grade year. He spent the majority of his time in that classroom, receiving nearly all of his academic instruction there and attending lunch, recess, phys-ical education, and art or music with the other students in what would be his regular class. Those times when he was with the other students had not always gone smoothly. His aggressive behaviors came and went with no predictable pattern, and though he made some progress with his grade-level curriculum, he was still falling behind his peers in math and reading.

After the midyear break, around Christmas, the teacher in the self-contained classroom had come to Mrs. Frayer with a request. The teacher, Ms. Carlow, had been in special education quite a while and was very well versed in working with students in the self-contained classroom. Her request was therefore a bit surprising to Mrs. Frayer. She asked if she could send four of the students from her self-contained classroom to Mr. Hammond's social studies class. One of those students was the boy with the history of aggression. "I'd like it to be his fifth-period class because he has low numbers in there currently," Ms. Carlow said. "We can transition these four students slowly, letting them spend half the class period in there the first week and then gradually increase it to the full period." When asked why she thought Mr. Hammond would accept the idea, Ms. Carlow said, "I've kept some informal tabs on him this year, and he seems to have the right disposition for this idea. He gets along well enough with the students but isn't a pushover. I think he's the right teacher."

Mrs. Frayer asked for a meeting with both Ms. Carlow and Mr. Hammond before she would approve such an arrangement and also told Ms. Carlow that the students' parents needed to be involved. After a week Ms. Carlow's plan was put into place, and those four students began attend-ing Mr. Hammond's fifth-period social studies class. At the start, the aide from the self-contained room went with the students, but after a few weeks she stopped. And the school year progressed.

WORKING WITH THE SCENARIO

Mrs. Frayer paused, giving Kortney time to process the story, before asking, "Any idea what we often call that kind of thing, taking students from a self-contained setting into a general education classroom?"

Kortney recalled the practice being discussed in one of her courses. "I think that's called main-streaming," she answered, "but I've heard some schools call it 'push-out,' I think."

"You're right on both counts there," Mrs. Frayer said. "Mainstreaming is an older term for it, but I do know a lot of schools are using that term 'push-out' and even calling their self-contained classes 'pull-in.' I'm glad you have a sense of that practice, but I need to run a few questions by you about the example I just shared, okay?"

"Yes, ma'am. I'm ready," Kortney answered.

"Very good," Mrs. Frayer responded. "Thinking about having students added to your class, what specific challenges might Mr. Hammond face when integrating the four students into his class? And who would be appropriate sources of support for Mr. Hammond to make Ms. Carlow's idea successful?"

Mrs. Frayer paused again to let Kortney absorb the questions before continuing. "How would you feel if you were asked to host, in your general education classroom, students from a self-contained classroom?" she asked. "And the last question is, how would you determine if Ms. Carlow's idea was successful or not? What criteria would you apply to determine if those students were being successful in Mr. Hammond's class?"

If you were Kortney, how would you respond to Mrs. Frayer's questions?

REFERENCES

Allan, J., & Brown, S. (2001). Special schools and inclusion. *Educational Review, 53*(2), 199–207. https://doi-org.libproxy.troy.edu/10.1080/00131910120055624

Certified Education Consultants. (2014). *Writing by design K8.* Certified Education Consultants.

Collins, B. C. (2012). *Systematic instruction for students with moderate and severe disabilities.* Brookes.

Cook, B. G., & Schirmer, B. R. (2003). What is special about special education? Overview and analysis. *Journal of Special Education, 37*(3), 200–205.

Eppler, P., & Ross, R. (2014). *Models for effective service delivery in special education programs.* IGI Global.

Hill, M. G. (2017). *Direct instruction in your classroom: 3 reasons to #teachwhatworks.* Medium. https://medium.com/inspired-ideas-prek-12/direct-instruction-in-your-classroom-3-reasons-to-teachwhat-works-e342adec142b

Hughes, C. A., Morris, J. R., Therrien, W. J., & Benson, S. K. (2017). Explicit instruction: Historical and contemporary contexts. *Learning Disabilities Research & Practice, 32*(3), 140–48. https://doi-org.libproxy.troy.edu/10.1111/ldrp.12142

McGraw-Hill. (2019). *Redbird language arts and writing.* McGraw-Hill.

Sayeski, K. L., Earle, G. A., Davis, R., & Calamari, J. (2019). Orton Gillingham: Who, what, and how. *Teaching Exceptional Children, 51*(3), 240–49. https://doi-org.libproxy.troy.edu/10.1177/0040059918816996

Scott Foresman. (2013). *Reading street.* Scott Foresman.

Scott Foresman. (2016). *Envision math 2.0.* Scott Foresman.

Scruggs, T. E., & Mastropieri, M. A. (1996). Teacher perceptions of mainstreaming/inclusion, 1958–1995: A research synthesis. *Exceptional Children, 63*(1), 59–74.

Smith, D. D., Tyler, N. C., & Skow, K. (2017). *Introduction to contemporary special education: New horizons.* Pearson.

Touch Math. (2019). Touch Math.

Turnbull, A. A., Turnbull, R., Wehmeyer, M. L., & Shogren, K. A. (2016). *Exceptional lives: Special education in today's schools* (8th ed.). Pearson.

U.S. Department of Education. (2017). Sec. 300.114 LRE requirements. https://sites.ed.gov/idea/regs/b/b/300.114

U.S. Department of Education, Office of Special Education Programs, Individuals with Disabilities Education Act (IDEA) database, retrieved February 20, 2020, from https://www2.ed.gov/programs/osepidea/618-data/state-level-data-files/index.html#bcc (See *Digest of Education Statistics 2019*, Table 204.60.)

Vaughn, S., Denton, C. A., & Fletcher, J. M. (2010). Why intensive interventions are necessary for students with severe reading difficulties. *Psychology in the Schools, 47*(5), 432–44. https://doi.org/10.1002/pits.20481

Zigmond, N. (2003). Where should students with disabilities receive special education services? Is one place better than another? *Journal of Special Education, 37*(3), 193–99.

Gifted Learners

By Dr. Shirley Farrell

> *What makes a child gifted and talented may not always be good grades in school, but a different way of looking at the world and learning.*
> —**Senator Chuck Grassley**

Setting the Classroom Scene

Mrs. Crawford is a fourth-grade teacher who has taught at the elementary school for 23 years. She has been in second, third, fourth, and fifth grades, but she prefers upper elementary because the students can work more independently. She always teaches the same way every year, with little variance. This year the principal has asked Mrs. Crawford to be a cluster teacher for gifted. She will have all five gifted students in fourth grade in her classroom. In previous school years, she may have had zero to two gifted students. Mrs. Crawford quickly agreed because who doesn't want the smartest students in their classroom!

She thought this year would be easy. She has five teacher helpers to work with the rest of the class. During group work, she is purposeful to put one gifted student in each group as the leader in learning. She finds, however, that the other students do not always get along with the gifted students, and the gifted students end up doing most of the work in the group.

When all students took the beginning-of-year progress-monitoring tests in reading and math, the scores were expected, except for the gifted learners. The scores of three of the five gifted students were at or below grade level:

- One scored at reading grade level 11.8 and math grade level 10.3

- One scored at reading grade level 8.3 and math grade level 8.8

- One scored at reading grade level 8.3 and math grade level 4.2

- One scored at reading grade level 4.1 and math grade level 8.8

- One scored at reading grade level 2.4 and math grade level 4.2

Mrs. Crawford was puzzled that all of the gifted students were not above grade level. She thought they were gifted. She also noted that the gifted students didn't always finish their work first in all subject areas. When they did finish first, they didn't want to do the extra work she had available. She wondered how these students were identified as gifted.

When she asked the gifted students to peer tutor with students who were struggling, they didn't want to help. As a matter of fact, one student asked her if a person has to go to college to be a teacher. Mrs. Crawford replied that she did have to have a college degree and was required to attend professional development every year to maintain her teaching certificate. That gifted student followed up with the question of why he was always asked to work with students who needed help when he had not been to college yet. He wanted to know when he was going to learn something new.

It is now November, and four of the five gifted students are not doing well in her classroom. Their grades have dropped from As to Cs and Ds. These gifted students have stopped turning in their homework but can take the tests and pass them. Two of the students have been acting out in class and creating discipline problems. One of the students cannot sit still but does complete his work. Mrs. Crawford thought this year would be easy, but that's not how it is working out.

Prereading Questions

1. How do you define gifted learners? What misconceptions did Mrs. Crawford believe about gifted learners?

2. If Mrs. Crawford continues to teach the way she always has, what will happen to the gifted learners? What strategies can Mrs. Crawford implement to motivate and engage the gifted learners? Is there anyone who could collaborate with Mrs. Crawford to help support the learning needs of the gifted learners?

3. How does your state define gifted, identify students, and provide services?

Introduction

Inappropriate education has been identified as the single most important cause of poor adjustment among gifted student ...

—Robinson (2002, p. 23)

Mrs. Crawford is learning that gifted students do not behave the way she thought they would. As a preservice teacher, she had a class on exceptional children, but teaching strategies for gifted students were not covered in the class. The gifted specialist at the school has talked about gifted learners during faculty meetings, but she was guilty of not always listening. How hard can it be to teach gifted students? She never had trouble before. Most teachers believe their own misconceptions about gifted learners and have had no training regarding the unique learning needs of gifted students. This chapter will start with a brief history of gifted, followed by characteristics of gifted students. The chapter will end with strategies to support gifted learners in the general education classroom.

What kind of students do you think learn the *least* during the school year? You might be surprised to learn it is the gifted learners, or the most able, who may learn the least if their learning needs are not met (Winebrenner, 1992). Gifted learners can be found in every classroom and come from all racial, ethnic, cultural, and economic groups. Many are well adjusted and involved in numerous activities; others may only focus on one interest. As a group, gifted learners are just as diverse as the wide range of students found in any heterogeneous general education classroom.

Preservice teachers often do not have any, or very little, coursework on gifted learners. Only one state currently requires preservice teachers to take one course in gifted education (NAGC & CSDPG, 2015). Teachers may believe that gifted students' educational needs are met because, overall, they do well on tests and assignments. Appropriate education for gifted students, however, may mean providing services beyond that which is normally offered in the general education classrooms. They have special needs that must be met, just as students with disabilities. As a matter of fact, gifted learners can sometimes be identified as a student with a disability (Baum & Owen, 2004).

As discussed in Chapter 2, teachers' attitudes and beliefs guide the instructional practices in the classroom (Bohner & Wänke, 2002). When teachers believed the myths of gifted learners, they did not see a need to adjust instruction for gifted because they didn't realize they held misconceptions about gifted students (Bohner & Wänke, 2002). The National Association for Gifted Children (NAGC, n.d.) published the top myths about gifted education and learners on its website (Table 7.1), and it appears that two myths in particular guide most teachers' perceptions of gifted learners.

One of the biggest myths is that teachers do not need to worry about gifted kids because they're going to be fine on their own. Gifted students may enter school with more than 50% of the grade-level content, skills, and objectives mastered (Reis et al., 1993; NAGC, n.d.). Giifted children who remain unchallenged, however, can become underachievers, with schools actually fostering this academic underachievement. Signs of underachievement may begin as early as second grade (Ford et al., 2004), and up to 50% of gifted learners will underachieve at some point in school (Siegle, 2013). These gifted learners can be discipline problems and may even drop out of school. Some gifted students coast along, making As with little effort. When they finally are challenged, they don't know what to do and are unable to cope. The good news is that this underachievement can be reversed (Rubenstein et al., 2012).

The other myth is that "all children are gifted." An agreement can be reached that all children can learn and all children have abilities. But not all children learn at an accelerated pace with depth and complexity. "Gifted" in the educational meaning compares children with their age peers for advanced abilities of learning and application of the learning in one or more school subjects, creativity, or the performing or fine arts. Gifted does not mean the child will have the golden ticket to success or is better than other children. Gifted means the child needs additional support for his or her unique learning needs.

TABLE 7.1 Myths About Gifted Students

Myth	Truth
Gifted students don't need help; they'll do fine on their own.	Would you send a star athlete to train for the Olympics without a coach? Gifted students need guidance from well-trained teachers who challenge and support them to fully develop their abilities. Many gifted students may be so far ahead of their same-age peers that they know more than half of the grade-level curriculum before the school year begins. Their resulting boredom and frustration can lead to low achievement, despondency, or unhealthy work habits. The role of the teacher is crucial for spotting and nurturing talents in school.
Teachers challenge all the students, so gifted kids will be fine in the regular classroom.	Although teachers try to challenge all students, they are frequently unfamiliar with the needs of gifted children and do not know how best to serve them in the classroom. A national study conducted by the Fordham Institute found that 58% of teachers have received no professional development focused on teaching academically advanced students in the past few years, and 73% of teachers agreed that "too often, the brightest students are bored and under-challenged in school—we're not giving them a sufficient chance to thrive." This report confirms what many families have known: Not all teachers are able to recognize and support gifted learners (Farkas & Duffet, 2008).
Gifted students make everyone else in the class smarter by providing a role model or a challenge.	Average or below-average students do not look to the gifted students in the class as role models. Watching or relying on someone who is expected to succeed does little to increase a struggling student's sense of self-confidence (Fiedler, Lange, & Winebrenner, 1993). Similarly, gifted students benefit from classroom interactions with peers at similar performance levels and become bored, frustrated, and unmotivated when placed in classrooms with low- or average-ability students.
All children are gifted.	All children have strengths and positive attributes, but not all children are gifted in the educational sense of the word. The label "gifted" in a school setting means that when compared with others their age or grade, a child has an advanced capacity to learn and apply what is learned in one or more subject areas or in the performing or fine arts. This advanced capacity requires modifications to the regular curriculum to ensure these children are challenged and learn new material. Gifted does not connote good or better; it is a term that allows students to be identified for services that meet their unique learning needs.
Acceleration placement options are socially harmful for gifted students.	Academically gifted students often feel bored or out of place with their age peers and naturally gravitate toward older students who are more similar as "intellectual peers." Studies have shown that many students are happier with older students who share their interest than they are with children the same age (Colangelo, Assouline, & Gross, 2004). Therefore, acceleration placement options such as early entrance to kindergarten, grade skipping, or early exit should be considered for these students.

National Association for Gifted Children, "Myths about Gifted Students," nagc.org. Copyright © by National Association for Gifted Children. Reprinted with permission.

(continued)

Gifted education programs are elitist.	Gifted education programs are meant to help all high-ability students. Gifted learners are found in all cultures, ethnic backgrounds, and socioeconomic groups; however, many of these students are denied the opportunity to maximize their potential because of the way in which programs and services are funded and/ or flawed identification practices. For example, reliance on a single test score for gifted education services may exclude selection of students with different cultural experiences and opportunities. Additionally, with no federal money and few states providing an adequate funding stream, most gifted education programs and services are dependent solely on local funds and parent demand. This means that in spite of the need, often only higher-income school districts are able to provide services, giving the appearance of elitism.
That student can't be gifted; he is receiving poor grades.	Underachievement describes a discrepancy between a student's performance and their actual ability. The roots of this problem differ, based on each child's experiences. Gifted students may become bored or frustrated in an unchallenging classroom situation, causing them to lose interest, learn bad study habits, or distrust the school environment. Other students may mask their abilities to try to fit in socially with their same-age peers, and still others may have a learning disability that masks their giftedness. No matter the cause, it is imperative that a caring and perceptive adult help gifted learners break the cycle of underachievement so they can achieve their full potential.
Gifted students are happy, popular, and well adjusted in school.	Many gifted students flourish in their community and school environment. Some gifted children, however, differ in terms of their emotional and moral intensity, sensitivity to expectations and feelings, perfectionism, and deep concerns about societal problems. Others do not share interests with their classmates, resulting in isolation or being labeled unfavorably as a "nerd." Because of these difficulties, the school experience is one to be endured rather than celebrated.
This child can't be gifted; she has a disability.	Some gifted students also have learning or other disabilities. These "twice-exceptional" students often go undetected in regular classrooms because their disability and gifts mask each other, making them appear "average." Other twice-exceptional students are identified as having a learning disability and as a result are not considered for gifted services. In both cases it is important to focus on the students' abilities and allow them to have challenging curricula in addition to receiving help for their learning disability (Olenchak *& Reis,* 2002).
Our district has a gifted and talented program: We have AP courses.	While AP classes offer rigorous, advanced coursework, they are not a gifted education program. The AP program is designed as college-level classes taught by high school teachers for students willing to work hard. The program is limited in its service to gifted and talented students in two major areas: First, AP is limited by the subjects offered, which in most districts are only a small handful. Second, it is limited in that, typically, it is offered only in high school and is generally available only for 11th- and 12th-grade students. The College Board acknowledges that AP courses are for any student who is academically prepared and motivated to take a college-level course.

| Gifted education requires an abundance of resources. | Offering gifted education services does not need to break the bank. A fully developed gifted education program can look overwhelming in its scope and complexity. Beginning a program, however, requires little more than an acknowledgement by district and community personnel that gifted students need something different, a commitment to provide appropriate curriculum and instruction, and teacher training in identification and gifted education strategies. |

(NAGC, n.d.)

Who Are the Gifted Learners?

According to the U.S. Department of Education, in the No Child Left Behind Act of 2001 (Title IX, Part A, Definition 22), gifted is defined as:

> Students, children, or youth who give evidence of high achievement capability in such areas as intellectual, creative, artistic, or leadership capacity, or in specific academic fields, and who need services or activities not ordinarily provided by the school in order to fully develop those capabilities.

Unlike Special Education under the IDEA, however, gifted is not federally mandated nor defined for the states. Each state must determine its own definition and laws for identification and services. In the most current State of the States survey (NAGC & CSDPG, 2015), of the 40 states responding, 32 states mandated gifted education. Of these 32 states, 28 mandated both identification and services for gifted learners, while four states only required identification of gifted learners.

The NAGC (2019, p. 1) developed a definition of gifted learners to summarize the research and to create a deeper understanding of the complexity of giftedness:

> Students with gifts and talents perform—or have the capability to perform—at higher levels compared to others of the same age, experience, and environment in one or more domains. They require modification(s) to their educational experience(s) to learn and realize their potential. Students with gifts and talents:

- Come from all racial, ethnic, and cultural populations, as well as all economic strata.

- Require sufficient access to appropriate learning opportunities to realize their potential.

- Can have learning and processing disorders that require specialized intervention and accommodation.

- Need support and guidance to develop socially and emotionally as well as in their areas of talent.

One of the keywords in these definitions is *capability*. Gifted learners may not always perform at high levels. They are children first and gifted second. When we look for giftedness, we need to look for the potential. Just as athletes and musicians have coaches to develop their potential and talent, gifted children need support and specialized instruction to reach their full potential and talent.

There are many issues within the field of gifted education. Some of these will be addressed in this chapter. Issues in gifted education include the following:

- Lack of funding for educational programs and gifted specialists
- Various definitions and identification methods of the gifted
- Training of all teachers to identify and meet learning needs of the gifted
- Underrepresentation of student populations in identification of students from culturally, linguistically, and economically diverse backgrounds
- Lack of differentiation in general education classrooms
- Lack of access to advanced courses and dual enrollment

Brief History of Gifted Education in the United States

Gifted education in the United States has been slow and sporadic. The first efforts to support gifted students in the country were established in 1868, in St. Louis, Missouri, by Superintendent William Torrey Harris, and a special school for gifted students was started in 1901, in Worcester, Massachusetts. The gifted education movement began in the 1920s with the work of Lewis Terman and Leta Hollingworth. Terman is known as the "father of the gifted education movement," and Hollingworth is known as the "mother of gifted education."

In 1916, Terman published the Stanford-Binet IQ test, which changed the testing of intelligence and American education. Terman (1925) began the now longest-running longitudinal study of gifted children with a sample of 1,500 children selected based on IQ scores. In 1922, Hollingsworth started a special opportunity class for gifted students in New York City. This class became the prototype for the Speyer School for gifted students, ages 7 to 9. Hollingworth (1926) published *Gifted Children: Their Nature and Nurture,* which became the first textbook on gifted education.

Theories about intelligence evolved from Terman's first identification of gifted students through high IQ scores. Although research in gifted constructs, identification, and services continued through the 20th century, it wasn't until 1957, when Russia launched the satellite Sputnik into space, that gifted education was noticed by the U.S. Department of Education. This created the Race to Space initiative, which provided funding for advanced science, math, and technology programs in public schools to develop the talents of the best and brightest students. The National Defense Education Act passed in 1958 as the first effort by the federal government to support gifted education. But once the United States achieved its goal to be the first nation to land on the moon, this funding was eliminated.

In 1972, the United States adopted the first federal definition of gifted and talented from the *Education of the Gifted and Talented*, better known as the Marland Report, which included multiple areas, including general intellectual ability, specific academic aptitude, creative or productive thinking, leadership, visual and/or performing arts, and psychomotor abilities (Marland, 1972). The current federal definition includes all areas except for psychomotor abilities. This report revealed that schools across America were failing gifted students and impairing their abilities by not meeting their learning needs and keeping services as a low priority (Farrell, 2016). After this report was published, gifted education exploded with multiple and diverse theories, constructs, identification methods, and services (Jolly, 2015; VanTassel-Baska & Johnsen, 2007).

Two later reports, *A Nation at Risk* (Gardner, 1983) and *National Excellence: A Case for Developing America's Talent* (Ross, 1993), exposed the low standards in schools and neglect of advanced students and the lack of educational opportunities for the top students, respectively. The latter report linked gifted education to economic loss in the United States because our brightest students could not compete globally compared with the brightest students from other countries (Ross, 1993). The report recommended challenging bright and gifted learners and removing barriers to include culturally, linguistically, and economically diverse students to be included in the advanced courses.

In 1988, Congress passed the Javits Gifted and Talented Act, which established national leadership in gifted education. The National Research Center for Gifted and Talented Children was established. Almost every year, Congress funds competitive grants for research to identify best practices for identification and service provisions. This research supports gifted education reform initiatives in the states.

In 2015, reauthorization of the Elementary and Secondary Education Act, known as the Every Student Succeeds Act (ESSA), was signed. For the first time, federal funds were allowed to be spent on gifted education in each school that receives these title funds. Title I funds could be used to support gifted education programs, and Title II funds can be used for professional development of faculty and staff members regarding the nature and needs of gifted learners. When *State of the States* (NAGC & CSDPG, 2015) was published, state funding for gifted education showed only four of 32 responding states provided full funding for gifted education, 20 states provided partial funding, and eight states provided no funding. Most gifted education is still funded through local school system monies. Wouldn't it be in the best interest of the United States to develop the abilities and talents of gifted learners to benefit society scientifically, aesthetically, and economically?

Based on what you have read about the history of gifted education in the United States, do you find it surprising that gifted education has lagged behind special education in terms of federal laws and guidelines? Why or why not? Do you believe more should have been done to address gifted education earlier? If so, what do you think should have been done?

Pause and Reflect

Identification

Identification of gifted learners varies from state to state. Of the 33 states that responded to the *State of the States* (NAGC & CSDPG, 2015) survey, 12 states required school districts to use identification criteria and methods established by the state department of education, while 21 states allowed the school district to determine the identification criteria and methods. Eight states responded that school districts were not required to use specific criteria or methods.

When a gifted student moves from one state to the next, the identification and eligibility for gifted services of one state may not meet the identification and eligibility for gifted services of the other state. In states where school districts determine gifted identification criteria, a student moving from one school district to another in the state would need to be identified again by that school system's identification procedures. The school system would determine whether the eligibility would be accepted or if the child would be identified with the new criteria.

An IQ composite or total test score was the first method of identification for gifted learners. The two main IQ tests used were the Stanford-Binet test and Wechsler Intelligence Scale for Children. Currently, there are multiple types of assessments for IQ with subscales and total scores, creative ability, nonverbal intelligence, and so on. An appropriate test must be chosen based on the strengths of the child. Current research for identification recommends the use of multiple criteria of aptitude, ability, and characteristics.

Referrals for gifted students are usually made by classroom teachers. Yet these teachers who are not trained in gifted behaviors and characteristics rely on their misconceptions of gifted to refer students. Usually, the bright students and teacher pleasers, not the gifted, are referred. Students from culturally, linguistically, and economically diverse populations are overlooked and underrepresented in gifted education programs. Giftedness is equally distributed among all populations. Across America, however, students from African American, Hispanic, Native American, and linguistically diverse populations are under-identified for gifted, while Caucasian and Asian students are overidentified. Lack of training about gifted learners, deficit thinking, hidden and/or institutional bias, disregard of cultural values, and discriminatory assessments create barriers to identification and services for these students (Foley-Nicpon, Assouline, & Colangelo, 2013; Ford, 2012). Training on identification of gifted learners is required to help teachers "see" giftedness.

Another method to remove or lower the hidden biases and/or barriers is to conduct a universal screening. This requires the administration of a group aptitude test to all students at a certain grade level, determined by the state or school system. This group aptitude test needs to be unbiased and include a nonverbal component. Some states go beyond the universal screening by requiring lessons taught to all students at that grade level to elicit gifted behaviors. These lessons are usually taught by the gifted specialist who assists in the observation of gifted behaviors. Although most universal screenings are completed during second grade with services starting in third grade, early identification is needed to develop the talents and abilities of gifted learners (Smutney, Walker, & Honeck, 2016).

Gifted students can be twice-exceptional, or 2e. They can be identified as gifted and have a disability at the same time. The giftedness can mask the disability, and the disability can mask the giftedness (Kaufman, 2018). These students may have physical or cognitive disabilities, including but not limited to visual and/or hearing impairment, a learning disability, and ASD. Sometimes, however, the gifted characteristics are not taken into consideration, and children may be misdiagnosed, such as ADHD, oppositional defiance disorder, or ASD. For example, John is a second-grade student who already knows his multiplication and division facts. He can work algebraic problems and is starting to learn geometry on a sixth-grade level. He readily participants in math and wants to share answers. But during reading class he becomes withdrawn and quiet. His reading level is at pre-reader. He doesn't know his sight words, and he struggles with simple sentences. If pictures are provided, he can figure out what is going on without reading the words; however, this strategy will not work much longer as the content of the text will continue to increase in difficulty. He has just been diagnosed with a learning disability and will receive services for this disability and receive services for his giftedness in math.

Characteristics

A class of gifted students is as different from one another as a heterogeneous general education class of students. Gifted students may not look gifted and may not look like what one would expect a gifted child to be. They are not always the highest achievers, leaders in the classroom, or extroverts. Gifted learners may range from gifted in one area to gifted in everything they do. A gifted learner may be performing well above his peers in one area but may still be deficient in some other areas of basic skills. For example, a child may be able to do geometry but still lack some of the basic addition or multiplication skills.

Gifted learners do not exhibit every gifted trait. Classroom teachers usually recognize the characteristics of high-achieving, bright students as gifted learners. An excellent comparison chart to show the differences between high-achieving students to gifted learners and creative thinkers was adapted by Bertie Kingore (2004) from J. Szabos (1989). Bright students work hard to earn As, perform at the top of the group, remember answers, are attentive and engaged in the lessons, enjoy age peers, and grasp meaning. Gifted learners tend to know answers without working hard to obtain them; pose unpredictable questions; perform beyond the group; need one to three repetitions for mastery; prefer the company of intellectual peers; comprehend and infer in-depth, complex ideas; and connect concepts. Creatively identified gifted learners are in their own group. They may daydream and seem off task, wonder why there is a need for mastery, ask a lot of what-if questions, play with ideas and concepts, prefer other creative gifted learners but like to work alone, and see exceptions.

Gifted learners prefer intellectual peers. Sometimes, they may appear to have no friends or cannot get along with others. It is difficult, however, for a gifted child to find an age peer who understands a conversation that includes the depth and complexity of subjects at which the gifted child discusses. Many age peers find gifted students weird or strange. For example, say a gifted student and a non-gifted student both like NASCAR. The non-gifted student may want to talk about how fast the cars go, the logos and sponsors, and trophies. The gifted student may want to discuss how to recalculate the ingredients of the fuel to make the car go faster. Both discussions are about the same subject, but they are on two totally different levels. Therefore, gifted students may not waste time trying to make friends with students who do not understand or "get" them.

Gifted characteristics vary according to the type of giftedness. For example, an indication of students who are gifted in languages, reading, and/or language arts is having a large, advanced vocabulary. Table 7.2 is adapted from multiple gifted characteristics lists. For a fully detailed list, go to the National Association of Gifted Children's website.

TABLE 7.2 Gifted Characteristics, Including Positive and Negative Behaviors

Gifted characteristics in and out of school	Positive manifestation	Negative manifestation, or flipside of the coin
Learns easily and rapidly	Finishes work quickly and accurately, acquires information quickly	Gets bored easily, resists drill and repetitions to practice, disturbs others, learns at a faster pace
Reads intensively	Reads many books, may always be reading	Neglects assignments or other responsibilities due to reading
Advanced vocabulary	Communicates ideas well, elaborates, uses large vocabulary in and out of school	Shows off, monopolizes the teacher by constantly talking, "turns off" age peers with high level of vocabulary, feels isolated
Retains information	Recalls and responds quickly; communicates physically, artistically, or symbolically	Monopolizes discussions
Long attention span	Sticks with projects	Dislikes interruption, may not transition to another activity well if not finished
Curious, variety of interests or intensity of interest	Advanced or unusual interests, intense interest in one or more areas, shows concern of local and global issues, asks lots of questions, may ask unusual questions, may be able to take apart and put back together items in school or at home	Reads all the time, dominates discussion with details, goes on tangents, may not have follow-through, likes to stump people with hard questions
Works independently	Goes beyond the classroom assignments, creates and invents	Refuses to work with others
Alert and observant	Recognizes problems, quick to see errors	May correct adults impolitely
Self-motivated	Requires minimal directions from the teacher; focuses on activities (may include nonschool activities); enthusiastic; completes tasks; may be culturally influenced	May want to do things his or her way, may challenge authority
Good sense of humor	Able to laugh at self, exceptional sense of timing, demonstrates unusual emotional depth	Plays cruel jokes or tricks on others, out of sync with classmates, class clown
Insight—recognizes relationships	Able to solve problems, change strategies if a solution fails, finds new ways to solve problems, draws inferences, sees unusual and diverse relationships	Interferes with others, perfectionistic, stubborn, may overlook details, out of sync with classmates
Logic, reasoning	Makes generalizations, uses metaphors and analogies, thinks things through, critical analysis	Notices too many details and may appear off task, does not readily follow directions, may tell adults better ways to do things

High academic achievement	Does schoolwork well	Brags, egotistical, impatient with others
Leadership	Forceful with words, leads peers in positive ways, quick to help others in school, home, and community	Bossy, unwilling to listen to others, leads others into negative behavior, tricks others into negative trick playing
Individualistic	Asserts self and ideas, unique sense of self	Stubborn in beliefs
Imagination/ creativity	Has wild, silly ideas; exceptional ingenuity with everyday items; nontraditional problem solving	Gets lost in thoughts, appears to daydream, may not have follow-through
Social/emotional	Asynchronous development, heightened imagination, emotional sensitivity, magnified sensation, high energy	Negative self-talk, perfectionistic, low self-image, hyperactive, fear of failure, unorganized, bullied for strengths and abilities
Asynchronous development	Uneven development between social, emotional, cognitive, intellectual, physical, and chronological age	May not fit in with age peers, may appear immature, frustrated with projects because manual skills are not developed to meet expectations, confused about where they belong

Brain research is showing that the gifted brain develops differently from the average brain. Gifted brains have faster movement of synapses (Eide & Eide, 2006; Singh & O'Boyle, 2004), both hemispheres communicating at a rapid pace (Eide & Eide, 2006; O'Boyle, 2008), more efficient processing of information (Geake, 2008), and different ages for brain growth and cortex pruning (Shaw et al., 2006). What does this mean? Gifted brains learn at a faster pace and need less repetition to master or remember information. Gifted students are multimodal, which means their senses are pulling information to the brain, and the brain is processing it without the students having to think about it. This is how they sometimes know things without knowing how they know it. Because of the different brain growth and pruning, gifted students are disorganized.

Creativity

Everyone can be creative, and creativity can be taught, but not everyone is creatively gifted. Creativity is a 21st-century skill, but what is it? Through analysis of multiple creativity research studies, creativity is defined as "the interactions among aptitude, process, and environment by which an individual or group produces a perceptible product that is both novel and useful within a social context" (Plucker et al., 2004, p. 90). Gifted learners must have the opportunity to express themselves creatively. Creativity is one of the constructs of giftedness. Renzulli (2005) uses it as one of three concepts to identify students—above average ability, motivation, and creativity. Gifted students need to develop their creativity or original thought for innovation and invention. Creative problem solving helps students solve problems and issues in different ways. Depending on how *gifted* is defined, and how students are identified, creativity can be performing or fine arts or academic creativity, which involves divergent thinking, evaluation, and redefinition. Creative thinking requires students to know the basic facts and content but then think about the content from different perspectives and time periods and imagine "what if" (Torrance & Goff, 1990).

Social-Emotional Support

Social-emotional support is needed for gifted learners. They perceive that others think "gifted" means they must always have the right answer for everything. Dr. Gatto-Walden refers to gifted as the "terrible toos" (Silverman, 2005, p. 4). Gifted individuals make things so complicated, take things so seriously, and view things as so important. These intensities can be too much for other people. Gifted learners think something is wrong with them because they do not fit in with their classmates (Silverman, 2005).

Asynchronous development is when social, emotional, cognitive, physical, and creative abilities are developing at uneven rates or are mismatched. In 1991, the Columbus Group—parents, psychologists, and educators who met to develop a gifted definition that reflected the inner experience of the individual—put asynchronous development at the center of their definition of gifted (Morelock, 1992). Asynchronous development is apparent when you have discrepancies between the chronological age of the child, IQ scores, social-emotional behaviors, and performance levels in academic subjects. For example, a gifted child is 9 years old, in third grade, and has an IQ score of 133. Her academic performance is 12th-grade reading level, first-grade spelling level, sixth-grade math level, and eighth-grade science level. Her fine-motor skills are at the kindergarten level, and she is socially at or below third grade. This is confusing not only for the gifted learners but also for parents and teachers. The more highly gifted a child is, the more pronounced the asynchronous development can be.

Overexcitabilities are defined as "a higher than average response to stimuli, manifested by either psychomotor, sensual, emotional, imaginational, or intellectual excitability" (Dabrowski, 1972, p. 303). It contributes to motivation, intensity, and complexity of feeling involved with the creative expression. Many gifted learners may have one or more overexcitabilities. When gifted learners exhibit these overexcitabilities, they feel and react with intensity. Table 7.3 is adapted from an article that describes overexcitablity manifestations and how these look in the classroom (Bailey, 2010).

TABLE 7.3 Overexcitability Characteristics With Classroom Strategies

Overexcitability	Characteristic	Classroom strategy
Psychomotor	Lots of energy	Opportunities for movement and speaking
Need to move and go	Loves movement	Hands-on learning
	Fast games	Allow fiddling with objects
	Talks a lot	May need to teach how to relax
	May bite their nails	Help students notice when their body is
	May look like ADHD	tired or they need quiet time

Sensory/sensual Heighted experiences from the senses	Appreciates music and languages early Need to be touched or to touch others Overeat Delight in pleasures from senses May hate the ways things feel (labels on shirts are irritating) Overstimulation can cause a student to lose focus	Keep visual clutter to a minimum Limit exposure to smells Reduce extraneous noises
Intellectual Intense need to understand	Search for answers and meaning Persistent questioning Heightened observational powers Earnest problem solving Loves learning Concentrate for long periods Always wants to be right	Provide time to explore and research topics Teach how to research and ask questions Differentiate instruction Service-learning projects Teach appropriate constructive criticism—how to give it and how to accept it.
Imaginational Vivid imagination—world in mind may seem just as real as the surrounding world	Metaphor and image use Detailed visualization Invention and fantasy Poor organizational skills May stretch the truth May have imaginary friends May worry a lot	Open-ended hands-on projects for writing and drawing Journaling Design own problem-solving system Help determine fact from fiction
Emotional Heightened intense feelings, extreme emotions, empathy	Strong physical response to emotions Develops relationships with strong attachments Compassion, empathy, sensitivity Deep sense of justice Heightened fears and anxiety May appear overdramatic or seeking attention	Compassion works better than punishment Accept all feelings, no matter the intensity Teach how to handle hurtful words Self-advocacy Help them anticipate physical and emotional situations and practice how to react Teach how to know when emotions are escalating Teach calming techniques Be alert for teasing and bullying

(Adapted from Bailey, 2010)

Pause and Discuss

In pairs or small groups, discuss the answers to the questions about gifted learners. Have you ever observed or interacted with a gifted learner? Describe your experience. Did you have misperceptions about gifted learners? What were they? What characteristics have you observed or experienced? How have your perceptions about gifted learners changed? How can this prepare you as an educator? Write and discuss your answers to the questions. Be prepared to present to the class.

Strategies for Gifted Learners

If we were TV sets, some of us would only get five channels. Others are wired for cable (the general population) and some of us (the gifted) are hooked up to a satellite dish. That makes these gifted children capable of making connections that others don't even know exist! Teaching those types of voracious minds in a regular classroom without enhancement is like feeding an elephant one blade of grass at time. You'll starve them.

—Elizabeth Meckstroth

To reach their potential, gifted students must have their unique learning needs met. Although many school systems may provide services through a pull-out program with a gifted specialist, the student spends more time in the general education classroom (Archambault et al., 1993). Therefore, gifted students need a continuum of services across all learning environments. Gifted students are gifted every day, not just the day they receive gifted services. Therefore, the general education teacher must differentiate the instruction to meet the learning needs of gifted learners. Collaborating with the gifted specialist, the general education teacher can develop appropriate activities for the gifted learners.

When the pacing is too slow, gifted learners can mislearn the information, and having too many repetitions creates a loss of the information (Stanley, 1993). Although his research was in math, additional research shows this can be applied to language arts, science, and social studies. Working below their ability levels can cause underachievement that leads to a resistance to challenge. Gifted students, in their area(s) of giftedness, need accelerated pacing, depth and complexity in the content, creative expression, and affective support met. Underachievement can be reversed through evidence-based practices (Siegle, 2013). Strategies to help classroom teachers meet these learning needs include grouping, differentiation, curriculum compacting, and acceleration.

Grouping

Grouping strategies range from between classrooms to within classrooms. The administrative decision to cluster gifted students together allows these students to become a group within a classroom instead of sprinkling the students among all of the teachers at a grade level. Cluster grouping, with no more than one-third of the class at an ability level, decreases the number of ability levels within a classroom and with differentiated instruction will increase achievement of all students (Winebrenner & Brulles, 2008). With a group of gifted students, instead of one or two, a teacher must provide activities for the students instead of having them read or help a classmate. Within the class, the teacher can use flexible, targeted, and temporary grouping to organize and work with students by skill level, interests, or needs. These groups are fluid, and group members change depending on the focus of the lessons (Rogers, 2006). Gifted students may be together sometimes and may not be together at other times. Remember that not all gifted students have high ability in every school subject.

Differentiation

Differentiation is tailoring the instruction to meet individual learning needs (Tomlinson, 1999). The teacher can differentiate content (what students learn), process (how students learn the content), product (assignments to demonstrate the learning), and the environment (where students learn).

1. Advanced content: Gifted learners may use advanced content, primary source documents, or listen to recordings of speeches instead of grade-level content for learning.

2. Most difficult first: Have gifted students complete the most difficult problems first. For example, in math, students complete the last five problems, which are the most difficult on the practice page. When the problems are successfully completed, students move to an enrichment activity (those advanced or enrichment activities in the math book), work on an independent study project, or move to the next lesson.

3. Preassessment: Give the end-of-the-chapter or unit test before teaching the lesson. Before giving the test, determine what percentage correct is needed for a student to be exempt from the test. For example, some teachers use 90% as passing. Then students who pass with the determined percentage or better are able to work on more advanced activities.

4. Grouping: Have gifted students work together on projects. They will challenge one another and bounce ideas off their classmates in unexpected ways.

5. Tiered learning: Having activities based on different ability levels. The teacher plans for the middle or average student, then tiers down for students who struggle or need remediation and tiers up to accelerate learning and/or add depth and complexity. This is a common practice when grouping students by ability. This takes time to plan, but it benefits all students.

6. Student choice: Provide open-ended activities for students to learn or create products. Choice boards can provide limits to what students may choose, yet students have a voice in their learning. Students may also choose to work in a group, with a partner, or by themselves. This choice gives ownership of learning to the students and allows them to use their strengths to show their learning. For example, students may be artistic and draw pictures to add to a PowerPoint/Google slide show.

When differentiating, don't assign more of the same work, use gifted learners as peer tutors, or give busywork. Differentiated activities need to advance the learning and be relevant and meaningful.

Curriculum Compacting

This strategy allows students to eliminate content already mastered and replace the original content with advanced or enrichment content (Reis et al., 1998). This eliminates content that must be relearned and replaces it with new learning opportunities for the students. Teachers must plan ahead on what content, skills, and objectives will be taught and mastered. Then the pre-assessment is developed, which can be the same as the post-assessment. Once the content is eliminated, the teacher and students can determine what the new content and activities will be, how they will present

Student Name: _____   Grade: _____   Subject: _____

Teacher Name: _____

Content/Skills/Objectives Mastered Documentation, such as, pre-test score	Content/Skills/Objectives Not Mastered Documentation, such as, pre-test score	Alternative assignment or project Deadline to complete

Teacher Signature: _____   Date: _____

Student Signature: _____   Date: _____

Parent Signature: _____   Date: _____
(when appropriate)

FIGURE 7.1 Example of a learning contract.

their learning, and the deadline to complete it. Students sign a compacting contract and work on the alternate projects; however, teachers should still periodically monitor the progress of the student(s). An example of a compacting contract is shown in Figure 7.1.

Acceleration

Some students may be beyond the grade-level content. When pre-assessments of the grade-level content (one or more academic subjects) are administered, gifted learners may demonstrate mastery of the content, skills, and objectives of one or all of the subject areas. This is when students may need to be accelerated to the next grade level. For subject acceleration, students take classes in the next grade level or enroll in online courses for the subject area. For example, if a student has mastered all of third-grade math on the grade-level pre-assessment, this student may be subject-accelerated to fourth grade for math. This student enters the fourth-grade classroom to learn math every day. If all subjects are mastered, then formal procedures may be implemented to grade accelerate the student. The teacher will need to follow school district guidelines for grade acceleration. Usually, teachers will use subject acceleration first to help determine whether grade acceleration is appropriate.

Write a short paragraph about your experience or observation of any of these strategies. It may be from elementary, middle, high school, or college level. What was the strategy? How well did it work? Explain why the strategy did or did not did work. What could have been done differently? Be prepared to share and discuss with the class.	**Pause and Reflect**

Conclusion

While this chapter covered a broad overview of gifted education, these topics are often covered in multiple courses with many textbooks. The goal is to provide a basic understanding of the gifted learner and evidence-based strategies used to challenge and engage them in learning, while attempting to remove the preconceived beliefs.

KEY CHAPTER TAKEAWAYS

Some important takeaways from this chapter include:

- Be a myth-buster! Preconceived beliefs and attitudes about gifted learners can prevent students from being referred for identification or from receiving appropriate services. Know the facts.

- Gifted definitions, identification methods, and services are specific to each state or school system. You must learn what is required in your school district.

- Gifted learners have a right to learn something new and have their unique learning needs of accelerated pacing, depth and complexity in the content, creative expression, and social-emotional needs supported.

- Gifted students need to work with intellectual peers.

- Peer tutoring is not the best use of time for gifted learners unless they want to help.

- Grouping, differentiation, curriculum compacting, and acceleration are strategies to help teachers meet the unique learning needs of gifted students.

- Collaborate with the gifted specialist in your school/district to help you meet the learning needs by developing appropriate lessons, centers, and activities for gifted learners.

CASE SCENARIO: THE INTERVIEW CONTINUES

"A special population of learners in classrooms are the gifted students," Mrs. Frayer said. "Have you ever worked with gifted learners?"

Kortney wondered where this was going. No one had ever asked her about gifted students before. She replied, "Yes, I believe I have worked with gifted learners. They are found in all classrooms."

Mrs. Frayer nodded her head in agreement as she presented a classroom scenario to Kortney to discuss. Mrs. Stephenson is teaching a third-grade class of 18 students, of which five are identified as gifted. The rest of the class, 10 students, fall within average to below average in ability range. She has three students with disabilities in the class, of which one is identified as gifted, and one of the students is non–English-speaking gifted. Her gifted learners are a diverse group, including two White students, one Asian student, one Hispanic ELL student, and one African American student. All of these students receive gifted pull-out services by the gifted specialist, Mrs. Hurst, for 4 hours every Tuesday. One student is 2e and struggles with reading, one is still learning the English language but is above grade level in math, one struggles in math but doesn't have a learning disability, and the other two are above grade level in all subjects.

These students will miss math, reading, and science when they are in gifted services. According to state law, students are not required to make up the class assignments missed when they are receiving the specialized instruction in their gifted class. Mrs. Hurst provides advanced learning using concept-based units and problem-based learning within their interest areas. In addition, Mrs. Hurst integrates social-emotional lessons into the unit, either in large or small groups, to meet their individual needs.

As part of ESSA and new reporting requirements, all students must show annual growth. This year the school district will add gifted learners as a subgroup on the district report card. This is the first time the school district will list gifted as a subgroup. Past data analysis of achievement scores showed gifted learners do not always show annual growth. Noticeably, their scores end up declining back to average, which is called regression to the mean.

The district clusters the gifted students into classrooms at each grade level so the classroom teacher has a group of students, and gifted students have intellectual peers within their classroom. All teachers with gifted students are quite nervous about this new pressure to show annual growth. Mrs. Stephenson has expressed concern about what to do to ensure gifted students show annual growth.

WORKING WITH THE SCENARIO

Mrs. Frayer paused briefly before asking, "Kortney, do you have any ideas about how Mrs. Stephenson can offer appropriate support for her gifted learners? What plan of action would you create to meet the learning needs of the clustered gifted students in that situation?"

Kortney also paused, once again trying to collect her thoughts and process all of the information before answering. The interview was proving to be more mentally challenging than she could ever have anticipated.

"And while you're considering your ideas, please keep a few things in mind," Mrs. Frayer added. "You need to be specific about how you would implement any plan you suggest, and also be considerate of other stakeholders who might be involved or able to support the plan. And as you consider strategies, also remember that those strategies will have to be evaluated. How would you go about determining whether they were successful for those gifted students?"

If you were Kortney, how would you answer the questions posed by Mrs. Frayer?

REFERENCES

Archambault, F. X., Westberg, K. L., Brown, S., Hallmark, B. W., Zhang, W., & Emmons, C. (1993). Regular classroom practices with gifted students: Findings from the classroom practices survey. *Journal for the Education of the Gifted, 16*, 103–19.

Bailey, C. L. (2010). Overexcitabilities and sensitivities: Implications of Dabrowski's theory of positive disintegration for counseling the gifted. *American Counseling Association.* https://www.counseling.org/resources/library/VISTAS/2010-V-Online/Article_10.pdf

Baum, S. M., & Owen, S. V. (2004). *To be gifted & learning disabled: Strategies for helping bright students with learning & attention difficulties.* Prufrock.

Bohner, G., & Wänke, M. (2002). *Attitudes and attitude change.* Psychology Press.

Colangelo, N., Assouline, S. G., & Gross, M. U. M. (2004). *A nation deceived: How schools hold back America's brightest students.* University of Iowa.

Dabrowski, K. (1972). *Psychoneurosis is not an illness.* Gryf.

Eide, B., & Eide, F. (2006). *Brains on fire: The multimodality of gifted thinkers. New horizons for learning.* School of Education, Johns Hopkins University. Retrieved March 2008 from http://education.jhu.edu/PD/newhorizons/Neurosciences/articles/30

Every Child Succeeds Act (ESSA) of 2015, Pub. L. No. 114-95, S.1177, 114th Cong. 2015. https://www.congress.gov/114/plaws/publ95/PLAW-114publ95.pdf

Farkas, S., & Duffet, A. (2008). Results from a national teacher survey. In T. B. Fordham Institute, *High achievement students in the era of NCLB* (p. 78). http://www.edexcellence.net/publications/high-achieving-students-in.html

Farrell, S. J. (2016). *An exploration of face-to-face and online professional development for gifted specialists* (Publication No. 10239650) [Doctoral dissertation, University of Alabama]. ProQuest.

Fiedler, E. D., Lange, R. E., & Winebrenner, S. (1993). In search of reality: Unraveling the myths about tracking, ability grouping, and the gifted. *Roper Review*, (16), 4–7.

Foley-Nicpon, M., Assouline, S. G., & Colangelo, N. (2013). Twice-exceptional learners who need to know what? *Gifted Child Quarterly, 57*(3), 169–80.

Ford, D. Y. (2012). Culturally different students in special education: Looking backward to move forward. *Exceptional Children, 78*(4), 391–405.

Ford, D. Y., Grantham, T. C., & Milner, H. R. (2004). Underachievement among gifted African American students: Cultural, social, and psychological considerations. In D. E. Boothe & J. C. Stanley (Eds.), *In the eyes of the beholder: Critical issues for diversity in gifted education* (pp. 15–31). Prufrock.

Gardner, D. P. (1983). *A nation at risk: The imperative for educational reform: A report to the nation and the secretary of education.* U.S. Department of Education. National Commission on Excellence in Education.

Geake, J. G. (2008, July 14–18). *The neurobiology of giftedness. Wystąpienie na konferencji 10th Asia-Pacific Conference on Giftedness, Singapore. Westminster Institute of Education.*

Hollingworth, L. S. (1926). *Gifted children: Their nature and nurture.* Macmillan.

Jolly, J. L. (2015). Historical perspectives: The gifted at risk. *Gifted Child Today, 38*(2), 124–27.

Kaufman, S. B. (Ed.). (2019). *Twice exceptional: Supporting and educating bright and creative students with learning difficulties.* Oxford University Press.

Kingore, B. (2004). High achiever, gifted learner, creative learner. *Understanding Our Gifted, 16*(3), 21.

Marland, S. P. (1972). *Education of the gifted and talented.* Report to Congress. Government Printing Office.

Morelock, M. J. (1992). Giftedness: The view from within. *Understanding Our Gifted, 4*(3), 1.

NAGC (National Association for Gifted Children). (2019). *A definition of giftedness that guides best practice.* Position statement. https://www.nagc.org/sites/default/files/Position%20Statement/Definition%20of%20Giftedness%20%282019%29.pdf

NAGC. (n.d.). *Myths about gifted students.* Retrieved May 4, 2020, from https://www.nagc.org/myths-about-gifted-students

NAGC & CSDPG (Council of State Directors for Programs of Gifted). (2015). *2013–2015 State of the states in gifted education.* https://www.nagc.org/resources-publications/gifted-state/2014-2015-state-states-gifted-education

Neihart, M., Reis, S., Robinson, N., & Moon, S. (Eds.). (2002). *The social and emotional development of gifted children: What do we know?* Prufrock.

No Child Left Behind Act of 2001. (2008). *20 U.S.C. § 6319.*

O'Boyle, M. W. (2008). Mathematically gifted children: Developmental brain characteristics and their prognosis for well-being. *Roeper Review, 30*(3), 181–186.

Olenchak. F. R., & Reis, S. M. (2002). Gifted students with learning disabilities. In M. Neihart, S. M. Reis, N. Robinson, & S. Moon (Eds.), *The social and emotional development of gifted children* (pp. 177–192). Prufrock.

Plucker, J. A., Beghetto, R. A., & Dow, G. T. (2004). Why isn't creativity more important to educational psychologists? Potentials, pitfalls, and future directions in creativity research. *Educational Psychologist, 39*(2), 83–96.

Reis, S. M., Westberg, K. L., Kulikowich, J., Caillard, F., Hébert, T., Plucker, J., Purcell, J. H., Rogers, J. B., & Smist, J. M. (1993). *Why not let high ability students start school in January? The curriculum compacting study* (Research Monograph 93106). National Research Center on the Gifted and Talented, University of Connecticut.

Reis, S. M., Westberg, K. L., Kulikowich, J. M., & Purcell, J. H. (1998). Curriculum compacting and achievement test scores: What does the research say? *Gifted Child Quarterly, 42*, 123–29.

Renzulli, J. S. (2005). The three-ring conception of giftedness: A developmental model for promoting creative productivity. In *Conceptions of giftedness* (2nd ed.) (R. J. Sternberg & J. Davidson, Eds., pp. 217–45). Cambridge University Press.

Robinson, N. M. (2002). *Assessing and advocating for gifted students: Perspectives for school and clinical psychologists*. Senior Scholars Series.

Rogers, K. B. (2002). *Re-forming gifted education: Matching the program to the child*. Great Potential.

Rogers, K. B. (2006). *A menu of options for grouping gifted students*. Prufrock.

Ross, P. O. C. (1993). *National excellence: A case for developing America's talent*. Office of Educational Research and Improvement, U.S. Department of Education.

Rubenstein, L. D., Siegle, D., Reis, S. M., McCoach, D. B., & Burton, M. G. (2012). A complex quest: The development and research of underachievement interventions for gifted students. *Psychology in the Schools, 49*(7), 678–94.

Shaw, P., Greenstein, D., Lerch, J., Clasen, L., Lenroot, R., Gogtay, N., & Giedd, J. (2006). Intellectual ability and cortical development in children and adolescents. *Nature, 440*(7084), 676–679.

Siegle, D. (2013). *The underachieving gifted child: Recognizing, understanding, and reversing underachievement*. Prufrock.

Silverman, L. K. (2005). *INTENSITIVE! Intensities and sensitivities of the gifted. Social and emotional needs of gifted children*. Tasmanian Association for the Gifted.

Singh, H., & O'Boyle, M. W. (2004). Interhemispheric interaction during visual information processing in mathematically gifted youth, average ability adolescents and college students. *Neuropsychology, 18*, 371–77.

Smutny, J. F., Walker, S. Y., & Honeck, I. E. (2016). *Teaching gifted children in today's preschool and primary classrooms: Identifying, nurturing, and challenging children ages 4–9*. Free Spirit.

Stanley, J. C. (1993). Boys and girls who reason well mathematically. In Ciba Foundation, *Ciba Foundation symposium, 178. The origins and development of high ability* (pp. 119–138). John Wiley & Sons. https://doi.org/10.1002/9780470514498.ch8

Szabos, J. (1989). Bright child, gifted learner. *Challenge, 34*(4), 3.

Terman, L. M. (1916). *The measurement of intelligence: An explanation of and a complete guide for the use of the Stanford Revision and extension of the Binet-Simon Intelligence Scale.* Houghton Mifflin.

Terman, L. M. (1925). *Genetic studies of genius. Mental and physical traits of a thousand gifted children.* Houghton-Mifflin.

Tomlinson, C. A. (1999). *The differentiated classroom: Responding to the needs of all learners.* Association for Supervision and Curriculum Development.

Torrance, E. P., & Goff, K. (1990). *Fostering academic creativity in gifted students.* ERIC Digest #E484.

VanTassel-Baska, J., & Johnsen, S. K. (2007). Teacher education standards for the field of gifted education: A vision of coherence for personnel preparation in the 21st century. *Gifted Child Quarterly, 51*(2), 182.

Winebrenner, S. (1992). *Teaching gifted kids in the regular classroom.* Free Spirit.

Winebrenner, S., & Brulles, D. (2008). *The cluster grouping handbook: A schoolwide model: How to challenge gifted students and improve achievement for all.* Free Spirit.

English-Language Learners

Setting the Classroom Scene

Larry Silver, the principal of North Street Middle School, a large school with more than 400 students in an urban school district, sat at his desk one afternoon. Across from him sat Carmen Espinoza, an assistant principal, and Stephanie Thorp, the school's guidance counselor. The three were meeting to discuss the upcoming parent-teacher conferences, an event held once in the fall and once in the spring of each school year.

"Before we get too far into this," Larry began, "I'd like us to start thinking about some of the obstacles we've encountered in past years and maybe lead with some ideas on how to avoid or overcome those, right out of the gate."

"Do you mean besides the usual?" Carmen asked.

"And by the usual I'm guessing Carmen means the frequent language barriers we've encountered the past few years," Stephanie added.

Larry did not answer right away and drummed the fingers of his left hand gently on top of his desk. It was a habit he displayed when he was thinking deeply on a particular subject. Both women knew not to interrupt this process. They let it play out for the few moments necessary. Larry stopped the drumming and looked at Carmen.

"In the problem-solving process that I was taught long ago and has been often used by this school district," he said, "two of the most important steps are to state the problem and then identify potential solutions. I think the phrase *language barrier* might be a pretty good two-word summation of a significant issue we've faced in years past, so with that in mind, we need to think about solutions."

"And as I recall about that problem-solving strategy, one of the initial points of discussion is if we are even able to solve the problem," Carmen said.

Stephanie smiled, and said, "But isn't that what modern education is all about? Solving the unsolvable problems?"

The three chuckled briefly at Stephanie's remark, but the moment of lightness was fleeting. Each knew that in their district the number of languages spoken at home had grown exponentially over the past 15 years. Gone were the days when a majority of the students who did not speak English at home at least spoke, in most cases, the same different language. All three were very well aware that, based on recent research into the number of languages spoken in their city, more than 50 dialects could be found among the homes of students in the school district. Although North Street Middle did not have a hard number for which dialects were spoken by the families of their students, the three educators knew from experience that the number was close to, if not just above, 20 in their school alone.

"I remember several years back when a state was pushing for a constitutional amendment to make English the official language," Larry said. "I know why it didn't pass and why it just wouldn't work, but there's a part of me that sympathizes with the gist. I mean, if someone who doesn't speak English is deathly sick and goes to the hospital, is it the hospital's responsibility to have someone on hand that speaks any and every possible language?"

"I'd tread pretty lightly on that type of thinking, Larry," Carmen said. "That kind of talk might not go over well with a lot of our constituents."

Larry held up his hands in mock surrender, and responded, "I know, I know. I was just saying I get it, not that I support it. And besides, I don't see any constitutional amendments helping us in time for our parent-teacher conferences. So, what are our potential solutions, because even if we can't solve this problem, we are going to have to face it."

"Well," Stephanie began, "maybe we can change how we're looking at it. Let's not treat it as a problem, but as an opportunity."

"How do you mean?" Larry asked.

"We know we'll need multiple interpreters, and getting some ELL teachers from other schools to volunteer and help us," Stephanie answered. "But maybe we can look at that as an opportunity to show how hard we try to support all of our students and their families. We go the extra mile to communicate, that sort of thing."

"I'm not usually so optimistic to buy the problem as opportunity ethos," Carmen chimed in. "That said, I think Stephanie makes a great point. And from a school leadership perspective, we need to model the kind of attitude we want our teachers to have."

"Excellent points, both of you," Larry said. "I think we need to do a quick survey with faculty members and see how many languages they can give us, that they know for sure are spoken by the parents of our students. That's a good first step, logistically, then we can start lining up the necessary resources as best we can."

"And one thing for sure we need to do is put together some great visuals," Carmen said. "I don't know as much as I need to about teaching English-language learners, but I do know from what I've seen they are heavy on visual supports."

"That they are," Larry added, as he wrote himself a brief note to email his teachers requesting the information just discussed. "And ultimately, we all need to remember that it doesn't matter what language they speak; if they come here to see how their child or children are doing, we need to be ready to communicate—in some form or fashion."

Prereading Questions

1. What are your experiences with friends or acquaintances whose primary language is not the same as yours?

2. Name at least three challenges you believe teachers face when trying to teach content and skills to students who are not native English speakers?

3. Do you believe it is important for teachers to have some training in effective methods for teaching students who do not speak English? Why or why not?

Introduction

Pause for a moment and think about what you just read. Consider how you read it. Did you progress fluently through the reading? Were you looking for key words and phrases? Did you notice shifts between the characters and when each was speaking? When you got to the prereading questions, did you again look for key words and phrases? If you answered yes to all of these questions, you should remember to thank all of those in your early life and school experience who helped you acquire language skills. Because without language skills, there would be no reading skills. Let that sink in for a moment.

When considering the importance of language, North Street Middle School is representative of many schools in the United States and around the world that find a large number of different languages spoken in the homes of their students. While the vast majority of schools do not have to be concerned with how to communicate with upward of 20 dialects, there are many school districts, particularly in large urban centers, that do indeed have more than 50 dialects spoken in the homes of their students. This array of home languages often presents unique challenges to schools and teachers. Students who are learning to speak English or who arrive at a school speaking no English at all are often referred to as "English-language learners," or ELL students. And the number of ELL students in the United States has increased dramatically in the past 30 years.

This chapter will seek to provide some information on ELL students, how many there are and the struggles they face, and also provide some general guidance on strategies for working with ELL students. But before diving into the specifics regarding English-language learners, it is important to consider a very brief overview of the significance of language in the learning process. Language is foundational to learning for many reasons, and the role of language in how students acquire new knowledge and skills cannot be overstated.

The Role of Language in Learning

> *There are, I think, three facets to language development: learning language, learning through language, and learning about language. In a sense, and from a child's point of view, these three are all the same. But in order to understand them properly, we need to consider them apart; this will enable us to see where each facet enters into the overall growth and development of a child.*
>
> **—M. A. K. Halliday**

Theories on how children learn abound. Educational psychology courses are quite common in teacher education programs, where well-known educational theorists such as Piaget, Vygotsky, Skinner, Gilligan, and Bandura, along with many others, are studied to help future teachers better understand the learning process. The theories developed by educational researchers have great validity and applicability, though to varying degrees based upon individual student needs and differences. One component that is vital to any learning theory, regardless of the theorist or application, is the role of language in the learning process.

Oral language acquisition actually begins before birth (e.g., Lecanuet, Granier-Deferre, & Busnel, 1989) and continues through infancy and early childhood. While the number of theories on how oral language is acquired and developed are quite numerous, perhaps equal to the number of learning theories referenced in the preceding paragraph, there are basic components of oral language development that are generally recognized as having great significance in how well oral language skills are developed in a child. These components are phonemic awareness, morphology, word recognition, semantics, and pragmatics (see Table 8.1). The reason oral language development is critical for learning is that oral language skills are foundational for understanding written language. While we all learn a great deal from listening, there is a tremendous amount of learning that occurs through reading, a fact that grows in importance as students progress toward higher elementary and secondary grades (e.g., Smagorinsky, 2001).

TABLE 8.1 Important Components in Language Development

Language component	Role
Phonemic awareness	Recognizing basic sounds in spoken language or basic gestures in sign language (Parrish-Morris, Golinkoff, & Hirsh-Pasek, 2013)
Morphology	In language, the mental system involved in formation of words, their internal structure, and how they are formed (Aronoff & Fudeman, 2011)
Word recognition	Closely linked to morphology, the active mental process of recognizing how letters combine to form words that convey specific meanings (Carreiras et al., 2014)
Semantics	The meaning of words in a language (Parrish-Morris, Golinkoff, & Hirsh-Pasek, 2013)
Pragmatics	How language is used in social contexts (Parrish-Morris, Golinkoff, & Hirsh-Pasek, 2013)

Taking into consideration the components of language presented in Table 8.1, it should be clear there is a progression from recognizing sounds to being able to form words to ultimately understanding how words are used in social contexts. While the progression of language acquisition is certainly important when linking language to learning, there are other lenses through which one can consider that critical relationship. For example, one way to think about language is to break it down into three distinct aspects: form, content, and use (Smith, Tyler, & Skow, 2017). Using those three aspects, *form* would include phonological awareness, *content* would include the meaning of statements using words, and *use* would link to semantics and pragmatics and the intention of communication in social contexts. In terms of learning new skills and knowledge, the form, content, and use of language will all play significant roles in the success of the learning process. Students must be able, whatever the language, to understand the words in a discussion, presentation, or lecture, and then recognize the content represented by those words before they can then be expected to use the content of the language in any meaningful way.

It appears impossible to separate language from learning. At its most fundamental stage, language involves sharing information. Whether that information is educative, informative, persuasive, entertaining, or rewarding is entirely dependent on the context, but the part that language must play in our lives and our learning cannot be understated. And yet we all, at some point or another, may take for granted that someone else is "speaking our language," that they are truly understanding what we are saying because they, presumably, understand the words we are saying or writing. But consider for a moment those unfamiliar with your language. When it comes to those individuals who speak another language, a group that in the United States will largely consist of those who speak primarily a language other than English, most assumptions about how we communicate are faulty and do not serve us well. This fact is one that teachers, in particular, must face as they attempt to teach all students, including those who are just beginning to learn English.

Although the preceding content was brief in regard to the role of language in learning (there are entire textbooks on that subject alone), with what content shared were you familiar? Do you believe you have a basic understanding of why language is so important to learning? Now think about how you learn new things. Do you ever pause to consider or note the role language plays in your own learning process? If so, what does this consideration tell you? And have you ever thought about how you use language when you are teaching others? Consider your own classroom. Is it language rich, in that it contains supports and activities that promote the acquisition and practice of language skills? How so, and if not, do you believe you can start taking steps to more explicitly honor language in your teaching?

Pause and Reflect

English-Language Learners

ELL: English language learner. A national-origin-minority student who is limited-English-proficient. This term is often preferred over limited-English-proficient (LEP) as it highlights accomplishments rather than deficits.
— **U.S. Department of Education**

The Numbers

Students whose native language is not English have steadily increased in number over the past few decades. This is in conjunction with data from 2012 that suggested 25% of children in America were from immigrant families whose primary language was not English (Samson, Collins, & Center for American Progress, 2012). Statistics on the percentage of students in America's public schools identified as ELL seem to lag in comparison with data on other categories of students, including those in poverty or those receiving special education services. For example, information published by the National Center for Education Statistics (NCES) in 2019 was for the year 2016. The data at that time noted that 9.6% (4.9 million) of students were identified as ELL, compared with 8.1% (3.8 million) of students in 2000 (NCES, 2019). Those numbers reflect a 29% increase in ELL students in just 16 years. Data for specific states revealed a range from 20% of students identified as ELL in California in 2016, to as low as 0.9% in West Virginia. By far the most common native language documented was Spanish, with other large numbers of native languages including Arabic, Chinese, Vietnamese, Somali, Russian, and Hmong (NCES, 2019). It is interesting to note that other sources suggest differing percentages, such as *Education Week*, which in a story from January 2018 stated that 44% of students in California and 2% in West Virginia were identified as ELL (Mitchell, 2018).

Regardless of the source, it is undeniable there is a significant percentage of students whose native language is not English. What explains the ever-increasing numbers of these students over the past 30 years? As covered in Chapter 3, the number of minority students in the United States has increased dramatically, and not including African American students in those minority numbers provides some evidence for the increase in students who do not speak English as their native language. Immigration, both legal and otherwise, has continued to bring an increasing variety of languages into American schools. Establishing concrete numbers for just how many languages and dialects are now present in schools across the country may be an impossible task—and this is not to venture into controversial matters—given the number of undocumented immigrants now in schools. Current estimates on the number of undocumented immigrants in the United states range from 10.5 million to 12 million (Kamarck & Stenglein, 2020), though it is difficult to find any reliable estimate on the number of undocumented immigrant students. While a student being an undocumented immigrant does not automatically mean they count as an ELL student, a reasonable assumption would be that many such students have a native language that is not English.

Given the dramatic increase in ELL students since 1990, it is important to consider the lack of federal guidelines for providing services for these students. The estimated percentage of ELL students, 10%, is roughly the same as the percentage of students who qualify for special education. Even with these similar percentages, there is no federal law in place guiding provision of services for ELL students (e.g., Ragan & Lasaux, 2006), while students receiving special education services have the protections afforded by the Individuals with Disabilities Education Act (IDEA; see Chapter 5). This lack of federal guidelines for ELL leaves it up to the states, and often individual school districts, to figure out the best way to educate ELL students.

So, to be clear, there are a significant number of students identified as English-language learners, yet despite the large number of these students, the guidelines for how best to instruct these students are quite variable based on state and local policies. Even considering this lack of consistent and standardized guidance, teachers are expected to educate these students, and furthermore, these students are not in any way exempted from standardized tests, no matter their difficulties with acquiring and practicing the English language. As the next section will address, both ELL students and the teachers tasked with educating them face some unique and significant challenges in successfully navigating the modern classroom.

Challenges for English-Language Learners

The limits of my language are the limits of my world.
—Ludwig Wittgenstein

Fêrbûna ger her kes bi heman zimanî diaxive pir hêsan e. Any idea what that means or even how to pronounce it? It is in Kurdish, if that helps any. If not, there is always Google Translate, but instead of taking a few moments to get the translation, here it is: Learning is a lot easier if everyone speaks the same language. That seems fairly obvious based on the earlier content on the role of language in learning. But if we believe that translated statement is true, do we also believe the opposite is also true? That learning is pretty difficult if everyone is speaking a different language? If that is the case, then students who do not speak English fluently are at a disadvantage as soon as they set foot in a classroom primarily taught in English. Moreover, it appears that students with limited or no English proficiency may take 5 to 7 years to achieve a functional level of English proficiency (Hakuta, Butler, & Witt, 2000).

Research has, not surprisingly, been fairly consistent in identifying that ELL students are performing academically at a level below their English-speaking peers. Those findings seem obvious on the surface, that students who do not speak English struggle in academics when the primary measures of achievement are from English-based assessments. It is very similar to research that demonstrates students with reading disabilities, as one example, perform poorly on standardized tests of reading achievement. These continuing trends are unfortunate, and what is more unfortunate is that little progress has been made in closing the achievement gap for ELL students. The first step in addressing the academic deficits often displayed by ELL students is to get a better sense of what factors contribute to those deficits. Table 8.2 provides an overview of the challenges often faced by ELL students.

TABLE 8.2 Challenges Faced by English-Language Learners

Challenge	Effect on education
Academic	Research in the early 21st century found that schools are not adequately prepared to support ELL students (Garrett & Holcomb, 2005), and there is a clear lack of resources provided for ELL instruction (Lee, 2012). These findings provide some explanation for the continued poor performance on standardized tests by the majority of ELL students (Shin, 2015).
Social-emotional	ELL students often face additional social-emotional stresses that may negatively affect academic performance. These include often having to serve as an interpreter for their parents (Kam & Lazarevic, 2014), having to provide child care at home, and contributing financially to their families (Perez, 2009). These added responsibilities often spark an early development of independence that may cause these students to feel resentments toward their families (Jaffe-Walter & Lee, 2011).
Socioeconomic	Approximately 75% of ELL students come from low-income families (Kanno & Cromley, 2015). As covered in Chapter 4, there are multiple negative effects on educational performance associated with living in poverty.
Parental involvement	Research suggests the majority of parents of ELL students have less formal education than the parents of non-ELL students (Kanno & Cromley, 2015). Because of this, parents of ELL students may not have the correct level of knowledge for how best to support their children's learning (Delgado, Huerta, & Campos, 2012).

It may be disheartening to consider the obstacles faced by many ELL students. They are at a disadvantage linguistically in many classrooms, a fact compounded by emotional stresses, socioeconomic factors, and varying degrees of parental involvement and support. Given these circumstances, the majority of ELL students clearly need a high level of support to be successful in school. Regarding the emotional challenges they face, many of the ideas presented in Chapter 4 to help promote a growth mindset may prove useful for ELL students. But ELL students are not the only ones facing challenges based on their limited English proficiency. Teachers working with ELL students also face some challenges when trying to effectively support these students.

Challenges for Teachers

The reality is that most, if not all, teachers have or can expect to have ELL students in their classroom and therefore must be prepared to best support these children.

　　　　　　—Samson, Collins, and Center for American Progress (2012)

English-language learners may often deal with unique challenges, but the teachers tasked with instructing these students also face specific challenges themselves. As previously noted, the regulations and supports for how states approach teaching ELL students vary, but there are some states that have taken a more direct approach. Florida, for instance, passed a provision that any teacher working with a student population that included 15% or more ELL students had to accumulate 600 hours of district training to earn an English for Speakers of Other Languages (ESOL) endorsement (Hite & Evans, 2006). While an admirable and direct approach to help teachers better support ELL students, research focused on first-grade teachers in Florida found that the average number of training hours accumulated was 60, only 10% of the requirement in the state mandate (Hite & Evans, 2006). The example provided by Florida is a good demonstration that even state mandates cannot solve the issue that the majority of teachers are not properly trained to support ELL students (e.g., Coady, de Jong, & Harper, 2011; de Jong & Harper, 2005).

Despite this lack of training and preparation, teachers are still called upon to teach all of their students. This is a core principle of education in America, that all students are indeed entitled to a free and appropriate public education. This entitlement does not mean that providing this equity in education is easy. Teachers must confront a host of needs and abilities in their classrooms on a daily basis and find ways to make things work. Finding a way often begins with recognizing the impediments that may lie in the path forward. This means that teachers should first acknowledge some of the difficulties they may encounter when working with ELL students.

Khong and Saito (2014) identified challenges teachers often face when working with ELL students and grouped them into social, institutional, and personal categories. Those three categories are outlined in Table 8.3.

TABLE 8.3 Challenges for Teachers of English-Language Learners

Challenge area	Description
Social	The dramatic increases in the number of ELL students has put pressure on society and, by proxy, teachers to better understand diverse cultures.
	Along with the growing number of ELL students is the increasing diversity among these students, meaning teachers need knowledge of even more cultures/ethnicities.
	Despite the increasing number and diversity of ELL students, neither federal, state, nor local education agencies have established consistent and proactive supportive regulations concerning ELL students.

(continued)

Institutional	Teacher education programs do not spend adequate time or include appropriate curriculum in training future teachers to work with ELL students.
	School districts do not provide consistent professional development focused on supporting ELL students.
	Although it is noted that ELL students learn differently than students whose primary language is English, school systems do not have sufficient materials or resources to differentiate instruction for these students.
	Teachers lack sufficient time to provide necessary supports and interventions to ELL students.
	There are significant communication challenges between teachers, ELL students, and the families of ELL students.
Personal	Teachers' beliefs, attitudes, and assumptions about ELL learners are often misinformed and inappropriate to supporting the needs of these students.
	From an emotional standpoint, teachers often experience frustration about the lack of progress by their ELL students or how long it may take these students to acquire adequate English skills.
	Teachers can also feel isolated and confused about how best to serve their ELL students based on the lack of consistent guidance from all levels of educational administration.

The contents of Table 8.3 represent a wide-ranging and diverse set of issues, many of which are out of a teacher's direct control. And there are some parallels to the challenges that were discussed in the chapters on students from poverty and from minority ethnic groups. These challenges do often exist on and stem from a societal level, which may make addressing them seem very daunting for educators. Can teachers truly change societal attitudes and beliefs? It is impossible to give that question a definitive yes, but teachers absolutely can control what they do in a classroom to address the challenges both they and their ELL students face. In the next section, strategies for supporting ELL students will be presented, and while meant for classroom implementation, these strategies may play some small part in addressing the social, institutional, and personal issues present in the challenges faced by teachers working with ELL students.

Pause and Discuss

In a small group, discuss what you believe are the most significant challenges faced by ELL students. Why are those particularly problematic or challenging? Also, discuss what you believe are the most significant challenges faced by teachers working with ELL students. Why are those particularly problematic or challenging? Share your own concerns or questions in regard to teaching ELL students. Do you have any instructional experience working with ELL students? If so, what was that experience like for you?

Supporting English-Language Learners

In earlier chapters, this text has covered the academic challenges faced by students with disabilities, students living in poverty, and students coming from diverse ethnic backgrounds. For each of those populations, suggestions have then been provided on how to begin to effectively teach those students. The same respect will be given to ELL students, as this section will present a few fundamental, evidence-based practices teachers can use to support ELL students.

For a more comprehensive yet still succinct overview of evidence-based practices for teaching ELL students, please refer to Richards-Tutor, Aceves, and Reese (2016). These authors compiled and detailed several strategies, including the ones that will be discussed next. Their work is available at https://ceedar.education.ufl.edu/wp-content/uploads/2016/11/EBP-for-english-learners.pdf. A sampling of the specific strategies these authors suggest, each followed by a brief description, follows:

- Provide designated time to develop English oral language proficiency.

Given the link between oral language skills and text-based skills, including comprehension (Lesaux & Geva, 2006), it makes sense that ELL students provided with a specific block of time to develop English oral language proficiency performed better than ELL students not provided that time (Saunders, Foorman, & Carlson, 2006). Teachers should explore scheduling options whereby small blocks of time can be given to ELL students during which they are provided direct instruction to improve English oral language proficiency.

- Provide sheltered instruction practices.

There are a variety of practices included in sheltered instructional techniques. A few examples include having clear content and language objectives, building background knowledge, and providing students with opportunities to interact with peers and teachers (Echevarria, Vogt, & Short, 2012). Such efforts, utilized consistently, have led to improved reading and writing performance (Echevarria et al., 2011), while building background knowledge through in-depth vocabulary instruction has also produced positive academic outcomes (e.g., August et al., 2009).

- Incorporate visual representations and multimedia into instruction.

Perhaps the simplest yet still powerful strategy teachers can use to support ELL students is to incorporate visual representations and multimedia resources into their teaching. There are many ways teachers can add visuals, whether it is during vocabulary instruction or reading text, though whichever method is chosen should be deliberate and strategic. Teachers can add visual images to the text, include objects that represent key terms, add visuals to graphic organizers, and even act out language through gestures and movements (Magnusson, 2017). These efforts can provide positive results beyond a student acquiring more English proficiency, as they can also help ELL students' self-confidence, concentration, and comprehension (Cook, 2012; Halwani, 2017; Vinisha & Ramadas, 2013).

- Use peer-supported instruction/learning.

Peer-support approaches to learning tasks have a strong research base as an effective instructional approach for many students, regardless of classification. Although it goes by many names, including cooperative learning, the fundamental idea is that students are paired with one or more peers to complete tasks. For ELL students, this provides them a chance to work with a student with a higher degree of English proficiency in a safe place (e.g., Echevarria, Vogt, & Short, 2012), and research suggests this approach, appropriately utilized, may yield increased academic achievement (e.g., Richards-Tutor, Aceves, & Reutebach, 2016).

- Teach explicit comprehension strategies.

There is abundant research evidence to support explicit strategy instruction as a means for helping students acquire and deploy various learning strategies. For ELL students, who are already dealing with limited English proficiency, the idea that teaching them comprehension strategies in a targeted and explicit manner makes sense. Comprehension strategies can involve previewing text, oral retells, summarizing, making inferences, and others. One specific approach is collaborative strategic reading, which was developed specifically for ELL students and struggling readers and has shown positive effects on comprehension (Klingner, Boardman, & Annamma, 2012).

- Teach high-utility academic words.

Teaching is full of "buzzwords" in regard to learning. They are commonly found in learning objectives, such as "The students will *analyze* the text and *summarize* the main ideas." Terms such as *analyze, summarize, understand, comprehend, explain, describe,* and many others are common in the language of teaching and are considered significant when determining whether a task requires a foundational skill, such as recall, or involves higher order thinking, such as synthesizing. For ELL students, the importance of understanding these words is critical to academic achievement. Teachers must also distinguish between general academic terms, such as *summarize, explain,* or *identify,* and domain-specific terms, such as *legislature, integer,* or *plasma* (Richards-Tutor, Aceves, & Reese, 2016). When considering which words to emphasize, teachers should be mindful of words central to understanding text, words that may have different meanings in other contexts, and words used frequently in text (Baker et al., 2014).

- Provide instruction with primary language support.

This may be the most challenging of the strategies shared in this section. Teachers may find it difficult to access and provide instructional materials in a student's primary language, but attempting to enrich content instruction with primary language can pay dividends. Research suggests that when ELL students receive accommodations and/or modifications to supplement the content in a class, there are positive effects on the students' content understanding (August et al., 2015; Echevarria, Vogt, & Short, 2012). Something as simple as finding vocabulary terms in a student's primary language and incorporating them strategically into instruction should be immensely helpful.

- Obtain additional formal and informal measures of student performance to clarify progress.

Using routine informal and formal assessment practices is important to monitor the progress of all students but can be especially important for ELL students. Researchers recommend that educators routinely monitor the progress ELL students are making toward proficiency (e.g., Hosp et al., 2011; Linan-Thompson & Ortiz, 2009), which can provide data to guide the provision of appropriate supports. These routine assessment practices should begin as soon as a student is identified as ELL to fully determine the student's linguistic background (Miller et al., 2006) and can include assessing linguistic practices in the home and community in order to begin provision of services based on the student's current level of English proficiency (Esparza-Brown & Sanford, 2011).

The preceding strategies are not the only ones available for supporting ELL students, but they do provide a good starting point for teachers working with ELL students. One point to consider when choosing among these or other strategies is time constraints. Any strategy chosen to implement as an intervention to support learners should be incorporated effectively and with appropriate attention to detail. Teachers will need to be mindful of schedule opportunities where effective strategies can be implemented.

Beyond these strategies are ones that focus on more intensive provision of services that will probably involve the ELL student receiving intervention services outside the general education classroom and also more formal strategies for using the student's primary language as part of instruction and assessment. There are also methods for creating more active collaborative partnerships with the parents of the ELL students. While these ideas certainly have validity and can yield positive results, their implementation will often require more time, effort, and external supports than most teachers can control.

As for strategies teachers can select and use independently, for the most part, Echevarria, Frey, and Fisher (2015) have divided the best practices for ELL students into four areas. Teachers should consider these as they begin to decide how they will work with and support ELL students. The first area is to be mindful that ELL students need access to the curriculum, the second is to ensure the classroom climate is accepting and inviting for ELL students, the third is maintaining equity in regard to expectations for ELL students, and the fourth is to help ELL student learning by paying particular attention to the language objectives within content teaching (as noted earlier). Keeping these four areas in mind when determining how to support ELL students should help teachers select and utilize appropriate strategies.

1. Which of the strategies presented in this section seems to be the most workable for you and your career as an educator?
2. Are you familiar with other effective strategies not covered in this text? If so, what are they?
3. Do you believe it is important for all teachers to have some working knowledge of teaching strategies to support ELL students? Why or why not?

Pause and Reflect

Conclusion

Teachers need to give encouragement and praise for what ELLs can do instead of focusing on all they can't yet do by providing frequent opportunities for their success.

—Judie Haynes, ELL teacher with 36 years of classroom and teacher-training experience (Ferlazzo, 2019)

The preceding quotation from Judie Haynes is a proper mindset to share as this chapter draws to a close. Although there are challenges faced by both ELL students and their teachers, there are also solutions, and these solutions can best be applied when teachers begin to recognize what ELL students truly can achieve. The strategies presented in the preceding chapter are, as noted, just a starting point for how teachers can support their ELL students. There are more available, and while not given significant attention in this text, the effort to establish good relationships with the families of ELL students is an effort all teachers should try to make. While the school-family relationship is obviously important for all students, it can be especially influential for ELL students when their families realize the school and teachers are being proactive to support these students. All of the information presented in this chapter should demonstrate that the English-language deficits displayed by ELL students should be addressed directly in all classes and that teachers do have methods available to help ELL students overcome these deficits and begin to find success in American schools.

KEY CHAPTER TAKEAWAYS

Some important takeaways from this chapter include:

- The number of English-language learners in American schools has increased dramatically over the past few decades.

- Language is an incredibly important part of learning. Phonemic awareness, morphology, word recognition, semantics, and pragmatics are particularly significant components of language development.

- When considering language in learning, it is important to keep in mind the form, content, and use of the specific language meant to impart knowledge and skills.

- Although specific data is hard to find on the number of ELL students in the United States, the available numbers indicate approximately 10% of students are identified as ELL, a percentage equivalent to the number of students receiving services for special education.

- Although a significant portion of the student population, ELL students do not have the same level of federal support guidelines as those provided for students in special education via the Individuals with Disabilities Education Act.

- ELL students have demonstrated difficulties in multiple areas related to their performance in school, including academics, social-emotional characteristics, socioeconomic characteristics, and parental involvement in education.

- Teachers working with ELL students have faced challenges in personal, institutional, and social areas when trying to effectively teach these students.

- There are multiple evidence-based strategies that teachers can utilize when working with ELL students. These include explicitly teaching vocabulary and comprehension strategies, finding time to support English oral language proficiency, teaching high-utility academic words, and using appropriate assessments to monitor the progress of ELL students.

- When selecting strategies, teachers should keep in mind that ELL students need access to the curriculum, should feel accepted in the classroom, and should be treated equitably, and teachers should also be very mindful of the role of language within content teaching.

CASE SCENARIO: THE INTERVIEW CONTINUES

"Kortney, did you take a foreign language in high school or college?" Mrs. Frayer asked.

"I took two years of French in high school," Kortney answered. "But I didn't have any language requirements for my undergraduate degree program."

"You're not alone in that," Mrs. Frayer said. "Very few first-year teachers that I interview had any type of foreign language class while in college. Some of them may have liked the classes in high school enough to take one or two to fill an elective, and some actually remember enough to be passably conversant in whichever language. But that's not the significant point of my question. I'm curious, do you have any idea how many languages are spoken in the homes of our students?"

"I don't," Kortney answered.

"It might surprise you to find we have identified 10 languages, and that includes multiple dialects from one language," Mrs. Frayer continued. "We have almost as many ELL students as we do students in special education."

"That surprises me a little," Kortney said. "We touched on ELL students briefly in my program, but I don't recall getting too deep into teaching them. I recall a lot about visual supports, I think."

Mrs. Frayer nodded before continuing. "Yes, visuals are very important. They're probably the biggest tool in the ELL strategy tool box, but far from the only one. Which leads me to another story that can give you some insight into our school, and a lot of schools around this country."

And with that, the principal told the following story:

Miss Sanford had been teaching fourth grade for 3 years when she got her first significant influx of ELL students. She never had more than one in her class during those first 3 years, but when her fourth year started, she began with two ELL students, one whose primary language was Spanish and one whose primary language was Cantonese. Only mildly flustered by this state of affairs, Miss Sanford continued to incorporate some basic ELL teaching strategies to support these two students. But then, during the first week of October, a student whose primary language was Russian enrolled at the school and was placed in Miss Sanford's class. And then just before Halloween she got her fourth ELL student, this one from a home where the primary language was Somali.

"It's starting to feel like a mini United Nations in my class," Miss Sanford shared with a colleague. "Having to cope with two languages besides English was a tall enough order, but now I've got five languages in my classroom. Five. Different. Languages. Think about that for a minute, the kinds of challenges that poses for me."

"I'll tell you what," her colleague, Mrs. Canon, answered. "I'll swap you straight up two of your ELL students for two of mine with these ridiculous IEP expectations. The number of accommodations I'm providing each day is ridiculous, but that's the law. What do you think?"

"I think you're really starting to lose your empathy skills," Miss Sanford answered sarcastically. "But please know my well of understanding never runs out."

"It's your true gift, and I'm sure it will get you through this new tribulation," Mrs. Canon said as she turned to walk away. "You'll think of something," she added, turning back to offer those parting words. "You always do."

I really hope I can this time, Miss Sanford thought. And she went back to her classroom to look over the paperwork on her new students.

She began by reviewing what had worked so far with Jaime, her Hispanic student, and Xian, her Chinese student. Miss Sanford had started to build in visual representations of new words and concepts on a routine basis, but even with those she had to help Jaime and Xian with extra practice in pronouncing new words and trying to use them in simple declarative sentences. She realized just how much extra time she was spending working with those two students. And now she would have to figure out ways to work with Illyana, her new student whose primary language was Russian, and Thok, her new student who spoke Somali.

As she reviewed the brief paperwork on Illyana and Thok, she found that each had only been in the country a few months and that there was no assessment data included in the files. In fact, the files were extremely thin, including very basic demographic information and a few notes from the school guidance counselor, who had met with the students and parents when the children were enrolled. The notes were not exactly inspirational, conveying that the students spoke little to no English, and the parents' English skills were also very limited. This was compounded by the fact, the guidance counselor had noted, that a translator familiar with Somali was not currently available in the district.

That must have been a fun meeting, Miss Sanford thought. And then she thought how much fun she had in store with trying to accommodate four foreign languages into her class. She sighed audibly.

WORKING WITH THE SCENARIO

"It seems like Miss Sanford has her hands full with that many different languages in her classroom," Kortney said when she sensed Mrs. Frayer was done sharing. She was starting to get a solid sense of the pattern the principal followed in relating these stories.

"Oh, assuredly," Mrs. Frayer said. "I know I'd struggle in those same circumstances. And I'm wondering how you might react given the same circumstances. Ready for more questions?"

"Yes, ma'am," Kortney answered. "I'll do my best."

"That is always appreciated," Mrs. Frayer responded. "Describe how you would feel if you were in Miss Sanford's situation. What emotions and thoughts might you be having about your role and ability as a teacher? Getting beyond your feelings, how would you start to plan supports for your new ELL students? What steps would you take with them very early in their time in your classroom? Would you explore how to communicate with the parents of these students?"

"That's a lot to consider," Kortney said, once again feeling the mental pressure of the questions.

"I agree, but interviews are tests, I think," Mrs. Frayer answered. "And here are the last two questions. Considering what you know about ELL students, what are some basic strategies Miss Sanford could have considered using in her class? Why do you think these would be appropriate and supportive of ELL student learning?"

If you were Kortney, how would you respond to the questions posed by Mrs. Frayer?

REFERENCES

Aronoff, M., & Fudeman, K. (2011). *What is morphology?* (Vol. 8). John Wiley & Sons.

August, D., Artzi, L., Kuchle, L., & Halloran, C. (2015). *Quality of English language proficiency assessments: Evaluation of state and local implementation of Title III assessment and accountability systems.* American Institutes for Research, U.S. Department of Education, Office of English Language Acquisition. https://ncela.ed.gov/files/15_2037_QELPA_ELSWD_Summary_final_dla_5-15-15_508.pdf

August, D., Branum-Martin, L., Cardenas-Hagan, E., & Francis, D. (2009). The impact of an instructional intervention on the science and language learning of middle grade English language learners. *Journal of Research on Educational Effectiveness 2*(4), 345–76. doi:10.1080/19345740903217623

Baker, S., Lesaux, N., Jayanthi, M., Dimino, J., Proctor, C. P., Morris, J., Gersten R., Linan-Thompson, S., Kiefer, M. J., & Newman-Gonchar, R. (2014). *Teaching academic content and literacy to English learners in elementary and middle school (NCEE 2014–4012).* National Center for Education Evaluation and Regional Assistance, Institute of Education Sciences, U.S. Department of Education. https://ies.ed.gov/ncee/wwc/publications_reviews.aspx

Carreiras, M., Armstrong, B. C., Perea, M., & Frost, R. (2014). The what, when, where, and how of visual word recognition. *Trends in Cognitive Sciences, 18*(2), 90–98.

Coady, M., de Jong, E., & Harper, C. (2011). From preservice to practice: Mainstream elementary teacher beliefs of preparation and efficacy with English language learners in the state of Florida. *Bilingual Research Journal, 34*(2), 223–39. doi:10.1080/15235882.2011.597823

Cook, M. (2012). Teaching with visuals in the science classroom. *Science Scope, 35*(5), 64–67.

de Jong, E. J., & Harper, C. A. (2005). Preparing mainstream teachers for English-language learners: Is being a good teacher good enough? *Teacher Education Quarterly, 32*(2), 101–24.

Delgado, R., Huerta, M. E., & Campos, D. (2012). Enhancing relationships with parents of English language learners. *Principal Leadership, 12*(6), 30–34.

Echevarria, J., Frey, N., & Fisher, D. (2015). What it takes for English learners to SUCCEED. *Educational Leadership, 72*(6), 22–26.

Echevarria, J., Richards-Tutor, C., Pham, V., & Ratleff, P. (2011). Did they get it? The role of fidelity in improving teaching for English learners. *Journal of Adolescent and Adult Literacy, 4*, 425–34.

Echevarria, J., Vogt, M., & Short, D. (2012). *Making content comprehensible for English learners* (4th ed.). Pearson.

Brown, J. E., & Sanford, A. K. (2011). *RTI for English language learners: Appropriately using screening and progress monitoring tools to improve instructional outcomes.* Portland State University.

Ferlazzo, L. (2019, July 31). Q&A collections: Teaching English-language learners. *Education Week.* https://blogs.edweek.org/teachers/classroom_qa_with_larry_ferlazzo/2019/07/qa_collections_teaching_english_language_learners_1.html

Garrett, J. E., & Holcomb, S. (2005). Meeting the needs of immigrant students with limited English ability. *International Education, 35*(1), 49–64.

Hakuta, K., Butler, Y. G., & Witt, D. (2000). *How long does it take English learners to attain proficiency?* University of California Linguistic Minority Research Institute. https://files.eric.ed.gov/fulltext/ED443275.pdf

Halliday, M. A. K. (1979/1980). Three aspects of children's language development: Learning language, learning through language, learning about language. In *Oral and written language development: Impact on schools. Proceedings from the 1979 and 1980 IMPACT conferences* (Y. Goodman, M., Hausser, & D. Strickland, Eds., pp. 7–19). International Reading Association and National Council of Teachers of English.

Halwani, N. (2017). Visual aids and multimedia in second language acquisition. *English Language Teaching, 10*(6), 53–59.

Hite, C. E., & Evans, L. S. (2006). Mainstream first-grade teachers' understanding of strategies for accommodating the needs of English language learners. *Teacher Education Quarterly, 33*(2), 89–110.

Hosp, J. L., Hosp, M. A., & Dol, J. K. (2011). Potential bias in predictive validity of universal screening measures across disaggregation subgroups. *School Psychology Review, 40*(1), 108–131.

Jaffe-Walter, R., & Lee, S. J. (2011). "To trust in my root and to take that to go forward": Supporting college access for immigrant youth in the global city. *Anthropology & Education Quarterly, 42*(3), 281–96.

Kam, J. A., & Lazarevic, V. (2014). The stressful (and not so stressful) nature of language brokering: Identifying when brokering functions as a cultural stressor for Latino immigrant children in early adolescence. *Journal of Youth and Adolescence, 43*(12), 1994–2011.

Kamarck, E., & Stenglein, C. (2020). *How many undocumented immigrants are in the United States and who are they?* Brookings Institution. https://www.brookings.edu/policy2020/votervital/how-many-undocumented-immigrants-are-in-the-united-states-and-who-are-they/

Kanno, Y., & Cromley, J. G. (2015). English language learners' pathways to four-year colleges. *Teachers College Record, 117*(12), 1–44.

Khong, T. D. H., & Saito, E. (2014). Challenges confronting teachers of English language learners. *Educational Review, 66*(2), 210–25.

Klingner, J., Boardman, A., & Annamma, S. (2012). Promoting high expectations with collaborative strategic reading. In *Places where ALL children learn: The power of high expectation curricula* (C. Dudley-Marling & S. Michaels, Eds., pp. 73–86). Teachers College, Columbia University.

Lecanuet, J. P., Granier-Deferre, C., & Busnel, M. C. (1989). Differential fetal auditory reactiveness as a function of stimulus characteristics and state. *Seminars in Perinatology, 13*, 421–29.

Lee, S. (2012). New talk about ELL students. *Phi Delta Kappan, 93*(8), 66–69.

Lesaux, N., & Geva, E. (2006). Synthesis: Development of literacy in language-minority students. In *Developing literacy in second-language learners: Report of the National Literacy Panel on Language-Minority Children and Youth* (D. August & T. Shanahan, Eds., pp. 53–74). Lawrence Erlbaum.

Linan-Thompson, S., & Ortiz, A. A. (2009). Response to intervention and English-language learners: Instructional and assessment considerations. *Seminars in speech and language, 30*(2), 105–120. Thieme Medical Publishers.

Magnusson, J. (2017). *Introducing non-EL teachers to visual learning strategies for beginning English learners: A proposal for workshop study.* Hamline University School of Education, Student Capstone Theses and Dissertations 4392. https://digitalcommons.hamline.edu/hse_all/439

Miller, J. F., Heilmann, J., Nockerts, A., Iglesias, A., Fabiano, L., & Francis, D. J. (2006). Oral language and reading in bilingual children. *Learning Disabilities Research & Practice, 21*, 30–43. doi:10.1111/j.1540-5826.2006.00205.x

Mitchell, C. (2018, January 17). Rising number of ESL students poses challenges for U.S. schools. *Education Week*. http://blogs.edweek.org/edweek/learning-the-language/2018/01/rising_number_of_esl_students_pose_challenges_for_schools.html

NCES (National Center for Education Statistics). (2019). *The condition of education 2019*. (2019–144). U.S. Department of Education.

Parish-Morris J., Golinkoff, R. M., & Hirsh-Pasek, K. (2013). From coo to code: Language acquisition in early childhood. In *The Oxford handbook of developmental psychology* (Vol. 1, P. Zelazo, Ed., pp. 867–908). Oxford University Press.

Perez, W. (2009). *We are Americans: Undocumented students pursuing the American dream*. Stylus.

Ragan, A., & Lesaux, N. (2006). Federal, state, and district level English language learner program entry and exit requirements: Effects on the education of language minority learners. *Education Policy Analysis Archives, 14*, 1–32.

Richards-Tutor, C., Aceves, T., & Reese, L. (2016). *Evidence-based practices for English learners.* (Document No. IC-18). University of Florida, Collaboration for Effective Educator, Development, Accountability, and Reform Center. http://ceedar.education.ufl.edu/tools/innovation-configurations/

Samson, J. F., Collins, B. A., & Center for American Progress. (2012). *Preparing all teachers to meet the needs of English language learners: Applying research to policy and practice for teacher effectiveness.* Center for American Progress.

Saunders, W., Foorman, B., & Carlson, C. (2006). Is a separate block of time for oral English language development in programs for English learners needed? *Elementary School Journal, 107*(2), 181–98. doi:10.1086/510654

Shin, N. (2015). *The effects of English language learner classification on students' educational experience and later academic achievement.* (Doctoral dissertation, University of California, Los Angeles). ProQuest. Shin_ucla_0031D_13985. https://escholarship.org/uc/item/0s90j2h0

Smagorinsky, P. (2001). If meaning is constructed, what's it made from? Toward a cultural theory of reading. *Review of Educational Research, 71*, 133–69.

Smith, D. D., Tyler, N. C., & Skow, K. (2017). *Introduction to contemporary special education: New horizons*. Pearson.

U.S. Department of Education, Office for Civil Rights Programs for English Language Learners. (n.d.). Retrieved June 25, 2020, from https://www2.ed.gov/about/offices/list/ocr/ell/edlite-glossary.html

Vinisha, K., & Ramadas, J. (2013). Visual representations of the water cycle in science textbooks. *Contemporary Education Dialogue, 10*(1), 7–36.

Teaching in the Digital Age: Creating Quality Learning Experiences With Technology

Dr. Shannon M. Bland

Setting the Classroom Scene

For 12 years, Ms. Somsen has been a science teacher primarily for sixth, seventh, and eighth grades in a small, rural community. She is beginning her fifth year teaching sixth grade and considers herself to be "tech-savvy," as well as an effective teacher.

A typical day for students in her classroom begins with a bell-ringer question in their science notebooks, then silent reading of the current topic in their science textbook, followed by a worksheet to answer content-related questions. Ms. Somsen typically wraps up the day by reviewing the worksheet answers and assigning homework. Weekly, however, she includes a "hands-on" lab or activity to go along with the content. She tries to include more engaging hands-on activities but typically has to stop due to student behavior disruptions. Therefore, her classroom is considered a more rigid learning environment compared with her colleagues' classrooms.

Her students' grades are below average to average, so she wants to find a better way to engage her students to make learning fun and potentially solve a few minor discipline issues. Her team teacher has recently told her about a new website that engages students in inquiry through the use of simulations. She checks out the site for herself and believes her students would like it. The problem: Her classroom only has one device, a computer with slow internet connection due to the school's rural location. Additionally, the school has one computer lab for all K–12 classes to use, which is typically booked. She lacks the support of professional development to help learn how to integrate technology more effectively and does not feel confident in her abilities. She ultimately decides not to use the lab and continues teaching as she typically does. The issue is not that Ms. Somsen does not care or does not want to engage the students, but feels defeated and unmotivated and decides, "It's just not worth the hassle."

Ms. Somsen is not alone. This is the case for many teachers around the country who are in poor, rural communities. They feel defeated by the barriers they encounter to effectively engage their students with technology to enhance their learning.

Prereading Questions

1. How do you define technology integration?

2. How do you envision integrating technology in your classroom?

3. What are some of the barriers affecting Ms. Somsen's ability to engage students with technology? What barriers might you encounter that may make technology integration difficult?

Introduction

Have you ever been as frustrated as Ms. Somsen? Do you deeply desire to engage your students with technology but feel overwhelmed or defeated by your school's lack of access to technology? Maybe you have access, but you are not sure what's the best way to engage students or don't know the best resources to assist you. In the 21st-century classroom, our students are more tech-savvy than ever, many having their own devices before they even entered the K–12 setting. Mobile devices and iPads have been placed in front of them from an early age for both learning and entertainment. They learn their ABCs by watching a sing-along video on YouTube or begin learning to read on the Kindle. Many of our students have only known a world in which these devices exist and are bringing these experiences with them into the classroom. Others, however, may only encounter technology through their school experiences.

Although students may be entering the classroom with a variety of technological experiences and abilities, one thing is certain—technology continues to advance and become more accessible globally, and our students need to be prepared for this consistent change in the 21st century. Integration through your instruction may be the first experience that students have with technology, and providing opportunities for them to develop positive attitudes with technology is more imperative than ever. Not only is it important, but students expect it.

What is educational technology and technology integration? If you scour the internet, you may find several definitions of technology. It is a broad term that is bigger than iPads, computers, and the latest social media application. This chapter will focus, however, on a more narrowed perspective of technology called educational technology, which is defined by the Association of Educational Communications and Technology as "the study and ethical practice of facilitating learning and improving performance by creating, using and managing appropriate technological processes and resources" (Richey, 2008, p. 24). In more simple terms, educational technology is the practice of implementing appropriate technological resources to improve student performance. True technology integration requires more than simply using a SMART Board to show a presentation or having students use Microsoft Word on a laptop to type an essay on World War II. True integration is more than just using devices as a "tool." To be effective, teachers must use these devices in ways that enhance the students' learning experience by engaging with the content in more meaningful ways, and this occurs across many different classroom environments.

Technology integration in classrooms has been present over the past few decades, but teachers continue to feel unmotivated or unprepared to engage their students. This chapter will begin with barriers teachers face implementing technology effectively in the classroom, followed by uses in the classroom. Additionally, the chapter will discuss the effects technology can have on both teachers and students, teaching in a crisis situation through e-learning, and concluding with strategies and best practices for using technology to create more meaningful experiences.

Barriers Teachers Encounter

Although using technology in the classroom setting proves to be advantageous, research has consistently shown that few teachers engage students in meaningful ways through the use of technology—in this case, digital technology, whether that includes computers, tablets, or mobile devices (Cuban, Kirkpatrick, & Peck, 2001). Based on the analysis of 48 empirical studies, the most frequently cited barriers affecting technology integration include resources, teacher knowledge and skills, and teacher attitudes and beliefs (Hew & Brush, 2007).

Resources

Lack of resources may include one or a combination of the following: technology, access to available technology, time, and support (Hew & Brush, 2007). Not every school or district has the financial ability to provide students with devices such as iPads or Chromebooks at a 1:1 ratio. How do you engage students when there is only one computer in the classroom, the school has only one computer lab/cart for the entire school, or you live in a rural community that has limited access to the internet? This is the case for some teachers across the nation; however, great strides are being made in helping districts across the nation close the connectivity gap. The Education Superhighway (2019), whose mission is to provide high-speed internet to every public K–12 school in the United States, reported that 99% of schools now have internet access, with only 743 schools remaining as of 2019. Also, in 2009, 97% of K–12 public school teachers reported they had one or more computers in their classroom, along with displays or projectors (84%), digital cameras (78%), and interactive whiteboards (51%). Despite the availability, however, only 69% reported that they were used during instruction (Gray, Thomas, & Lewis, 2010).

School access is not the only barrier to consider—students from a variety of socioeconomic backgrounds also have limited access to the internet, devices, or both. According to the Federal Communications Commission (2019), there are reportedly 21 million Americans without access to high-speed internet. Additionally, a 2018 report found nearly one in five students in K–12 schools do not have access to both computers and an internet connection (Anderson & Perrin, 2018). No matter the demographic background of your school's population, it is important to consider the needs of each student and their ability to access the internet and devices on an individual level.

Knowledge and Skill Level

Another two barriers to consider are knowledge and skill level. Teachers may lack the support of professional learning opportunities due to budget, time, or typical teacher responsibilities. Technological skill level may also have an effect on teacher self-efficacy and motivation to integrate technology in lessons (Lai, Pratt, & Trewern, 2001). Studies conducted over the past 20 years found that specific technology knowledge and skills—such as using databases and spreadsheets, logging on to networks, opening and closing files, and other basic word processing tasks—are the most common reasons teachers do not use technology (Hughes, 2005; Snoeyink & Ertmer, 2001–2002; Williams et al., 2000). In addition, teachers are unfamiliar with the pedagogy of integrating technology with students and need to have "technology-supported-pedagogy knowledge" (Hughes, 2005, p. 284) in which they can draw upon to plan integrated lessons.

Although studies have reported teacher knowledge and skill level as barriers, student knowledge and skill level must also be taken into consideration. If your students lack access in their home environment, this may also hinder their own abilities when beginning to use technology in the classroom environment. While some students may have had access to computers and tablets from a young age and have a fair grasp on how to use them, other students will not come into contact with such technological devices until they enter the classroom; therefore, teachers should take into consideration students' abilities when using technology and should accommodate accordingly.

Lastly, digital technology itself can also be a challenge. According to Koehler and Mishra (2009), digital technology can be used in a variety of ways, is opaque (inner workings are hidden), and is considered unstable (continuously changing), thus creating challenges for teachers desiring to integrate technology.

Technology Attitudes and Beliefs

Another pair of major barriers to consider are teacher attitudes and beliefs toward technology integration (Hermans et al., 2006). Teacher attitudes toward integration is defined as liking or disliking the use of technology, while beliefs regarding technology integration is defined as premises believed to be true about teaching and learning, and the technology itself—and teachers' beliefs can determine their attitude (Bondur, Brinberg, & Coupey, 2000; Ertmer, 2005; Windschitl & Sahl, 2002). Several studies worldwide investigated whether technology integration was dependent upon teacher attitudes and beliefs. One study in the United States found that teachers' beliefs about technology shaped their goals. For example, teachers who viewed technology as a way to keep kids busy did not find it relevant in the curriculum. Similarly, studies in other countries revealed that teachers believed technology would not aid in deeper understanding or faster learning and were unconvinced that technology could help in education (Ertmer et al., 1999; Karagiorgi, 2005; Newhouse, 2001). Ertmer (2005) concluded that the technological attitudes and beliefs teachers hold ultimately influence their decisions on planning and integration.

Consider your own skill level with technology. How does this influence your beliefs regarding technology integration in your classroom?

Pause and Reflect

Overcoming Barriers

With STEM jobs and the advancement of technology on the rise, it is more important than ever to help teachers overcome the barriers of technology integration and provide students with technological experiences. Although there are many barriers—123 were listed in 48 empirical studies—the most prevalent ones frequently cited included resources (access, time, support), teacher knowledge and skills, and teacher attitudes and beliefs (Hew & Brush, 2007). Several strategies can be implemented to help teachers increase technology integration, including the following:

1. Lack of technology and access: Use laptop carts with wireless connections to save on computer lab space. Also, introduce technology in one content area at a time to ensure students and teachers have adequate access (Lowther, Ross, & Morrison, 2003; Tearle, 2004). If your classroom only has access to one computer and projector, create whole-class opportunities to engage students with technology by having a student demonstrate the website, game, or activity. Call on student volunteers to participate in front of the class. Having students actively participate with the single computer or device provides technological opportunities, no matter how limited. Additionally, in a single-device classroom, teachers can create a center, or station, that students rotate through, giving all students a chance to engage with technology.

2. Lack of time: Teachers need time to plan and collaborate to create integrated lessons (Dexter, Anderson, & Ronnkvist, 2002; Lim & Khine, 2006). As a new teacher, you may be paired with a mentor teacher in your school. Plan a time weekly, biweekly, or monthly with your mentor to collaborate. If you are not paired with a mentor teacher, reach out to veteran teachers to ask for ideas and guidance.

3. Lack of technical support: Find students in your class or school who have greater technological abilities to help (Cuban, Kirkpatrick, & Peck, 2001; Lim et al., 2003). When all else fails, find a tutorial on YouTube.

4. Attitudes/beliefs: Institutional support such as having a technology vision and plan, providing ongoing professional development, and encouraging teachers will help promote positive attitudes and beliefs (Lawson & Comber, 1999; Sandholtz & Reilly, 2004). Ask your administration about its vision for utilizing technology in the classroom, and begin a dialogue that can lead to supporting your technology goals.

5. Knowledge and skills: Providing opportunities for professional development and training that focuses on content-connected technology examples can positively influence teacher attitudes, beliefs, and relevance (Hughes, 2005). If your school provides opportunities, do not

hesitate to sign up. The more knowledge and skills you gain, the more comfortable you will be integrating technology. But if you are limited to professional development opportunities provided by your school or district, many organizations host conferences or workshops that discuss technology integration. Research professional development opportunities through your state's education department site. This is a great initial place to search due to teacher certification and renewal guidelines. Also, search workshop opportunities through state and national teacher organizations, education blogs, and teacher social media accounts. Many veteran teachers share their knowledge through their own education social media accounts about lessons they have implemented.

Uses of Technology in the Classroom

From student engagement to classroom management, there are multiple uses for technology in the classroom. Consider how you are currently using technology in the classroom, if you are. Do you use it for typical teacher tasks such as attendance and grades? Do you use it in ways to enhance the content? There are a variety of ways to integrate technology, including assessing students, promoting inquiry through simulations and virtual/augmented reality, managing your classroom, communicating and collaborating with both parents and students, supplementing your lesson, and assisting learners with different needs.

Assessment

Currently, one popular way teachers are integrating technology into their classroom is through the use of formative assessment tools to generate feedback and assess learning occurring in the classroom. Teachers can use technology to administer quizzes and polls, to have students demonstrate conceptual knowledge through drawing and discussion boards, or to collaborate on digital mind-mapping tools—all to assess current student understandings. These tools can be a great way to enhance a lesson and gauge whether students are progressing toward learning outcomes. Tools such as Plickers and FlipGrid bring classroom learning into the digital age and provide a means to reach a variety of learners. Consider using the following tools for assessment:

- Plickers, or "paper clickers," is a student response tool that allows students to respond to multiple-choice questions by holding up a QR-style code. The teacher, using the downloaded Plickers app on a device, is able to scan student responses, collecting real-time feedback.

- FlipGrid is a video discussion platform that allows students to respond to a topic by creating videos ranging from 15 seconds to 5 minutes by using either the desktop version or the application version for mobile phones and tablets. Student video responses appear on the classroom "grid," giving the application a social media feeling, a concept with which students are familiar. Students and teachers can "like" shared videos, comment, or respond with video feedback, fostering a collaborative learning environment.

Simulations for Inquiry

Bell and Smetana (2008) broadly define computer simulations as "computer-generated dynamic models that present theoretical or simplified models of real-world components, phenomena, or processes … [which] can include animations, visualizations, and interactive laboratory experiences" (p. 23). In content areas such as math and science, simulations allow students to visualize content that may be abstract and hard to understand from reading a text or allow students to manipulate variables in a simulated lab that could be too dangerous in real life.

There have been many studies over the past several decades aimed at determining the effects simulations have on student achievement. Research shows that simulations help students learn how to solve problems and make decisions rather than just learn facts and increase achievement more than hands-on labs. One particular study found that simulations are beneficial in "developing content knowledge and process skills, as well as in promoting more complicated goals such as inquiry and conceptual change" (Bell & Smetana, 2008, p. 23).

Using simulations in a classroom setting can be a great learning tool; however, there are guidelines that should be followed to achieve the most success. The following guidelines were developed by Bell and Smetana (2008):

- Use computer simulations to supplement, not replace, other instructional modes.

- Keep instruction student-centered. Challenging students to think more critically is important, and using simulations can help facilitate this.

- Point out the limitations of simulations. Students should understand that some aspects of simulations are not factual and are only there to make the concept easier to understand or see.

- Make content, not technology, the focus. Students should focus on what the simulation is trying to teach them. If the software or program is complicated and hard to use, they may miss what is most important.

Using simulations can visually enhance the learning experience and reach a variety of learners. Consider using the following simulation tools:

- Explore Learning Gizmos are interactive math and science simulations that allow students to engage in inquiry through graphing, measuring, comparing, predicting, and proving at both the elementary and secondary level. These gizmos provide experiences that enhance content in a virtual environment through the manipulation of variables.

- Google Earth is a computer program that renders a three-dimensional representation of the Earth, the sky, the moon, and Mars. Most commonly used for the Earth, the satellite imagery allows students to freely explore oceans and continents, use time-history imagery, create tours around the world, and utilize measurement tools to calculate distances from one country to another or the height of the Great Pyramid. This software has been shown to support spatial thinking and develop critical technology and thinking skills (Patterson, 2007). Although great for a geoscience class, this tool can be implemented across the curricula for math, science, English, and history lessons.

Classroom Management

There is an array tools allowing teachers to more easily manage their classroom. These tools can be implemented in a way that not only allows teachers to track behavior and manage day-to-day tasks but also engages students to make learning fun. There are tools, websites, and applications that allow teachers to manage point-and-reward systems or call on students for participation. Consider using the following tools to ease classroom management:

- Class Dojo is a free, positive classroom management program that engages teachers, students, and parents by generating a digital equivalent of a behavior management chart commonly seen in many elementary classrooms. Teachers are able to create a class using their roster of students, each assigned an editable avatar. The teacher can reward students for positive behavior by assigning points to desirable traits (e.g., +1 point for being on task) or deduct points for less desirable behavior (e.g., -1 point for being off task). The program includes a default of positive and less-positive behaviors but can be edited by the teacher. Parents can also connect with the mobile application to monitor their child's behavior. The platform, however, is more than a behavior management platform. It has a variety of tools for both teachers and families that foster community through photos, videos, and messages.

Collaboration

Today we are more connected than ever. There are numerous tools that allow us to connect with anyone and anything with the touch of our fingers, and many of these tools can be utilized in the classroom to foster collaboration between students, teachers, and parents and to connect with other classrooms on a global scale. Consider using the following tools to foster collaboration and communication:

1. Digital concept mapping tools, such as Bubbl, Popplet, and Lucidchart, allow students to digitally create concept maps in real time that showcase their current understandings. Students can collaborate together as a class or in pairs/groups to work on brainstorming sessions for group projects, research papers, or chapter outlines.

2. Google Classroom is a learning management system (LMS) that is part of the Google Apps for Education suite that allows teachers, students, and parents to be involved in the learning process. This platform provides a central location to assign homework and quizzes, collect student work, and provide feedback in a timely manner. It interfaces with Google Drive, allowing teachers and students to easily collaborate and upload stored documents. Many schools use this due to cost efficiency (free) and usability.

3. Social media tools have changed the way teachers, students, and parents communicate and collaborate. Many use social media in their daily personal lives, but these tools are quickly transforming education as a way to stay connected beyond the school day. Teachers use apps such as Facebook and Instagram to showcase their students' work or show the daily activities of their students. Twitter is used as a way to ignite discussion on important topics. Not only do schools utilize it as a way to disseminate information to the community, but teachers are

beginning to utilize these tools in projects and assignments as an alternative means to assess student understandings and foster collaboration among peers.

Accommodation

Meeting students' individual learning needs can be more easily accomplished with the integration of technology. There are many resources that allow teachers to accommodate students based on their language needs and comprehension needs. Consider the following resource to meet students' learning needs:

- Newsela is a database of current events articles allowing teachers to connect content and relevance while simultaneously meeting the language and comprehension needs of individual students. The database allows teachers to search for articles based on grade level, content, and language. Each article has the ability to be modified based on Lexile level to adjust vocabulary and word count for students who are below reading level, at reading level, or above reading level. Many of the articles also come with a Spanish version for ELL students.

Distance Learning

Distance education, or e-learning, has many names and has been on the rise over the past several decades. Many college campuses have been utilizing distance-learning platforms to increase enrollment, improve accessibility, and provide more flexible options for students (Toppin & Toppin, 2016). Over the years, K–12 schools have begun providing distance-learning options for their students to provide flexibility for highly mobile families or provide alternative options for families dealing with social concerns such as safety, bullying, and other types of peer pressures (Toppin & Toppin, 2016). Distance-learning platforms have been transforming education for decades, and though they are not considered the "norm" in K–12, these platforms can still be used to enhance the learning experience and engage students outside the classroom for a blended educational experience.

Distance learning allows students the opportunity to repeat instruction to gain understanding as often as needed. It allows students to work at their own pace and spend more time on topics that are difficult to understand. Studies have shown that distance learning leads to higher retention of material because of the consistency and accessibility of repeated material. Students, however, must have self-discipline to succeed in a virtual learning environment.

Learning management systems provide a method of delivering instruction through a virtual environment. As a college student, your campus may use or have used Blackboard, PowerSchool©, or Canvas. Many K–12 classrooms are also switching to similar platforms as an easy way to display grades for parents or distribute homework. These systems do not come without a price. But there are also free, or nearly free, LMS platforms available for teachers, such as Google Classroom, Moodle, or Schoology, and they have many of the same capabilities for providing a quality virtual learning experience.

Resources Wrap-Up

Consider using the previous resources as a way to layer technology in your classroom. This is not an exhaustive list but a list of resources with which many teachers have had great experiences. With technology changing at a rapid pace, more resources for student engagement are sure to come. If you do not know where to begin, ask your colleagues, your students, your mentors, or your school's technology coordinator for ideas. Refer to trusted organizations such as the International Society for Technology in Education (ISTE), an organization that promotes a global collaboration among educators who believe technology has the power to transform education. This organization provides professional learning, technology standards, and a sense of community for educators incorporating technology into their instruction. Whether joining an organization, asking colleagues, or scouring the internet yourself, making the decision to be more intentional with technology integration is the first step.

Pause and Discuss	In a small group, discuss your ideas on how you plan to use technology in your future classroom. Make a list of one idea per use (assessment, inquiry promotion, collaboration, classroom management, accommodation, and distance learning), and share your ideas with your group.

Creating a Technology-Integrated Environment

Now that you are aware of your own beliefs regarding technology or the barriers you may personally have to overcome in your school, let us think about how we can effectively begin engaging our students with technology. This section will discuss levels of technology integration and guidelines to create a technology-integrated environment.

SAMR

If you are considering beginning integration of technology into your lessons, you may lack confidence to jump in and fully integrate, or your students may not have developed the skills necessary to make them successful for a fully integrated lesson. A framework that can help aid and scaffold your lesson is the SAMR model. SAMR, an acronym for substitution, augmentation, modification, and redefinition, is a model for technology integration into teaching, developed by Dr. Ruben Puentedura (2010). SAMR provides a strategy for moving through levels of integration to find more meaningful uses of technology in teaching and move away from simply "using tech for tech's sake." This model also serves as a way to assess how you are currently implementing technology into your lessons.

Think of the model as a spectrum, beginning with *substitution* on one end and *redefinition* on the other. As you move from one level to the next, technology integration is strengthened, completely transforming the lesson and providing more meaningful experiences to enhance the content.

Consider Ms. Somsen's classroom from earlier in the chapter. In *substitution*, an assignment, such as students reading the hard copy of their science textbook to learn about mitosis, is simply substituted with an online version of the textbook. The technology in this case acts as a direct substitute for the traditional format, providing no meaningful enhancement of the original assignment. The students are using the technology in the same way as they would the textbook. No matter how small the scale, it is an opportunity for Ms. Somsen, and other teachers, to begin integrating technology and providing experiences for their students.

Next, in *augmentation*, there is slight enhancement of the original assignment, but the technology continues to serve as a direct substitute. For example, instead of Ms. Somsen's students only reading the online version of the textbook, now students use the highlight tool to highlight key terms or the digital textbook's glossary to study key terms being learned throughout the chapter. They also click on video links embedded throughout the digital textbook to watch videos of mitosis in action. In this stage, the digital version of the textbook is being used in the same way a traditional textbook would be used. The digital version, however, allows students to access tools and videos to enhance the experience.

As you move across the spectrum, you begin to truly transform your lesson with technology. In *modification*, the learning task is completely altered, or modified. To continue the previous example, instead of reading the digital textbook or highlighting key terms with tools, Ms. Somsen instructs students to create their own video using a multimedia tool that illustrates the process of mitosis. The task has been redesigned to be more than reading, and the technology is now modified to be utilized in such a way that students' learning experience is not only enhanced but transformed.

Finally, on the end of the spectrum, is *redefinition*. At this level, technology allows for the complete transformation of an assignment that would not have previously been possible. Referring to the previous scenarios, Ms. Somsen's students use 3-D sketch software to design a device that will prevent rapid mitosis (tumors/cancer). Their designs will then be printed using a 3-D printer. At this level, the task has been completely transformed so that students construct knowledge through the integration of technology. They now apply what they have previously learned about mitosis to solving a problem through the use of innovative technology.

Not every lesson calls for *redefinition*, and some lessons are best suited for paper and pencil. It is important to consider not only the needs of students and their grade level/abilities but also what makes sense for the current objective, topic, or activity.

Additionally, consider using this model as a way to differentiate the activity for students with different needs. Some students may need technology as a direct substitute for writing their notes, while other students may learn best with the traditional paper and pencil. Use Table 9.1 to evaluate your previous lessons and enhance your future plans to provide your students with opportunities to experience technology.

TABLE 9.1 Questions to Ask Yourself When Using SAMR

SAMR Level	Questions
Substitution	What will be gained by replacing the current task with the new technology?
Augmentation	Does the technology add new features that improve the original task?
Modification	Does the task significantly change with the use of the new technology?
Redefinition	Does the technology allow for creation of a new task that was previously unconceivable?

(Brown, 2015)

Consider a lesson you previously taught. How can you move through the
levels of the SAMR model to integrate technology? Take a moment to mod-
ify your original lesson and determine where technology integration could
be most beneficial.

Pause and
Reflect

Guidelines for Integration

Flick and Bell (2000) proposed a set of guidelines aimed at providing guidance for science teachers to design instruction supported by technology; however, these guidelines are relevant to all content areas and can be slightly modified for all educators. Consider the following proposed *modified* Flick and Bell guidelines for using technology:

- Technology should be introduced in the context of the content. Many teachers may find a great technology resource or application and try to fit it into their standards and objectives; however, this is inappropriate. It is important to begin first with your content. What objectives and standards must your students achieve? Then find technology to create opportunities for your students to achieve those standards and enhance learning, as opposed to the content being an afterthought (Flick & Bell, 2000).

- Technology should address worthwhile content with appropriate and effective pedagogy. If teachers do not effectively teach, then the technology accompanying the lesson will not be effective either. For example, teachers must learn what content is best suited with technology and what is not. Harder concepts that can be made clearer through technology can have an effect on student learning if incorporated appropriately. If the teacher does not choose wisely, students may think, "What was the point of that?" In this case, they may fail to make connections. Choose technology that not only helps students with foundational knowledge, such as the rote memorization of vocabulary, but also helps them engage in inquiry and critical thinking. It is also important to model how to utilize this technology for your students (Flick & Bell, 2000).

- Technology instruction should take advantage of the unique features of technology but not replace hands-on learning. Instead, use technology to help students explore content more interactively, when appropriate. It is important to remember that technology is not the only answer for learning. Where does it make sense to incorporate technology? Consider looking at the stars. There are interactive websites, such as Google Earth, that allow students to explore space. It is equally important, however, for students to physically go out and look at the night sky and orient themselves with different structures so that when they go outside again, they are able to find what they are looking for. Studying the stars by only looking at an interactive map may not be the most effective. Using technology to perform tasks that can be as easily accomplished without it may actually hinder student learning (Flick & Bell, 2000).

- Technology should make content more accessible. Flick and Bell (2000) state that "appropriate educational technologies have the potential to make scientific concepts more accessible through visualization, modeling, and multiple representations" (p. 45). This is true not just for science content but for any content area. Using simulations or virtual reality is a great example of using educational technology to model a phenomenon or bring the world into the classroom.

- Technology instruction should develop students' understanding of the relationship between the content and technology. For example, it is important for students to understand how history and new discovery influence the advancement of technologies. Also, as technology advances, it influences progress and leads to more discovery (Flick & Bell, 2000).

Flick and Bell's ideas provide guidance for educators in the traditional classroom setting. Additional guidelines must be considered when conducting distance learning or blended learning opportunities. The National Science Teaching Association (NSTA) provided a position statement on key elements of high-quality, effective e-learning experiences, many of which are applicable to any discipline area. The NSTA (2008) states that e-learning experiences should reflect current research on how people learn. Also, e-learning experiences should be designed to reflect what research says is most effective for the learning environment with the goals and outcomes clearly stated. The courses should also be accurate, interesting, engaging, relevant, and standards-based while being facilitated by instructors skilled in both content and pedagogy in an e-learning environment. E-learning should also incorporate instructional design practices that allow for individual decision making and to accommodate differences among learners and their contexts while conducting ongoing evaluation and assessment to guide continuous improvement of instruction. Additionally, it is important to promote frequent interaction between teacher and learner to allow continuous monitoring and adjustment of the dynamic learning environment.

Integration Wrap-Up

Use the SAMR framework or the modified guidelines, whether for traditional or distance-learning environments, as a way to begin assessing, planning, and integrating technology into your classroom. Consider your students' needs and abilities. Consider what makes sense for the desired outcome. Integration should be intentionally designed or structured for particular subject matter ideas in specific classroom contexts (Flick & Bell, 2000; Koehler & Mishra, 2009). Effective integration is achieved when students select tools to help them obtain information, analyze the information, and present it in a professional manner. Success is achieved when technology is utilized seamlessly in the everyday classroom (ISTE, 2000). When integrated successfully, technology enhances students' learning experiences in powerful ways.

Conclusion

According to the 2012 *NMC Horizon Report*, "digital media literacy continues its rise in importance as a key skill in every discipline and profession," and educators have started "to realize that that they are limiting their students by not helping them to develop and use digital media literacy skills across the curriculum" (Johnson, Adams, & Cummins, 2012, p. 3). Educators are beginning to understand how the influence of integrated technology encourages critical thinking and problem solving, collaboration and communication, and technological literacy to provide students with 21st-century skills that will be essential in current and future work environments (Buchem & Hamelmann, 2011; Rotherham & Willingham, 2010; Dohn, 2009; Dowling, 2011).

Many barriers must be overcome at the individual, district, and state levels to provide students with meaningful experiences in technology. Teachers are faced with lack of access to sufficient tools, time, and professional learning opportunities to develop their technology literacy and skills. Similarly, students from a variety of socioeconomic backgrounds lack access to devices and internet connection. Utilizing frameworks such as Puentedura's (2010) SAMR model or Flick and Bell's (2000) guidelines is a step closer in overcoming these challenges while simultaneously motivating teachers to create more integrated opportunities.

Although challenging, integrating technology in your classroom is critical to student outcomes. Students need experiences with technology to prepare for the future workforce. It is not only imperative for teachers to provide these opportunities, it is expected!

KEY CHAPTER TAKEAWAYS

Some important takeaways from this chapter include:

- Technology integration is more than using a tool as mere substitution. True integration is when technology enhances the content and provides students with quality learning experiences through the use of technology.

- Barriers (access, time, knowledge, skills, beliefs) prevent teachers from providing integrated experiences.

- Technology can be used for assessment, inquiry, classroom management, collaboration, accommodation, and distance learning.

- Use the SAMR (substitution, augmentation, modification, redefinition) framework to assess and plan for future technology integration.

- Consider the modified guidelines modeled from Flick and Bell's (2000) original technology guidelines.

- Not every learning experience requires technology. Consider learning outcomes and students' abilities when planning for technology.

- Technology integration has an effect on both students and teachers and is a great way to create quality learning experiences.

CASE SCENARIO: THE INTERVIEW CONTINUES

"I want to discuss technology," Mrs. Frayer stated. Kortney perked up. Finally, an area in which she felt confident. She had various experiences in both her personal and professional life with technology, but she wondered exactly where the principal was going with this topic.

Mrs. Frayer continued, "I'm an advocate for integrating technology for instruction in the classroom. I find that much of my staff struggles with implementing technology into their lessons, but one teacher here is very innovative! Let me tell you an example of what I mean."

Kortney was intrigued. She wondered whether other teachers loved using technology as much as she did. She listened for Mrs. Frayer to continue.

The educator began with a story about Mr. Andrews, a sixth-grade reading teacher. Mr. Andrews found that using iPads, for example, proved a great way to provide students with accessible experiences to learn fluency and comprehension. It has enabled him to engage students on a deeper level and develop skills that go beyond the classroom.

Mr. Andrews had a student who was considered a "struggling reader" and reading well below grade level. He found that sometimes he was unable to give this student the help he needed due to the pacing of the material. He had worked with him as much as class time allowed but wanted to provide more opportunities to assess and give feedback. He began to think creatively on how he could continue to help when the student wasn't always accessible during instruction.

Finally, he came up with an ingenious idea of using the class iPads to assess the student's reading, as opposed to using a paper copy of the book. He had the student record himself with a screen-casting application while reading a story. Afterward, Mr. Andrews was able to go back and watch the student's video to pinpoint specific areas of strengths and weaknesses. Having the student record himself allowed him to continue to work on his reading and also allowed Mr. Andrews more time to provide specific feedback. Additionally, it allowed the student to learn a new skill to assess his own reading while at home. Mr. Andrews was a believer in the power that technology can provide to students and their learning, and he continued to provide opportunities as much as possible.

WORKING WITH THE SCENARIO

"I want you to imagine Mr. Andrew's classroom and his beliefs regarding technology. What are your beliefs in regard to learning and technology integration? Furthermore, follow that up with an example of a time you implemented technology to improve student learning through assessment," Mrs. Frayer stated.

"My beliefs?" Kortney said, looking puzzled. She had never associated a belief system with using technology before. Technology was just something that was always around. A tool that she had always known and never really experienced a life without.

"I'd also like to hear an example of how you would use technology to help manage your classroom and how you plan to use technology to promote inquiry through collaboration."

Put yourself in Kortney's position. How would you answer Mrs. Frayer's question, and which example would you use?

REFERENCES

Anderson, M., & Perrin, A. (2018). *Nearly one-in-five teens can't always finish their homework because of the digital divide.* Pew Research Center. https://www.pewresearch.org/fact-tank/2018/10/26/nearly-one-in-five-teens-cant-always-finish-their-homework-because-of-the-digital-divide/

Bell, R. L., & Smetana, L. K. (2008). Using computer simulations to enhance science teaching and learning. *National Science Teachers Association, 3,* 23–32.

Bondur, H. O., Brinberg, D., & Coupey, E. (2000). Belief, affect, and attitude: Alternative models of the determinants of attitude. *Journal of Consumer Psychology, 9*(1), 17–28.

Brown, P. (2015, February 6). A guide for bringing the SAMR model to iPads. *Edsurge News.* https://www.edsurge.com/news/2015-02-06-a-guide-for-bringing-the-samr-model-to-ipads

Buchem, I., & Hamelmann, H. (2011). *Developing 21st century skills: Web 2.0 in higher education—A case study.* eLearning Papers 24 (April), 1–4. http://www.elearningeuropa.info/files/media/media25535.pdf

Cuban, L., Kirkpatrick, H., & Peck, C. (2001). High access and low use of technologies in high school classrooms: Explaining an apparent paradox. *American Educational Research Journal, 38,* 813–34.

Dexter, S. L., Anderson, R. E., & Ronnkvist, A. M. (2002). Quality technology support: What is it? Who has it? And what difference does it make? *Journal of Educational Computing Research, 26*(3), 265–285.

Dohn, N. B. (2009). Web 2.0—Mediated competence: Implicit educational demands on learners. *Electronic Journal of e-Learning, 7*(2), 111–18.

Dowling, S. (2011, September). Web-based learning—Moving from learning islands to learning environments. *Teaching English as a Second or Foreign Language—Electronic Journal, 15*(2). http://www.teslej.org/wordpress/issues/volume15/ej58/ej58int/

Education Superhighway. (2019). *State of the states: Education superhighway's fifth annual report on the state of broadband connectivity in America's public schools.* https://stateofthestates.educationsuperhighway.org/#national

Ertmer, P. A. (2005). Teacher pedagogical beliefs: The final frontier in our quest for technology integration? *Educational Technology Research and Development, 53*(4), 25–39.

Ertmer, P. A., Addison, P., Lane, M., Ross, E., & Woods, D. (1999). Examining teachers' beliefs about the role of technology in the elementary classroom. *Journal of Research on Computing in Education, 32*(1), 54–71.

Federal Communications Commission. (2019). *Inquiry concerning deployment of advanced telecommunications capability to all Americans in a reasonable and timely fashion.* https://www.fcc.gov/document/broadband-deployment-report-digital-divide-narrowing-substantially-0

Flick, L., & Bell, R. (2000). Preparing tomorrow's science teachers to use technology: Guidelines for science educators. *Contemporary Issues in Technology and Teacher Education, 1*(1), 39–60.

Gray, L., Thomas, N., & Lewis, L. (2010). *Educational technology in U.S. public schools: Fall 2008.* NCES 2010–034. National Center for Education Statistics. https://nces.ed.gov/pubs2010/2010034.pdf

Hermans, R., Tondeur, J., Valcke, M. M., & Van Braak, J. (2006). *Educational beliefs as predictors of ICT use in the classroom* (Paper presentation). Annual Meeting of the Association for Educational Communications and Technology, Chicago.

Hew, K. F., & Brush, T. (2007). Integrating technology into K–12 teaching and learning: Current knowledge gaps and recommendations for future research. *Educational Technology Research and Development, 55,* 223–52.

Hughes, J. (2005). The role of teacher knowledge and learning experiences in forming technology-integrated pedagogy. *Journal of Technology and Teacher Education, 13*(2), 277–302.

ISTE (International Society for Technology in Education). (2000). ISTE national educational technology standards (NETS).

Johnson, L., Adams, S., & Cummins, M. (2012). *Technology outlook for Australian tertiary education 2012–2017: An NMC Horizon report regional analysis* (pp. 1–23). The New Media Consortium.

Karagiorgi, Y. (2005). Throwing light into the black box of implementation: ICT in Cyprus elementary schools. *Educational Media International, 41*(1), 19–32.

Koehler, M., & Mishra, P. (2009). What is technological pedagogical content knowledge (TPACK)? *Contemporary Issues in Technology and Teacher Education, 9*(1), 60–70.

Lai, K. W., Pratt, K., & Trewern, A. (2001). *Learning with technology: Evaluation of the Otago secondary schools technology project.* Community Trust of Otago, Dunedin, FL.

Lawson, T., & Comber, C. (2000). Censorship, the internet and schools: A new moral panic? *The Curriculum Journal, 11*(2), 273–285.

Lim, C. P., & Khine, M. (2006). Managing teachers' barriers to ICT integration in Singapore schools. *Journal of Technology and Teacher Education, 14*(1), 97–125.

Lowther, D. L., Ross, S. M., & Morrison, G. M. (2003). When each one has one: The influences on teaching strategies and student achievement of using laptops in the classroom. *Educational Technology Research and Development, 51*(3), 23–44.

Newhouse, C. P. (2001). A follow-up study of students using portable computers at a secondary school. *British Journal of Educational Technology, 32*(2), 209–19.

NTSA (National Science Teachers Association). (2008). *NSTA position statement: The role of e-learning in science education.* https://www.nsta.org/nstas-official-positions/role-e-learning-science-education

Patterson, T. C. (2007). Google Earth as a (not just) geography education tool. *Journal of Geography, 106*(4), 145–52.

Puentedura, R. (2010). *SAMR and TPCK: Intro to advanced practice.* http://hippasus.com/resources/sweden2010/SAMR_TPCK_IntroToAdvancedPractice.pdf

Richey, R. C., Silber, K. H., & Ely, D. P. (2008). Reflections on the 2008 AECT definitions of the field. *TechTrends, 52*(1), 24–25.

Rotherham, A., & Willingham, D. (2010, spring). 21st-Century Skills—Not new but a worthy challenge. *American Educator.* http://www.aft.org/pdfs/americaneducator/spring2010/RotherhamWillingham.pdf

Sandholtz, J. H., & Reilly, B. (2004). Teachers, not technicians: Rethinking technical expectations for teachers. *Teachers College Record, 106*(3), 487–512.

Snoeyink, R., & Ertmer, P. A. (2001–2002). Thrust into technology: How veteran teachers respond. *Journal of Educational Technology Systems, 30*(1), 85–111.

Tearle, P. (2004). A theoretical and instrumental framework for implementing change in ICT in education. *Cambridge Journal of Education, 34*(3), 331–51.

Toppin, I. N., & Toppin, S. M. (2016). Virtual schools: The changing landscape of K–12 education in the US. *Education and Information Technologies, 21*(6), 1571–81.

Williams, D., Coles, L., Wilson, K., Richardson, A., & Tuson, J. (2000). Teachers and ICT: Current use and future needs. *British Journal of Educational Technology, 31*(4), 307–20.

Windschitl, M., & Sahl, K. (2002). Tracing teachers' use of technology in a laptop computer school: The interplay of teacher beliefs, social dynamics, and institutional culture. *American Educational Research Journal, 39*(1), 165–205.

Students' Mental Health

Setting the Classroom Scene

"I'm worried about him," said Carlos Ramirez, an algebra teacher at Iron Bridge High School, a medium-sized suburban school with approximately 800 students in grades nine to 12.

"Who, Dylan?" responded Cheryl McTiernan, a freshman English teacher who shared planning time with Carlos and worked with him on the grade-level planning team focused on interdisciplinary planning and student support.

"Yes, he just seems off lately. I mean, he's always been on the shy side, pretty quiet in general, but here lately he seems to be very withdrawn," Carlos said.

Cheryl nodded. "That happens frequently with teenagers," she said. "They are moody. And I mean that with a capital M."

Carlos nodded before continuing. "I know. I've been at this long enough to see the highs and lows and everything in between, but with Dylan, this time, it's been going on for a few weeks. Maybe even a month. It's enough that I notice, and based on what we've been taught about watching out for warning signs, well, like I said, I'm worried about him."

The two teachers had been at the school when, two years ago, a student had attempted suicide. Aftershocks of that horrific event were still reverberating throughout the school. The entire faculty had been provided ongoing professional development focused on supporting students holistically, meaning the teachers were to be mindful of the students' lives in a scope larger than the teacher's specific classroom. As much as possible, anyway. Both Carlos and Cheryl believed in the value of the training they had received; they both also held some doubts whether teachers could realistically be expected to know each and every student quite as well as the training suggested.

"How many students do you have this semester, 70? 80?" Cheryl asked. "I've got 67 total across my three classes, and the number is only that low because I've got a section of Honors English with only 16. I try to get to know them all a little beyond the classroom, but it's tough. And it's even tougher since we're on the block schedule and only have these students for 18 weeks before they rotate out."

"Yeah, I agree," Carlos said. "It's hard to discuss much beyond equations and all that, given the curriculum and amount of time, and thinking we can know enough about these students to recognize when one of them is having an emotional problem is a pretty tall order. Still, Dylan stands out to me. The more I think about it, the more drastic the change seems to be. What about in your class?"

"I guess now that we're talking it about it, I can see he has been extra quiet lately," Cheryl answered. "But I've honestly been busy trying to get those two new ELL students settled in. Don't even get me started on what a challenge that has been. Anyway, maybe we just need to pay a little more attention to Dylan, talk to him more and see what we can discern."

Carlos smiled. "Discern?" he asked. "Are you getting your students prepped for the vocabulary on the next test or what?"

Cheryl gave him a playful punch on the arm before going back to her class, and over the next week both teachers did pay closer attention to Dylan. Despite their efforts to get him engaged and talkative, Dylan remained quiet and even put his head down several times. Carlos and Cheryl talked to his other teachers and found the behaviors were occurring across all classes. And then not even two weeks after that initial conversation, Dylan missed school. That by itself was not a huge issue; when he missed 3 consecutive days with no contact from home, both Carlos and Cheryl agreed it was indeed a significant issue.

Before school started on what would be Dylan's fourth consecutive absence, Carlos and Cheryl went to the school's guidance counselor to see if he knew anything about Dylan's situation. Both had meant to ask after Dylan's second absence but the counselor, Mr. Atherton, had been at the district office. He was sitting in his office when the two teachers walked in.

"I've got a feeling I know why you're both here," he said as a greeting. "I'm getting an email together now to let Dylan's teachers have some idea what's up with him."

"Can we get a short version now?" Carlos asked.

"Hard to put all of this in a short version," Mr. Atherton answered. "But here's a quick rundown. Dylan's dad lost his job a month ago, and hasn't been able to find work. Add to that Dylan's mom left the family two months ago, and that Dylan's grandmother has been going downhill fast with pancreatic cancer, and, well, she passed away a few days ago."

"We honestly had no idea," Cheryl said.

Mr. Atherton sat further back in his chair and folded his hands together in front of his chest, a habit he had when he was about to make a significant point. "And that's the rub right there," he said. "Too many times in situations like this we have no idea."

Prereading Questions

1. In regard to knowing students outside the classroom, how much do you think it is reasonable to expect teachers to know about their students' lives?

2. If a student has a dramatic change in behavior, what do you believe is an appropriate response from that student's teachers? What kinds of questions should teachers ask when they have concerns about a student's behavior or mood?

3. If Dylan was in your class, how long would you have waited before trying to contact his parents or guardians when you noticed his behavior had changed? Who would you have spoken to first, and why?

Introduction

> *A child's mental health is just as important as their physical health and deserves the same quality of support. No one would feel embarrassed about seeking help for a child if they broke their arm—and we really should be equally ready to support a child coping with emotional difficulties.*
> **—Kate Middleton, from a public service announcement**
> **for the United Kingdom's first Children's Mental Health Week (2015)**

An interesting phenomenon occurred in the southeastern United States in the latter months of 2005. Researchers noted a significant increase in the number of adolescents being diagnosed with post-traumatic stress disorder (PTSD), and research conducted in the years after 2005 noted that the PTSD symptoms in many of those diagnosed were not decreasing at an expected rate given the passage of time (e.g., Osofsky et al., 2009; Weems et al., 2010). What makes this an interesting trend is that the spike in PTSD diagnoses could predominantly be traced to children from one state, and more specifically to one city. That city was New Orleans, and the event that precipitated the rise in PTSD cases among children (and many adults, for that matter) was Hurricane Katrina.

While admittedly a dramatic example, the traumatic effects Katrina had on many children in and around New Orleans does offer lessons on how children can be negatively affected by life's events. And the children of New Orleans, in some cases, took that emotional damage far and wide in the United States as many were displaced and homeless after the hurricane and sent hundreds of miles away to stay with family or friends. Students coping with PTSD from Katrina ended up attending schools in Omaha, Nebraska, as one example, meaning the educational effects of the catastrophic hurricane were felt far and wide indeed.

Estimates of the number of children with a treatable mental disorder are shocking, as some research suggests approximately 16% of children between the ages of 6 and 17 meet the diagnostic criteria for a mental disorder (Whitney & Peterson, 2019). Researchers analyzing the data citing that percentage also noted that approximately half of the children with a treatable mental health disorder do not receive treatment from a qualified mental health professional (Whitney & Peterson, 2019). These numbers may be particularly troubling to teachers, who are already tasked with working with students representing a wide range of cultures, abilities, and socioeconomic situations. Adding students with mental health concerns into the mix gives teachers one more thing to consider when pondering how best to instruct all of their students.

But even if it is daunting for educators to consider teaching children with mental disorders, the fact is that nearly every teacher will eventually experience having such a student in their classroom. A teacher's ability to connect with and support these students will be of great importance when considering the student's emotional health, which can play a part in the student's academic success. All of this means a teacher needs more than just a passing knowledge of children's mental health, as the teacher may one day be in a position first to recognize the presence of a possible mental disorder in a student and then to do what is possible to help that student in school.

Specific Issues

> *A recent analysis (jamanetwork.com) of 2016 National Survey of Children's Health data published online in JAMA Pediatrics indicated that as many as one in six U.S. children between the ages of 6 and 17 has a treatable mental health disorder such as depression, anxiety problems or attention deficit/hyperactivity disorder (ADHD).*
>
> **—Devitt (2019)**

One in six. That is a staggering percentage of school-age children to consider having a treatable mental health disorder. While daunting, it is important to remember there is a wide range of effects associated with various mental disorders, some of which are more harmful than others. Not every child who meets the diagnostic criteria for a mental disorder will have the same level of impairment. Regardless of the level of severity, teachers will be well served to have some basic idea of what behaviors and symptoms may be associated with particular disorders.

The exact number of students who may be experiencing a specific disorder is hard to pin down, though research can provide some good, if variable, estimates. For example, the number of students diagnosed with ADHD is believed to be approximately 5% (APA, 2017), though the Centers for Disease Control and Prevention (2019) has reported estimates that 11% of children between the ages of 3 and 17 have been diagnosed with ADHD at least once. ADHD is a particularly interesting mental disorder, as research further suggests nearly 60% of children with ADHD meet the diagnostic criteria for at least one other disorder (Danielson et al., 2018).

When considering the number of students with a mood disorder, which includes anxiety and depression, Twenge and colleagues (2019) found that from 2005 to 2017 the percentage of 12- to 17-year-old students who reported a major depressive episode rose from 8.7% to 13.2%. While an episode does not automatically indicate a diagnosis, that upward trend in depressive episodes among adolescents should be cause for concern. Research is ongoing regarding anxiety, an often "hidden" disorder that can manifest in children as young as 4 years, and which appears to be negatively affecting a growing number of school-age children (Ghandour et al., 2019).

Other examples of common mental disorders children experience include obsessive-compulsive disorder, oppositional defiant disorder, and as referenced at the beginning of this section, PTSD. Mental disorders can be characterized by either internal or external behaviors, or a combination of both (Smith, Tyler, & Skow, 2017). External behaviors are much easier to recognize as symptoms of a disorder and include aggression, belligerence, impulsivity, and noncompliance. Internal behaviors are much harder to discern, as they are distinguished by withdrawn actions (Smith, Tyler, & Skow, 2017). Anxiety and depression are referred to at times as hidden disorders because it is very difficult to "see" internal worry or sadness. Table 10.1 lists some of the most common childhood mental disorders and includes a brief overview of their key characteristics.

TABLE 10.1 Common Childhood Mental Disorders and Key Characteristics

Disorder	Key characteristics (Paraphrased from the DSM-V)
Attention deficit/hyperactivity disorder (ADHD)	–ADHD is characterized by symptoms involving attention or impulsivity, or a combination of the two. • Inattention symptoms include frequent careless mistakes, being disorganized, and failure to stay focused while completing tasks. • Impulsivity symptoms include excessive fidgeting or talking, interrupting others, and leaving one's seat frequently.
Depression (major depressive disorder)	–Depression is characterized by: • A constant feeling of sadness • Frequently feeling worthless • Feelings of guilt • Lack of interest in most daily activities • A reduced ability to concentrate or focus • Indecisiveness • Feeling tired or lacking appropriate energy • Frequent thoughts of death, including the consideration of suicide

Adapted from: American Psychiatric Association, "Common Childhood Mental Disorders and Key Characteristics," *Diagnostic and Statistical Manual of Mental Disorders (DSM–5)*. Copyright © 2017 by American Psychiatric Association Publishing.

Anxiety (generalized anxiety disorder)	–Anxiety is characterized by: • A significant degree of worry or concern over a variety of daily events • An inability to control worry –Anxiety may be evidenced by: • Irritability • Inability to sleep • Difficulty concentrating on tasks • Feeling restless • Soreness related to muscle tension • Rapidly leasing energy and becoming tired
Obsessive-compulsive disorder (OCD)	–OCD includes feelings of emotional distress based on persistent obsessions or compulsions. –Obsessive behaviors include: • Repeated thoughts/impulses that infringe on clear thinking and cause obvious anxiety. These thoughts are not reasonable concerns with real-life issues and occur despite attempts to suppress them. • A person suffering these obsessive thoughts is aware of them, rather than the thoughts being the result of delusions. –Compulsive behaviors include: • Repetitive, often stereotypical, behaviors that a person feels driven to perform, such as excessive washing of hands, putting objects in order, or following one exact route to a location. • The repeated behaviors are performed to ward off or diminish stressful thoughts or impede the occurrence of a stressful situation.
PTSD	–PTSD may begin after an individual experiences, witnesses, or learns about a traumatic event that included or threatened harm or death. –Symptoms of PTSD include: • Repeated distressing memories of the event. • Troubling dreams about the event. • Avoiding anything associated with the event. • Obvious emotional reactions to anything pertaining to the event. • Flashbacks in which a person feels as if they are going through the event again. • Impaired thinking when anything pertaining to the event is present.

(APA, 2017)

The symptoms of the mental disorders listed in Table 10.1 are indeed troubling, and it is interesting to note that the clinical guidelines from the APA for a diagnosis commonly require the presence of these symptoms for 6 months or longer. That seems a long time to wait for a teacher to express concern. If a student suddenly began to display signs of excessive and uncontrollable worry, the appropriate response would not be, "Well, I see Ivy is having some serious worries. Let me note this observation in my calendar and check back in 6 months to see if she's still anxious to a serious degree." A better response would be to follow the vigilance advice that law enforcement agencies often suggest: "If you see something, say something." In the next section some specific warning signs related to mental disorders will be addressed.

What are your experiences with individuals with a mental disorder? Did that person display any of the symptoms listed in Table 10.1, or was the disorder not listed in the table? If so, what was the disorder, and what do you remember about its effects on the individual? Now put yourself in the position of a teacher. How worried would you be if a student began to display any of the behaviors from the table? Why? What are some ways you believe those behaviors could affect a child in your classroom?

Pause and Reflect

Warning Signs

Although teachers are not diagnosticians in matters of their students' mental health, they can still be on the lookout for patterns of behaviors that may suggest a child is dealing with a mental or emotional problem. MentalHealth.gov (n.d.) provides the following list of student behaviors that should spark concern in teachers:

- Feeling very sad or withdrawn for more than 2 weeks
- Seriously trying to harm oneself or making plans to do so
- Sudden overwhelming fear for no reason, sometimes with a racing heart or fast breathing
- Involvement in many fights or desire to badly hurt others
- Severe out-of-control behavior that can hurt oneself or others
- Not eating, throwing up, or using laxatives to make oneself lose weight
- Intense worries or fears that get in the way of daily activities
- Extreme difficulty concentrating or staying still that puts the student in physical danger or causes problems in the classroom
- Repeated use of drugs or alcohol
- Severe mood swings that cause problems in relationships
- Drastic changes in the student's behavior or personality

A quick comparison of the contents from Table 10.1 and the preceding list reveals these warning signs have much in common with the symptom profiles associated with mental disorders. Something that must be stated is that any of these warning signs should be viewed, as much as possible, through a clinical lens. This means that everyone displays some warning sign behaviors from time to time. We are all going to feel anxious, depressed, impulsive, or find it difficult to concentrate at some point. What matters is the degree to which these behaviors affect our functionality. When the behaviors in the listed warning signs begin to inhibit or impede a student from successfully engaging in the learning process, proper attention must be paid.

If any of the behaviors cited here begin to be displayed suddenly or are extremely out of character for a student and occur at a level that causes obvious impairment, teachers should consult with the appropriate personnel at their school to determine next steps. In reviewing the list of warning signs, it should be obvious that these would be extreme changes from normative behavior, and it does not require much in the way of imagination to consider how these behaviors could have a drastic effect on a student's academic performance. In fact, research consistently points to negative educational outcomes for students dealing with emotional or behavioral disorders.

For example, Nelson and colleagues (2004) conducted research on K–12 students with a diagnosed emotional-behavioral disorder (EBD) and found significant academic achievement deficits across content areas, particularly in mathematics. These results mirrored those found by Reid and colleagues (2004) that same year. These academic deficits have been found in more recent research (e.g., Ysseldyke et al., 2017), suggesting that students with EBD are not making significant gains in catching up with their nondisabled peers. Additionally, and sadly, the academic deficits these students demonstrate appear to continue to have negative personal, professional, and social consequences following graduation (e.g., Davis & Cumming, 2019). The reason mental disorders may negatively affect a student's class performance is often tied to the student's inability to maintain focus on the classwork or to demonstrate the impulse and emotional control to properly engage in the classroom (e.g., Vaughn & Bos, 2020). Fortunately, as the next section will cover, there are evidence-based methods with which teachers can support students experiencing a mental disorder.

External events can obviously have an effect on students' mental health. In 2020, when COVID-19 led to the closure of schools and a dramatic and sudden shift to online learning, there was suddenly a new sort of stress for students. The quote that follows from Richards (2020) is a summation of the trials experienced by many students.

> With the sudden halt to in-person learning, many students missed their friends, yearned to be out of the house, developed erratic sleep habits and drove their (often working) parents crazy. On top of that, many were dealing with the trauma of sick or dying family members, economic hardship and disruption to the life they once had.

Based on the preceding sentiments, it is no surprise that in a survey administered in May 2020, 29% of parents responded that their children were experiencing some degree of harm to emotional or mental health based on social distancing measures and school closures (Calderon, 2020).

| Pause and Discuss | How much responsibility do you believe teachers have in regard to monitoring students for signs of a mental disorder? If you believe there is a degree of responsibility for teachers, why do you think that? Briefly review the warning signs shared in the preceding section. Do you believe these are appropriate, or should there be more? If you think there should be more, what might you add to the list? If you were a teacher, would you feel comfortable sharing concerns if you noticed a child displaying troubling behaviors to a very significant degree? Why or why not? |

Ways to Help

A child whose behavior pushes you away is a child who needs connection before anything else.
>   —**Kelly Bartlett,** *Encouraging Words for Kids (2012)*

Teachers wear many professional hats. They are educators, guides, advisors, disciplinarians, cheer-leaders, counselors, data analysts, and more. One thing they are not is a licensed mental health practitioner, meaning that if they suspect a child is dealing with a mental or emotional disorder, or demonstrating the symptoms of such a disorder, they should seek guidance and support via their school's established protocols. But just because a teacher is not allowed to provide formal mental health support services does not mean he or she cannot utilize strategies in the classroom to accommodate students dealing with such issues. What follows is a list of ideas that teachers can use to help improve the classroom experience and performance of students dealing with mental health issues.

Strategies to Support Students Experiencing a Mental Health Issue

- Promote self-regulation strategies.

  - Self-regulation involves the concept of being mindful of one's actions and behaviors, especially in service to accomplishing a goal. Duckworth and Carlson (2013) defined self-regulation as "the voluntary control of attentional, emotional, and behavioral impulses in the service of personally valued goals and standards" (p. 209). Teachers can help students improve self-regulation by incorporating self-monitoring, self-evaluation, and self-management techniques by which students directly focus on their efforts, actions, and behaviors in regard to accomplishing classroom or homework activities (e.g., Popham et al., 2018).

- Utilize positive reinforcement and motivational practices.

  - Many students coping with mental health issues need some extra support in terms of motivation and praise. Research has indicated these students may require as much as a 9:1 ratio of positive to reprimand comments (Caldarella et al., 2019). This means that for each reprimand or negative comment, nine positive comments are needed to fully encourage students dealing with mental health issues. Teachers need to be deliberate and strategic, putting these students in positions in which positive reinforcement and praise are more likely, or simply be almost hyperaware of when to use praise with these students.

- Incorporate peer-mediated interventions.

  - Peer-mediated intervention approaches are centered on cooperative learning. They include class-wide peer tutoring, peer-assisted learning strategies, peer assessment, peer modeling, and peer reinforcement. Research has indicated positive outcomes on the academic and social performance of students with mental health issues when peer-based methods are incorporated into instruction (e.g., Dunn et al., 2017).

- Focus on antecedent manipulation.

  - When focusing on antecedents, teachers are assuming responsibility for manipulating the actions that precede a student's behavior. In this case, interventions are teacher-mediated and involve direct actions by the teacher to better influence a student's behaviors toward an academic or behavioral goal. Teachers can manipulate antecedents by having students verbalize math problems, having students complete work in a cubicle or at their desk, using structured planning that requires students to complete a sequence of tasks for an assignment, using modeling and rehearsal strategies, using previewing, teaching test-taking strategies, and teaching mnemonic strategies for remembering strategies (see Ryan, Pierce, & Mooney [2008] for a review of these strategies). There are other ways for teachers to manipulate antecedents, but all of them involve the teachers using instructional methods meant to specifically direct behaviors and thus possibly eliminate negative behaviors before they occur.

- Be clear and specific with directions.

  - While on the surface this may seem a blatantly obvious teaching practice, appropriate for all students, students with mental health concerns need abundant clarity with routines and expectations. Research has consistently noted that when teachers are clear with rules, expectations, and procedures, and extend that clarity to directions and expectations for classroom activities, students with mental health issues respond positively (Niesyn, 2009). Being clear and specific with routines and expectations can help students feel more confident, a natural extension of them being familiar with how a classroom is organized and managed.

All of the strategies just cited may produce positive results for students dealing with mental health issues, but none of them will really be effective if a teacher does not lead with empathy and understanding. Students believe caring relationships with teachers are important (Cothran, Kulinna, & Garragy, 2003), and teachers are in unique positions where they are well suited to be relationship builders (Walker, Shea, & Bauer, 2007). If a student trusts that a teacher has their best interests at heart, then the student is much more likely to engage and be receptive to the strategies reviewed above. For students with mental health concerns, teachers often have to make establishing that level of trust a first priority. Once it is established the benefits can be immense, especially for the students.

Do you believe any of the strategies presented in this section have particular value or would be more effective? Why or why not? Do you have any experience implementing any of the preceding strategies? If so, what was that experience like? Look back at the strategies. Why do you believe there is a focus on promoting self-regulation and using positive reinforcement for students experiencing mental health issues? Do you agree that these should be part of the methods for working with these students?

Pause and Reflect

Conclusion

"They don't care what you know until they know that you care" is a phrase commonly heard in the teaching profession. It is especially true for teachers working with students dealing with emotional or behavioral issues that are significant enough to indicate the presence of a mental disorder. Teachers can be great sources of support for these students but first must be on alert for the signs of a mental disorder. If they suspect one is present, they should follow the protocols established by their schools and then begin to provide accommodations and use teaching strategies that are effective for these students. While never expected to treat a mental illness, teachers will nevertheless be called upon to educate these students to the best of their ability.

KEY CHAPTER TAKEAWAYS

Some important takeaways from this chapter include:

- The number of students who experience a treatable mental illness may be nearly 17% of the student population, and research suggests approximately half of those students do not receive treatment from a licensed mental health professional.

- Some of the most common mental health impairments affecting students include ADHD, depression, and anxiety. Other disorders may be less frequent but still have significant negative effects on a student.

- Mental health issues often negatively influence a student's academic achievement, and personal, social, and professional aspects of postsecondary life may also be affected negatively.

- Symptoms of mental health issues affecting students are often present for longer than 6 months, though teachers should not wait that long to seek guidance once troubling behaviors are observed.

- Teachers should be mindful of both externalizing behavior symptoms, which are much more obvious, and internalizing behavior symptoms, such as a student becoming suddenly withdrawn, to be mindful of the presence of a possible mental health issue.

- There are warning signs that, when displayed prominently, may indicate the presence of a mental health issue.

- Strategies to support students experiencing emotional or behavioral disorders include a focus on promoting self-regulation, practicing strategic positive reinforcement, and providing clear directions and a structured environment in which a student feels confident and secure.

CASE SCENARIO: THE INTERVIEW CONTINUES

Kortney felt herself tensing up. The interview with Mrs. Frayer had already run much, much longer than she had anticipated. *Doesn't she ever run out of stories,* she thought, as Mrs. Frayer glanced at some papers on her desk. *I don't know if I sold her on being good with technology or not, and I wonder what she's going to talk about next,* she thought.

Mrs. Frayer turned her attention back to Kortney. "My apologies if I got a little distracted there," she said. "It's just that we're coming to the end of this interview and this last topic is one I find particularly challenging to discuss during interviews."

Kortney's tension ratcheted up a notch. *THIS last topic,* she thought, *like all the rest haven't been challenging enough?* Not wanting to give away her stress level, she asked, "And what topic is that, Mrs. Frayer?"

Mrs. Frayer picked up the papers she had been glancing toward. "This is our school improvement plan, or SIP," she said. "You may be familiar with how teachers have to have professional development plans, or PDPs, every year. We do love our acronyms in education. And the SIP is like the PDP for the entire school. We have to set goals and establish procedures for how to implement and monitor them. I'm curious if you have any guesses as to what our plan might include?"

Kortney remembered how in her student teaching seminar she had been required to complete a professional development plan, and she felt her tension lessen noticeably. Her cooperating teacher had worked on the SIP committee at Kortney's student teaching placement, so she felt pretty confident she could handle this line of questioning. "I would have to guess attendance is a part of it, and most likely test scores, particularly in reading," she said.

"Very good and accurate guesses," Mrs. Frayer said. "It seems we address student attendance nearly every year, and we can't escape state testing, so those are logical things to include in an SIP. But the part of this that concerns me more than anything," she paused to hold up the papers for emphasis, "is how we want to start being more mindful of our students' mental health."

Kortney had not expected that to be part of the school's SIP, so she said, "That seems like a pretty tough thing to measure, given how children can be up and down emotionally. Why is that going to be part of your plan?"

"Because it's a topic that every school in this country should be considering," the principal answered. "We want our kids to be physically and emotionally healthy, because we know that's when they learn the best. When there is any kind of mental issue at play it can be harmful to a student's progress. Let me give you a specific example of what I mean."

And with that she told this story:

Jasmine Amos was by all accounts a very normal and average fourth-grade student. Her attendance was solid and consistent, and her grades were all As and Bs. She socialized appropriately with her classmates and played with them at recess. She had demonstrated a few struggles in reading earlier in school but had made good progress in that area, though she was continuing to show some deficits in terms of math skills. In math class her grade had fallen to a C, and her teacher was getting very close to calling in the parents to discuss Jasmine's issues in math.

And then one Wednesday everything seemed to change. Jasmine became suddenly argumentative. She fussed at her classmates during lunch and on the playground, and during class she seemed resentful when given work to complete. During lunch she would refuse to clear away her dining ware, a routine practice for the entire class, and she would sulk when pressed to follow the rules. Her behavior change came to a head one day 2 weeks later when she got into an argument with another student and pushed the girl to the floor in the hallway.

In the office after the pushing incident, Jasmine sobbed uncontrollably but would not admit that she had done anything wrong. When her teacher asked her repeatedly why she was acting so differently, Jasmine folded her arms across her chest and put her head down, refusing to answer. Exasperated by it all, the teacher and assistant principal called Jasmine's mother and asked her to come to the school for a conference. Ms. Amos was at first reluctant but decided to come to the school when the assistant principal mentioned the chance for a suspension if Jasmine's behavior did not improve.

When Jasmine's mother arrived at the school for the meeting, Jasmine did not get up to meet her. Instead, she continued to sit with her head down as her mother walked through the reception area and into the assistant principal's office. Over the course of the next 30 minutes, Ms. Amos outlined many new circumstances in Jasmine's life. These included Ms. Amos's ending a long-term relationship that also ended Jasmine's time with her ex-boyfriend's children, how the family had recently moved into a new rental property on the other side of town away from most of Jasmine's friends, and how Jasmine's father had become even more insistent on sharing custody of Jasmine and her younger sister despite the fact that he lived 3 hours away.

The last thing Jasmine's mother shared was that the Department of Health and Human Services had just paid her a visit the previous day.

WORKING WITH THE SCENARIO

"This may be one of the toughest sets of questions I've given you," Mrs. Frayer said. "I mentioned this was a delicate example."

"I think I understand why you feel that way," Kortney said. "But I am interested to see what kind of follow-up questions you have."

"All right then, here they are," Mrs. Frayer said. "Should Jasmine's teacher have taken action earlier in regard to contacting Jasmine's mother? Why or why not? In your opinion, were the struggles in math enough of an indication that a larger problem might have been looming? Do you think the teacher should have contacted Jasmine's mother sooner about the math concern? And lastly, based on the brief description of Jasmine's changed behaviors, what are some strategies you might suggest that the teacher could start using to help her? Why do you think those would be practical?"

If you were Kortney, how would you answer the questions posed by Mrs. Frayer?

REFERENCES

APA (American Psychiatric Association). (2017). *Diagnostic and statistical manual of mental disorders* (5th ed.). American Psychiatric Association.

Bartlett, K. (2012). *Encouraging words for kids: What to say to bring out a child's confidence.* Bartlett.

Caldarella, P., Larsen, R. A., Williams, L., Wills, H. P., & Wehby, J. H. (2019). Teacher praise-to-reprimand ratios: Behavioral response of students at risk for EBD compared with typically developing peers. *Education and Treatment of Children, 42*(4), 447–68.

Calderon, V. J. (2020, August 19). *U.S. parents say COVID-19 harming child's mental health.* Gallup. com. news.gallup.com/poll/312605/parents-say-covid-harming-child-mental-health. aspx?_ga=2.260213325.1307683930.1597937491-678598535.1597937491

Centers for Disease Control and Prevention. (2019). *Data and statistics about ADHD.* https://www.cdc.gov/ncbddd/adhd/data.html

Cothran, D. J., Kulinna, P. H., & Garragy, D. A. (2003). "This is kind of giving a secret away …": Students' perspectives on effective class management. *Teaching and Teacher Education, 19*, 435–44.

Danielson, M. L., Bitsko, R. H., Ghandour, R. M., Holbrook, J. R., Kogan, M. D., & Blumberg, S. J. (2018). Prevalence of parent-reported ADHD diagnosis and associated treatment among US children and adolescents, 2016. *Journal of Clinical Child & Adolescent Psychology, 4*(2), 199–212.

Davis, M. T., & Cumming, I. K. (2019). Practical strategies for improving postsecondary outcomes for students with EBD. *Preventing School Failure, 63*(4), 325–33. https://doi-org.libproxy.troy.edu/10.1080/1045988X.2019.1608898

Devitt, M. (2019). *Study: One in six U.S. children has a mental illness.* https://www.aafp.org/news/health-of-the-public/20190318childmentalillness.html

Duckworth, A. L., & Carlson, S. M. (2013). Self-regulation and school success. *In Self-regulation and autonomy: Social and developmental dimensions of human conduct, 40,* 208–9.

Dunn, M. E., Shelnut, J., Ryan, J. B., & Katsiyannis, A. (2017). A systematic review of peer-mediated interventions on the academic achievement of students with emotional/behavioral disorders. *Education & Treatment of Children, 40*(4), 497–524. https://doi org.libproxy.troy.edu/10.1353/etc.2017.0022

Ghandour, R. M., Sherman, L. J., Vladutiu, C. J., Ali, M. M., Lynch, S. E., Bitsko, R. H., & Blumberg, S. J. (2019). Prevalence and treatment of depression, anxiety, and conduct problems in US children. *Journal of Pediatrics, 206,* 256–257. doi: 10.1016/j.jpeds.2018.09.021

MentalHealth.gov. (n.d.) *For educators.* Accessed May 5, 2020. https://www.mentalhealth.gov/talk/educators

Nelson, J. R., Benner, G. J., Lane, K., & Smith, B. W. (2004). Academic achievement of K–12 students with emotional and behavioral disorders. *Exceptional Children, 71*(1), 59–73.

Niesyn, M. E. (2009). Strategies for success: Evidence-based instructional practices for students with emotional and behavioral disorders. In *Preventing school failure: Alternative education for children and youth, 53*(4), 227–34.

Osofsky, H. J., Osofsky, J. D., Kronenberg, M., Brennan, A., & Hansel, T. C. (2009). Posttraumatic stress symptoms in children after Hurricane Katrina: Predicting the need for mental health services. *American Journal of Orthopsychiatry, 79*(2), 212–20.

Popham, M., Counts, J., Ryan, J. B., & Katsiyannis, A. (2018). A systematic review of self-regulation strategies to improve academic outcomes of students with EBD. *Journal of Research in Special Educational Needs, 18*(4), 239–53.

Reid, R., Gonzalez, J. E., Nordness, P. D., Trout, A., & Epstein, M. H. (2004). A meta-analysis of the academic status of students with emotional/behavioral disturbance. *Journal of Special Education, 38*(3), 130–43.

Richards, E. (2020, August 2). Kids' mental health can struggle during online school. Here's how teachers are planning ahead. *USA Today*. Gannett Satellite Information Network. www.usatoday.com/story/news/education/2020/07/31/covid-online-school-kids-mental-health-teachers/5529846002/

Ryan, J. B., Pierce, C. D., & Mooney, P. (2008). Evidence-based teaching strategies for students with EBD. *Beyond Behavior, 17*(3), 22–29.

Smith, D. D., Tyler, N. C., & Skow, K. (2017). *Introduction to contemporary special education: New horizons*. Pearson.

Twenge, J. M., Cooper, A. B., Joiner, T. E., Duffy, M. E., & Binau, S. G. (2019). Age, period, and cohort trends in mood disorder indicators and suicide-related outcomes in a nationally representative dataset, 2005–2017. *Journal of Abnormal Psychology, 128*(3), 185.

Vaughn, S., & Bos, C. S. (2020). *Strategies for teaching students with learning and behavior problems* (10th ed.). Pearson.

Walker, J. E., Shea, T. M., & Bauer, A. M. (2007). *Behavior management: A practical approach for educators* (9th ed.). Pearson.

Weems, C. F., Taylor, L. K., Cannon, M. F., Marino, R. C., Romano, D. M., Scott, B. G., Perry, A. M., & Triplett, V. (2010). Post-traumatic stress, context, and the lingering effects of the Hurricane Katrina disaster among ethnic minority youth. *Journal of Abnormal Child Psychology, 38*(1), 49–56.

Whitney, D. G., & Peterson, M. D. (2019). US national and state-level prevalence of mental health disorders and disparities of mental health care use in children. *JAMA Pediatrics, 173*(4), 389–91.

Ysseldyke, J., Scerra, C., Stickney, E., Beckler, A., Dituri, J., & Ellis, K. (2017). Academic growth expectations for students with emotional and behavior disorders. *Psychology in the Schools, 54*(8), 792–807.

The End of the Interview

"How do you feel?" Mrs. Frayer asked.

"Drained," Kortney answered. "Honestly, this has been draining. But it's also been very ..."

"Enlightening?"

"I was going to say educative," Kortney said. "But definitely enlightening as well. Your questions and stories have given me so much to think about."

The principal stood and came around the desk. She sat in the chair next to Kortney's and smiled.

"You've actually handled this process better than a lot of newly minted teachers," she said. "I admit it can be a lot to process and isn't really anyone's definition of a normal interview. I address a lot of topics other principals steer clear or, for whatever reason. And one thing I can assure you, I have yet to interview a candidate who had experience with all of the matters I presented to you."

This information did not surprise Kortney. She had been thinking to herself more than once as the interview rolled on that no one could possibly have a good answer for the majority of questions and scenarios Mrs. Frayer was throwing at her. That thought had given her a bit of comfort in the midst of the interview, a sense she was not alone in being overwhelmed by the interview approach Mrs. Frayer was using. Pondering this for a moment, a question came to Kortney.

"Mrs. Frayer," she began, "if I might ask, what's the best anyone has ever done in one of your interviews? I wouldn't pry and expect a name or anything; I'm just curious what might have impressed you the most from a candidate?"

Nodding, Mrs. Frayer did not immediately answer. Instead, she appeared to be taking a moment to collect her thoughts. She put her hands together briefly, as if she were about to pray, and then nodded.

"Yes, that's a fair question," she said. "The truth is there are really two ways to look assessing how well anyone does in my interview. Or two time frames. I'd say I've had the whole catalog of example stories I used with you for the past three, maybe four years. Before then I was building the collection, so to speak. Candidates who came through 5 or more years ago got small doses of what you experienced, and truthfully they didn't exactly set themselves apart as being ready to deal with the uniqueness of a given situation. So the first way to assess would be how someone did as I was developing this approach, and the second would be to assess how well someone does facing the final product. Does that make sense so far?"

"Yes, ma'am, it does," Kortney said.

"Good, because this is a complex process to describe," Mrs. Frayer continued. "The candidates from 5 or more years ago had good ideas and sound pedagogy and talked up classroom management, but they didn't really grasp the increased diversity in schools. And how many types of diversity there are these days. One or two had some personal experiences that related, but that was about it. Those scant few did stand out, just because they could have a conversation about one, maybe two aspects of diversity that were becoming significant here."

Kortney interjected, "So it wasn't necessarily their college educations that set them up to be able to answer your questions, then? They had life experience that set them apart?"

"Yes, that's exactly it. But don't take that as an indictment of your teacher preparation, or theirs. Some things don't fit naturally in a college classroom."

"That reminds me of something one of my professors said," Kortney responded. "She would talk to us before about what it would be like during our student teaching, and she emphasized repeatedly that the college couldn't re-create, or *emulate* was her word, what it would be like for us to have to run a classroom all day 5 days a week. That we got small doses during our field experience, but that it would get ramped up big time when we got our classrooms for that final semester."

Mrs. Frayer nodded. "I'd say she was spot-on," she said. "And just like a college can't replicate a running classroom for 7 hours for 5 straight days, they also can't replicate what it's like to deal with diversity on so many levels and in so many forms. They can talk about it but really, unless you get out and experience true diversity, you won't have the proper frame of reference."

"So what about the applicants in the past few years?" Kortney asked. "Have they gotten better for your interviews? I'd think word would have gotten out about how you do interviews, though it surely didn't make it to me."

"You know, I'm surprised that word hasn't spread more, but some things just take time to get really out there," Mrs. Frayer answered. "I know some of the candidates I interviewed had to go back and tell their friends what it was like, but I still get applicants who are clearly caught off guard by my approach. And that brings me to your question, about whether or not I've seen improvement in the past few years, in how people handle my interviews. The honest answer is there hasn't been that much improvement. The ones who stand out are the ones who, just like before, had some personal experiences or relations with the diversity concepts I present, and therefore, they could fashion a better response than those who did not."

What Mrs. Frayer was saying gave Kortney a brief pause. She was thinking about the course evaluations she had completed in the past and even the one she had done for her student teaching seminar. Her seminar instructor had encouraged the students to be honest and forthright with stating areas for improvement in the teacher education program. Kortney had offered a few suggestions, mostly dealing with classroom management and how to communicate effectively with parents, but she had not said anything about improving diversity education.

"I'm wondering then," Kortney began, "what you might recommend to universities and colleges to help them better prepare their future teachers for the types of stories you've shared with me? I mean, I've heard about advisory councils where my school is supposed to talk to administrators about what my school is doing well but where we could improve."

"You're right about those councils," Mrs. Frayer answered. "Schools have to involve external partners, including school districts, as part of their accreditation process. But that's a whole different matter. Your question is good, though. What could your program have done better in regard to diversity? My first thought relates to your field experiences. How diverse were they? Did you have to go to urban, suburban, and rural schools? Did you have to go to multiple grade levels? But that's just the first part. What kind of documentation did you have to keep besides an attendance log? What kind of reflections were required, and what kind of discussions did you have about your field experiences?"

At that, Mrs. Frayer stopped, clearly expecting Kortney to answer.

"Well, we would have debriefings in class where we shared our experiences," Kortney answered. "We would talk about what we saw and how we interacted with the teachers and students. If we taught lessons, we would analyze them a little. But I don't remember much conversation at all about race, poverty, gifted learners, hardly any of the topics we touched on today."

"There you go," Mrs. Frayer said. "Your program needed to be more strategic in how it approached diversity in the field. I'm sure you and your peers were circling around a lot of examples of what we talked about during this interview, but if your attention wasn't on them, and you didn't have to formally reflect on them or discuss them, they probably slipped right on by."

"So you think they need to add that more formally to what we're told to look for in the field?" Kortney asked. "Aren't some of these issues a little delicate, even for teachers already working?"

"Oh, most certainly," Mrs. Frayer answered. "But we can't shy away from them, and you have to be better prepared for them. I'm not saying you need to walk into a school and demand to see an example of everything we've discussed. I'm saying your program needed to teach you more mindfulness about diversity."

"Mindfulness?" Kortney asked, just a bit perplexed. She was not familiar with the term.

"Another word for it might be self-awareness," Mrs. Frayer said. "It ties back to emotional intelligence, another topic that could fill a book or five, but the gist is you are aware of your surroundings at a higher level and are strategic about where you put your focus. Your program should be promoting awareness because that can lead you to my final three pieces of advice."

"And those would be?" Kortney asked, feeling as if the interview had been inverted and she was now the interviewer rather than the interviewee.

Mrs. Frayer stood and went back around her desk but did not sit back down. "Kortney, you've been pretty good during this interview. You've held your composure well, and even though I could sense you were caught off guard, your responses to the situations I described didn't give me a negative impression. You actually demonstrated an open mind. And you've asked some great follow-up questions. So, with that said, my advice to you and any teacher education program is to build on three particular skills in regard to diversity. And those are acknowledge, accept, and embrace."

Mrs. Frayer then briefly described each of those three terms in regard to diversity before telling Kortney she had another meeting lined up.

"I appreciate your time today," Kortney said as she got to the door and shook Mrs. Frayer's hand. "You've given me a lot to think about, and I do hope I'm in consideration for the position."

"You certainly are," Mrs. Frayer answered. "As with most elementary school jobs this time of year, there are several applicants, and we have to interview a few. I can never promise anything after an interview, but I can say you've done nothing in this interview to eliminate yourself. I appreciate your interest and your time. Thank you for coming in today."

Kortney thanked her in return and then made her way out of the school and back to her car. She got in and started the engine but did not leave immediately. She took several minutes to think about the interview experience and what Mrs. Frayer had asked and shared concerning not just teaching but the wide variety of diversity teachers could encounter. Kortney realized she did not feel badly about the interview at all; it had indeed been a good learning experience. And she knew that whatever job she ultimately took, she would keep the open mind Mrs. Frayer had noticed and do her best to practice the three pieces of advice Mrs. Frayer had given her about diversity.

Mrs. Frayer's Three Words of Advice

Mrs. Frayer talked to Kortney about three terms—*acknowledge*, *accept*, and *embrace*—and what follows is what Mrs. Frayer had to say about each. These words are meant to be viewed in a wide context, to help guide thoughts and feelings toward diverse students. They represent a three-step approach to first seeing diversity, then noting its existence and place, and finally giving value to what diversity has to offer, not just to educators but to the world.

Acknowledge

Mrs. Frayer told Kortney the first step in understanding how to work with diverse students and diverse situations was to **acknowledge** them. "We can't pretend these things aren't a part of education," she said. "Acknowledging them is the first step toward working with them in the right way. We have to recognize that our students come from different backgrounds and have different experiences, strengths, and needs. Recognizing is acknowledging." There is no "head in the sand" option in modern education. It is one thing to admit that diversity is ever increasing in schools but another to acknowledge it. How teachers react to various types of diversity will reveal their level of acknowledgment. Supporting all students begins with recognizing the diversity so many of them represent.

Accept

"And it's not enough to acknowledge diversity," Mrs. Frayer continued. "I can acknowledge that the sky is blue and the grass is green, but I also have to accept those as facts." To **accept** diversity in our schools is the next step after acknowledge. Many teachers go through educator preparation with an idea that they will teach in a school very similar to those they attended. That is not necessarily the case in this ever-changing world, so teachers need to accept the ever-increasing diversity in their classrooms, in whatever form that diversity takes. Acceptance goes beyond acknowledgment. It is a higher level of understanding how things are in a particular situation. "But it's not necessarily the accept you hear in the serenity prayer," Mrs. Frayer said. "You know, 'the wisdom to accept the things I cannot change.' That's a bit defeatist from an educator's standpoint. I mean accept in the way that you say these are the cards I've been dealt, now how is the best way to play them." To Mrs. Frayer's point, accept diversity and be willing to work with diversity in ways that will support students.

Embrace

"And the last part is embrace, which may be the toughest one," Mrs. Frayer concluded. In this context **embrace** is to cherish the diversity in the world and in particular the classroom. Embracing a concept, idea, or practice means holding it in high regard and seeing its inherent value. In order to be a force for good for all of their students, teachers must embrace diversity. Carrying banners in parades or become activists for culturally responsive pedagogy is not the idea here. Teachers have the most influence in their own classroom and in their own schools, and that influence can spread to the community through a natural osmosis. Students will carry home with them the fact that their teachers do embrace diversity and respect it in their teaching practices. "You can't fool your students," Mrs. Frayer added. "They'll know if you care about something by how you act and your attitude. It all matters, which is why I want my teachers to embrace diversity. It really is so very important."

Acknowledge, accept, and embrace; simple practices in the grand scheme, but somewhat more complex when applied to education. Those three words are quite important in regard to a teacher's ultimate success in working with a diverse student population. And while this book did not address every type of diversity a teacher may encounter, it did cover many of the common forms of diversity in the modern world and in modern classrooms. The content and ideas presented are meant to help teachers acknowledge, accept, and embrace diversity.

Final Thoughts

This book has presented a great deal of information concerning the wide-ranging diversity in modern classrooms. Some of the topics have treaded on controversial and sensitive grounds, yet those sensitive areas will only become less sensitive when they are openly studied, discussed, and addressed in meaningful ways. The adage "food for thought" comes to mind when discussing issues of diverse student populations. It is hoped the food for thought presented here will become "fuel for action," to add to and complete the adage. Teachers must take action to support their students, and having knowledge of which supports may be most helpful for particular groups of students is important.

Summarizing the content of the preceding chapters in a succinct manner would be difficult, and the "Key Chapter Takeaways" at the end of each chapter should serve as a nice encapsulation for each chapter. The "Setting the Classroom Scene" vignettes and "Working With the Scenarios" in each chapter were designed as opportunities to engage more deeply with the ideas presented. And still, all good lessons feature a proper conclusion that briefly summarizes the key points, and so should any book trying to impart knowledge. With that in mind, the subsequent sections will review some of the most critical content presented.

The Goal

To begin, a reiteration of this book's overall goal is necessary. The author began writing wanting to create a text that was user-friendly, practical, and aimed at helping future educators better understand the diverse student populations in modern classrooms. With that goal in mind, the content of each chapter focused on a particular group of students and the aspects of those groups that would influence their educational performance. But the information presented should not have been viewed solely from an academic perspective. The characteristics, strengths, and even needs of a particular group of students will always go beyond the classroom and school. Teachers should not limit their increased awareness of diversity to their classrooms. After all, teachers are working to help students achieve at a high level and to apply skills and knowledge beyond the classroom. Teachers should in turn apply their knowledge of diversity beyond the classroom as well.

As the chapters progressed, and Kortney's long interview continued, readers should have engaged in critical thinking about the content. The opportunities to pause and consider the reading were designed to help the information presented be processed more fully. The vignettes to begin each chapter were meant to establish a context for learning for each chapter, and the concluding stories from Mrs. Frayer were meant to provide further opportunity to engage with the material. It is hoped that engagement was on a personal level and readers were able to view those situations based, as much as possible, on readers' own experiences. No matter the particular subject of a given chapter, the goal remained to expand knowledge and understanding of that subject. And that leads to a final goal that encompasses the entire reading, promoting the power of an open mind.

In her 2012 book *Stay Positive: Daily Reminders from Positively Present,* author Danielle DiPirro listed the following seven benefits of having an open mind (a brief summation of each is provided):

1. **Letting go of control:** The idea that you do not have to be in control of your thoughts at all times, which opens you to new ideas.

2. **Experiencing changes:** New ideas you encounter may lead to changes in how you think and what you believe.

3. **Making yourself vulnerable:** Not to be viewed negatively, this concept is an acceptance that you do not know everything and are therefore willing to learn.

4. **Making mistakes:** An open mind allows you to view errors as learning opportunities, not failures. Failures are truly destructive when we do not learn from our mistakes.

5. **Strengthening yourself:** Having an open mind allows us to see new ideas that we can use to build our mental, emotional, and social skills.

6. **Gaining confidence:** An open mind can increase your sense of self-confidence because as you learn more you can do more.

7. **Being honest:** This gets back to the notion that you do not know everything, and this is an authentic attitude that helps you be willing to learn and seek improvement.

Clearly, these benefits of an open mind are valuable, and teachers should realize these benefits are available when they keep an open mind about diverse student populations. One critical takeaway from this book should be the willingness to acknowledge, accept, and embrace the diversity in the world. Those three important steps cannot be accomplished without an open mind. It is hoped the information from these pages has helped broaden your thinking in regard to diversity, and that is significant because diversity is here to stay.

The Future of Teaching Diverse Populations

Teaching increasingly diverse student populations is not going to get easier. There are no doubts that the world is becoming increasingly diverse. And diversity itself is becoming more diverse in regard to race, religion, socioeconomic status, gender identity, achievement levels, and numerous other categories. It is therefore imperative that both current and future teachers continue to gain a better understanding of and respect for the diversity that surrounds us. That understanding and respect may at times require a certain level of vigilance. Take the following example:

> In a town hall meeting on May 28, 2019, then-Congressman Steve King, of Iowa, said, "If we presume that every culture is equal and has an equal amount to contribute to our civilization, then we're devaluing the contributions of the people that laid the foundation for America, and that's our Founding Fathers" (Watkins, 2019). This comment came at the end of an argument he was having with a constituent who had challenged some of his earlier remarks as "dehumanizing" toward certain races. King went on to say he was not talking about race, that he does not deal in race, and "It is not about race. It's never been about race. It is about culture" (Watkins, 2019). This from a member of the U.S. Congress, who apparently was attempting to praise the culture of the Founding Fathers, men who lived and worked in a new country largely devoid of the diversity in today's world. His comment might elicit the following question: "Who has the right to judge or establish the value of any particular culture?"

The preceding example is not meant to denigrate King but rather to show an example of how a skewed view on the value of cultural diversity can be presented in modern times. The efforts of the Founding Fathers should be lauded; their courage in the face of tyranny laid the foundations for our modern democracy. But by praising the Founding Fathers, are we automatically saying their culture was superior to the British Empire from which they broke away? This line of thinking crosses into somewhat dangerous philosophical grounds in regard to diversity. Do we have to respect and therefore implicitly support all parts of a particular culture? The answer is no, but we must tread lightly in this area. Just as the Founding Fathers could justly rebel against the obvious oppressive actions of Parliament and king of England, anyone has the right to defend themselves against oppressive or abusive actions and not have to stop and think about cultural implications in the process. But as with all things, we cannot judge an entire culture based on the actions of a few.

For teachers, all of this means they must learn to respect the individual student and the culture that student represents in the right way. It is not to say that teachers should think, "Student A comes from an impoverished, racial minority, and gender-nonconforming household, therefore I can assume that ..." This type of thinking is what perpetuates stereotypes and implicit bias. Having some fundamental knowledge of a culture is all well and proper; making automatic judgment calls on a person from that culture is not. See the person and the culture holistically. Appeal to the multicultural nature of your classrooms by building on the strengths those cultures share with the world. Learn and appreciate what your diverse students have to offer, but do not judge.

The future of teaching in an increasingly diverse world requires teachers to continue to develop their "cultural consciousness," their awareness of and sensitivity to the ever-evolving nature of their diverse student populations. This will take a willingness to learn from teachers, an attitude they should be modeling for their students. To help future educators begin to grow more comfortable in accepting and supporting diversity, especially in their classrooms, the next section should be useful. It introduces briefly some strategies for becoming more culturally sensitive and responsive.

Next Steps

Allow this book to serve as a starting point as you move forward toward stronger skills in supporting students from diverse backgrounds. Although the chapters provided broad overviews of different facets of diversity, there are a few key strategies, presented in Table 11.1, that you can utilize to take the spirit of this text and put it into practice. These strategies do require an open mind and willingness to learn. Part of the learning process is acknowledging what we do not know; the subsequent methods will help you learn more about being responsive to diversity.

TABLE 11.1 Strategies to Improve Responsiveness to Diversity

Strategy	Brief description
Develop cultural critical consciousness. (Gay & Kirkland, 2003)	This practice requires self-analysis and monitoring of one's personal beliefs about different cultures and how those beliefs affect instructional practices. Are your attitudes toward and understanding of diverse cultural groups helping you effectively teach members of that group?
Develop an affirming attitude toward students from culturally diverse backgrounds. (Villegas & Lucas, 2002)	Teachers who take an affirming, positive view of their diverse students demonstrate respect for validity of a multitude of ways of learning, thinking, speaking, and engaging in the school environment. This respect will be demonstrated by teaching in a manner that supports diversity.

Learn about your students' lives outside of school. (Moll & Gonzalez, 1997; Ladson-Billings, 1994)	The more you know about your students' lives outside of school (the "funds of knowledge" their families possess and their interests, motivations, and activities), the more you can design your instruction to build on that knowledge and appeal to the strengths your students have developed.
Strengthen your empathy. (Warren, 2014)	Simply put, empathy is your ability to relate to the thoughts and feelings of others. Researchers have theorized that teachers who can empathize properly with their students can better respond to their educational needs. Please note this should not be confused with sympathy; empathizing with your students fundamentally means understanding, as much as possible, why they act and feel the way they do and adjusting your actions accordingly.
Embrace a constructivist view of learning.	The constructivist theory of learning states that students build knowledge and skills by interacting with materials and new knowledge and developing links to existing knowledge they already possess (e.g., Piaget, 1997). Knowing that your culturally diverse students will possess different background knowledge will help you design learning experiences that help these students connect new knowledge to their existing schema.

Perhaps you already engage in some of these strategies. If so, you are on the right path and should keep going in the direction that will best support your diverse students. If not, the majority of these strategies begin with self-reflection and self-analysis. Taking the time to critically assess how you think about diversity and how you view diverse cultural groups is a positive first step in using these methods effectively. They are starting points on your way toward becoming "diversity responsive" and becoming truly effective in today's diverse classrooms.

Faith in Educators

An individual has not started living until he can rise above the narrow confines of his individualistic concerns to the broader concerns of all humanity.
                                                                    —Dr. Martin Luther King, Jr.

Diversity requires commitment. Achieving the superior performance diversity can produce needs further action—most notably, a commitment to develop a culture of inclusion. People do not just need to be different, they need to be fully involved and feel their voices are heard.
                                                                    —Alain Dehaze (2014)

The preceding quotes reflect very well the aspirations of this book. As King notes, a person needs to have an expanded focus on the needs of everyone—not necessarily all the time but often enough to demonstrate an understanding that we are all truly in this together. And as Dehaze stated, dedicating ourselves to a culture of inclusion allows everyone to feel involved and that they have a say in events surrounding them. All students want that sense of involvement and to know they are respected, meaning teachers can go a very long way in helping the words of the above quotes become a reality in our classrooms.

The author has tremendous faith in educators and incredible respect for the power teachers have in their students' lives. Teachers can be, and often should be, change agents, promoting equity and inclusion in the classroom so students can learn these powerful values and carry them out into the world. And teachers must acknowledge that with power comes responsibility. When teachers recognize their power and use it to properly educate the students of today, those students can go on and create a future society in which the many types of diversity are recognized and respected. When teachers acknowledge, accept, and embrace diversity, they are truly better prepared to reach all learners.

References

Dehaze, A., & Adecco Group. (2014). *The path to a shared future is built on diversity and inclusion.* World Economic Forum. https://www.weforum.org/agenda/2018/01/here-s-why-diversity-is-more-important-than-talent/

DiPirro, D. (2012). *Stay positive: Daily reminders from positively present.* Lulu.

Gay, G., & Kirkland, K. (2003). Developing cultural critical consciousness and self-reflection in preservice teacher education. *Theory into Practice, 42*(3), 181–87.

Ladson-Billings, G. (1994). *The dreamkeepers: Successful teachers of African American children.* Jossey-Bass.

Moll, L. C., & Gonzalez, N. (1997). Teachers as social scientists: Learning about culture from household research. In *Race, ethnicity, and multiculturalism: Policy and practice* (P. M. Hall, Ed., pp. 89–114). Garland.

Piaget, J. (1977). *The development of thought: Equilibrium of cognitive structures* (A. Rosin, Trans.). Viking.

Villegas, A. M., & Lucas, T. (2002). Preparing culturally responsive teachers: Rethinking the curriculum. *Journal of Teacher Education, 53*(1), 20–32.

Warren, C. (2014). Towards a pedagogy for the application of empathy in culturally diverse classrooms. *Urban Review, 46*(3), 395–419. https://doi-org.libproxy.troy.edu/10.1007/s11256-013-0262-5

Watkins, E. (2019). *Steve King warns against presuming "every culture is equal."* CNN. https://www.cnn.com/2019/05/29/politics/steve-king-culture-founding-fathers-iowa/index.html

CPSIA information can be obtained
at www.ICGtesting.com
Printed in the USA
BVHW011153270122
627377BV00008B/80